BIRD CONSERVATION ON GOLF COURSES

A DESIGN AND MANAGEMENT MANUAL

Scott W. Gillihan

Colorado Bird Observatory

United States Golf Association

Ann Arbor Press
Chelsea, Michigan

Illustrations by Jeff Lakey, Assistant Professor of Landscape Architecture at Colorado State University
Cover Photo courtesy of Wendy Shattil and Bob Rozinsky

Library of Congress Cataloging-in-Publication Data

Gillihan, Scott W.
Bird conservation on golf courses : a design and management manual / Scott W. Gillihan.
    p. cm.
    ISBN 1-57504-113-8
    1. Birds, Protection of. 2. Bird attracting. 3. Golf courses. I. Title.
QL676.5.G55   1999
639.9'78—dc21   99-11903
                                                                    CIP

ISBN 1-57504-113-8

© 2000 by Sleeping Bear Press
Ann Arbor Press is an imprint of Sleeping Bear Press

PRINTED IN THE UNITED STATES OF AMERICA
10 9 8 7 6 5 4 3 2 1

Acknowledgments

Guidance for this project came from Jim Snow (USGA Green Section) and Peter Stangel (National Fish and Wildlife Foundation).

An editorial advisory board reviewed the manuscript and offered many helpful suggestions, which resulted in a much stronger final product:

Michael J. Benkusky, Lohmann Golf Designs, Inc., Marengo, IL
Michael Carter, Colorado Bird Observatory, Brighton, CO
Darren Davis, Olde Florida Golf Club, Naples, FL
Mark Hostetler, Department of Zoology, University of Florida, Gainesville, FL
William Iko, U.S. Geological Survey, Biological Resources Division, Ft. Collins, CO
Jeff Lakey, Landscape Architecture Program, Colorado State University, Ft. Collins, CO
Robert Lohmann, Lohmann Golf Designs, Inc., Marengo, IL
Jean Mackay, Audubon Cooperative Sanctuary Program, Audubon International, Selkirk, NY
Charles Nilon, School of Natural Resources, University of Missouri–Columbia, Columbia, MO

Additional editorial advice came from the USGA's Wildlife Links Advisory Committee:

Ron Dodson, Audubon International
Paul Engman, Fairfax County Park Authority
Jim Felkel, U.S. Forest Service
Mike Lennartz, U.S. Forest Service
Dan Petit, U.S. Fish and Wildlife Service

Colorado Bird Observatory staff also reviewed the manuscript:

Jim Bradley, Joanne Carter, Scott Hutchings, Tony Leukering

Other individuals generously contributed time and information:

Marla Briggs, Audubon International
Louise Chambers and James R. Hill III, Purple Martin Conservation
    Association
Angela England, Bat Conservation International, Inc.
Marlin Ewing and Glenn Smickley, Robert Trent Jones Golf Club,
    Gainesville, VA
Nathan Farmer, Applewood Golf Course, Golden, CO
P. Stan George, Prairie Dunes Country Club, Hutchinson, KS
Gary Grigg, Royal Poinciana Golf Club, Naples, FL
Scott Hamm, Riverwood Golf Club, Port Charlotte, FL
Tim Hiers, Collier's Reserve Country Club, Naples, FL
Tony Koski, Colorado State University
Scott Mac Ewen and Tony Stepik, TPC of Tampa Bay, Lutz, FL
George McBath, Naples, FL
Ed Miller, South Florida Superintendent's Association
Randy Roth, University of Florida
Rich Roth, Cocoa Beach Country Club, Cocoa Beach, FL
Roe Sherbert, Arrowhead Golf Club, Littleton, CO
David Stubbs, European Golf Association Ecology Unit
Don Tolson, Fox Hollow at Lakewood, CO
Chip Winslow III, Kansas State University
David Worthington, U.S. Fish and Wildlife Service

Highest praise and deepest gratitude goes to my wife, Brenda Martin

About the Author

Scott W. Gillihan, Forested Ecosystems Program Coordinator for the Colorado Bird Observatory, received his B.S. in wildlife biology from Colorado State University and his M.A. in zoology from the University of Montana. His very first job was as a caddie at a country club; later positions included horticulture and landscape construction and maintenance. Scott has been a wildlife technician and biologist for state and federal natural resource agencies since 1983, working on research and management projects directed primarily at birds, but also at small mammals, fish, and amphibians. His work at the observatory has included analyzing the effects of forest management practices on bird populations, studying habitat use by bald eagles nesting at the edge of an urban area, and writing management guidelines for the conservation of forest and grassland birds. His current research interests include winter ecology of birds and small mammals, landscape-level natural disturbances and their effects on forest bird communities, and bird conservation in forest areas.

About the Colorado Bird Observatory

Founded in 1988, the Colorado Bird Observatory's mission is the conservation of Rocky Mountain and Great Plains birds and their habitats through research, monitoring, and public education. The CBO's work is designed to increase the understanding of birds—what habitats they use, what roles they play in healthy ecosystems, and what factors threaten their survival. The CBO accomplishes its goals through the education of children, teachers, natural resource managers, and the general public. The CBO also conducts on-the-ground conservation work and research in cooperation with agencies such as the U.S. Forest Service, National Park Service, U.S. Fish and Wildlife Service, Bureau of Land Management, Colorado Division of Wildlife, Instituto de Ecología in Mexico (where many western birds spend the winter), and others responsible for managing areas and programs important to birds.

Foreword

I grew up on a golf course. Our front yard was just a short chip shot from the first green of the Rockport Country Club. Leaving the car parked in the side driveway was risking a nasty dent from an errant slice, and I had to scour the yard for golf balls each week before mowing commenced. After school on most days I would come home, grab a quick snack, and head over to the course—to go birding.

The Rockport Country Club was great birding. Woodcock flew from nearby woods to the roughs along the second hole each spring, drawn by the short grass that allowed potential mates to better witness their elaborate courtship display. The open fairways attracted eastern bluebirds, which at that time were still quite uncommon. During migration, a sora or common snipe would sometimes lurk in the cattails bordering the small stream that bisected the course. Barn swallows nested in the utility barn, rocketing in and out through a small hole carved in the door by the caring groundskeeper. Golfers would often yell to me, sharing their recent sightings, and asking me in return for news of good birds.

The Rockport Country Club had no special management programs to benefit birds and other wildlife, but both were abundant. Many of the members, and certainly the groundskeepers, were aware of wildlife, appreciated birds, and did their best to conserve habitats that benefitted our local fauna. Even without special management, the club was attractive to both common and unusual birds.

The features typical of any course—water hazards such as streams and ponds, brushy edges where rough meets wood, and even the wide-open fairways—offered habitats important to both migratory and resident birds. As a tecnager, I would walk my favorite routes, watching for birds, fantasizing about what I would do, given the chance, to make the course even better for wildlife. By planting emergent vegetation along streams, I was sure that red-winged blackbirds could be enticed to nest. Sparrow populations could be doubled by adding native brush under taller-canopy trees. Hairy and downy woodpeckers would excavate cavities in dead limbs and snags retained in the abundant forest surrounding the course. I was sure my improvements would not only attract more birds, but also make the course more beautiful and challenging for golfers.

This book by Scott Gillihan, of the Colorado Bird Observatory, represents the most significant step to help make fantasies like mine a reality. Contained in the following pages are dozens of practical, inexpensive ideas that golf course superintendents and architects can use to conserve, maintain, and restore valuable bird habitats, while enhancing the playing experience for golfers.

The idea for this book—which is really a management manual—came from a group of professional biologists and managers who make up the Wildlife Links Advisory Committee. Wildlife Links is a joint venture of the United States Golf Association (USGA) and the National Fish and Wildlife Foundation (NFWF). It was created to provide funding for priority research and management projects aimed at enhancing wildlife habitats on golf courses. USGA generously funds the program, which is coordinated by NFWF through the Advisory Committee.

At an early meeting, the Advisory Committee recommended that one of the most important projects for Wildlife Links was to make biologically credible information on wildlife management available in a practical form to those with responsibility for designing and managing golf courses. This manual by Scott Gillihan fulfills the Committee's recommendation, as it applies to birds.

Scott's manual is a first in many ways. It is the first book, to my knowledge, that brings together the latest and best information on bird and bird habitat management as it applies to golf courses and similar settings. It is the first book that provides this information in a format that is easy to understand and use—an absolutely critical feature. Golf course superintendents and architects are professionals, as witnessed by the superior playing conditions maintained on a daily level at even the busiest courses. Most, however, don't have the time to wade through technical journals in search of hints on how best to provide habitat for birds. Scott has filled this role for the golf industry, and the result is one of the clearest, most practical presentations of bird management techniques that I have ever seen. Superintendents will find Scott's recommendations and illustrations easy to understand and implement.

Most important, Scott's manual is the first to elevate golf courses as important—and in some cases essential—components of the conservation landscape. This manual was conceived by the Wildlife Links Advisory Committee in recognition of the fact that golf courses can provide important habitats for a wide variety of both resident and migratory birds. Although playing conditions will dictate most course features, there are many, many things that can be done to conserve and restore essential habitats for birds. Properly designed and maintained, almost any golf course can complement the conservation role played by bird sanctuaries and wildlife refuges.

Readers should also be aware that information in this manual will be valuable to a wide diversity of conservationists not associated with golf courses. Local planning commissions, park managers, and conservation activists will find indispensable information for improving the quality of habitats at a variety of urban and rural sites. In fact, I predict that distribution of this manual to interests outside of golf will far outstrip that to the industry itself. That this manual will provide valuable information to an audience far beyond golf is a credit to both USGA and Scott Gillihan.

I would like to personally thank USGA for funding this important manual, and for its support of the Wildlife Links Program. I am inspired by the commitment of Jim Snow, Kimberly Erusha, and their colleagues within USGA to making golf courses an important part of the conservation landscape. The Wildlife Links Advisory Committee has provided leadership and expertise to this project and others, despite many other competing demands. At NFWF, Alison Dalsimer and Katie Distler have smoothly managed contracts and finances. Scott Gillihan has done a thorough job synthesizing the frequently complex and confusing information on bird management, and presented it clearly. His legacy through this book will be an abundance of birds and their habitats on golf courses across the continent.

Peter Stangel
National Fish and Wildlife Foundation

Preface

This book is a hands-on manual for designing and managing golf courses to benefit birds. It grew out of a belief that golf courses can and should play a significant role in bird conservation. As urbanization and land development rapidly replace natural features with artificial ones, golf courses often stand alone as the only pockets of natural habitat for birds in otherwise inhospitable urban landscapes of concrete and asphalt. The presence of these habitat remnants, along with low levels of human disturbance, place golf courses in a unique position to contribute to bird conservation. The golf course industry has accepted this role of environmental steward and conservator of birds and other wildlife, but lacks critical information needed to effectively fulfill that role. The purpose of this book is to fill the information gap by presenting the latest findings from the sciences of landscape ecology, conservation biology, wildlife management, and ornithology, adapted for practical application on golf courses.

This manual was written primarily for golf course architects and course superintendents. However, other people could benefit from this information, including landscape architects, city planners, real estate developers, and managers of open space areas, parks, cemeteries, industrial and municipal complexes, college campuses, school grounds, and estates—in short, anyone whose design, planning, or maintenance work affects birds and their habitats in developed areas.

Material in this book is directed toward the habitat needs of songbirds, hummingbirds, woodpeckers, raptors, shorebirds, and wading birds. Most game birds, waterfowl, and gulls are omitted because their numbers are generally stable and their management is usually a priority for state wildlife agencies. Habitat needs during the breeding season (spring and summer) are emphasized because of that season's importance in the life cycle of birds, and because it overlaps with the golfing season. Some information on migrating and wintering birds is also included. The geographic scope of the manual includes the continental United States, but the basic principles are applicable anywhere that birds and golf courses coexist.

This manual's organization goes from general concepts to specific suggestions. Throughout, terms that may be unfamiliar to readers are in boldface, and are defined in a glossary. Chapter 1 presents arguments for conserving birds on golf courses. Chapter 2 covers the basic principles of bird biology, including general habitat requirements. Chapter 3 is directed toward architects interested in incorporating bird habitat into a course design, and course managers who want to improve conditions for bird communities in general. Principles presented in this chapter include creation and preservation of habitat patches of suitable size, quality, and arrangement. Chapter 4 is directed toward course superintendents interested in managing specific bird species or groups of birds. Topics covered in this chapter include managing small-scale habitat characteristics such as vegetation layers, snags, and nest boxes. Chapter 5 covers issues of course maintenance, and Chapter 6 offers suggestions for dealing with problem birds. Chapter 7 presents detailed management information for species in particular need of conservation efforts, and Chapter 8 introduces other golf course residents. Supplemental material includes a glossary, a list of pertinent reference materials, helpful contacts for additional information, a list of plants of particular value to birds, guidelines for artificial nest structures, regional bird lists, and a list of more than 400 North American breeding birds with their habitat requirements and conservation status.

Contents

BIRD CONSERVATION ON GOLF COURSES

A DESIGN AND MANAGEMENT MANUAL

CHAPTER ONE

WHY SHOULD GOLF COURSES BENEFIT BIRDS?

Why birds?

Birds are an obvious choice for enhancement activities on golf courses. They are the most conspicuous wildlife, easily seen and heard by golfers. For example, to find out which wildlife group was most likely to be encountered by visitors to **urban** parks, a biologist made careful notes of all the wildlife he saw in 15 parks for one year. By the end of the year, he had made 20,000 observations, of which *96% were birds* and only 3% were mammals. Birds are also the most species-rich wildlife group. A golf course might be home to 5 to 10 mammal species, which remain mostly hidden from people. But the same course might be used by more than 100 bird species, each with unique habits and characteristics. Birds interest people because of their singing, their color, their interactions with each other, and their food-gathering and nesting activities. Also, they are relatively free from objectionable traits—with few exceptions, birds are harmless to humans and their property. In addition, bird **habitat** overlaps with habitat for other wildlife species, so protecting bird habitat also protects the homes of many other forms of wildlife. Healthy populations of birds indicate a healthy environment and a healthy golf course.

Birds need help

Populations of many bird species are declining at an alarming rate. Many of the species with the steepest declines are long-distance migrants—birds that breed in the United States and Canada, but spend their winters in the southern United States and the tropical regions of Central and South America and the Caribbean. These declining migratory species are primarily insect-eaters—birds that could be helping to control insect pests on golf courses. Because the time required for migration leaves less time for breeding, many of these birds build simple, cup-shaped nests, often in a low bush or on the ground. Such exposed nests are more susceptible to destruction by weather or predators. On the other hand, birds that do not migrate at all, or migrate only short distances, have the time to create more elaborate nests—including excavating a cavity in a tree—which offer added protection. If the eggs of a long-distance migrant are destroyed, there often isn't enough time to try to nest again. So not only do these birds face a greater risk of losing their nest to predators, they often don't have the opportunity to build another nest to make up for the loss.

One way that migrants have compensated for exposed nests is by placing those nests deep in the heart of woodlands, away from predators (such as raccoons, jays, and snakes), which favor more open areas and habitat **edges**. Unfortunately, the extensive woodlands in many areas of North America have been fragmented into smaller woodlots. This occurs when parts of the woods have been converted to agriculture, housing, or other human uses. In many places there are no longer any large tracts of woods where migrants can get away from predators. Instead, the forest is subdivided into small woodlots, which do not provide enough internal area for birds to get away from the habitat edges. These factors, combined with the loss of their winter habitat due to conversion of forests and other natural areas to other uses, are believed to be responsible for the declines in this group of birds.

Another hazard faced by many songbirds is nest parasitism. The brown-headed cowbird is a **nest parasite**—a bird that lays its eggs in the nests of other birds for them to raise, rather than building its own nest. Often these other birds fail to notice the cowbird egg, and accept it as one of their own, even though it is often larger and colored differently. Once hatched, the young cowbird pushes the other eggs or nestlings out of the nest, and becomes the sole beneficiary of its adoptive parents' feeding efforts. In many cases, the young cowbird grows larger than its new parents, which continue to feed it despite the extra work and obvious size discrepancy. Freed from any parental responsibilities, adult cowbirds can range over four miles from their feeding sites in search of nests in which to lay their eggs. And cowbirds are prolific—a female can lay 20 to 40 eggs per year. The brown-headed cowbird is a **native** North American species, and it has been parasitizing nests for thousands of generations without jeopardizing the populations of other birds. However, it is a species of open country and habitat edges where fields and forests meet. Forest clearing in recent history has created more habitat, allowing the cowbird to move into areas of the continent where it did not live before and increase its populations beyond historical levels. As a result, cowbirds are now having a larger impact on bird populations than ever before. Migratory species are hit harder than resident species because the migrants usually only have enough time to nest once, while resident species can renest later in the season, and cowbirds rarely parasitize late-season nests.

One example of a migratory bird in need of conservation efforts is the wood thrush. This bird nests in forests of the eastern United States and spends its winters in Central America. Its populations have declined by 40% over the past 25 years, due in part to habitat loss, but also due to extremely high rates of cowbird nest parasitism. In scientific studies that sought the causes of this bird's decline, practically every wood thrush nest contained at least one cowbird egg. Wood thrushes are putting all of their time and energy into raising cowbirds rather than more wood thrushes—it's no wonder their populations are declining.

Another reason that some bird populations are declining is that their habitat is being lost to urbanization. When natural areas are converted to urban areas, the bird species that decline are those with specialized habitat needs—such as a particular vegetation type or only one kind of food—while the species that increase are birds that can live in a variety of habitats and eat a lot of different foods. In general, birds that eat insects decline, while birds that eat seeds increase; birds that nest on the ground or in tree cavities decline; and birds that prefer to live along habitat edges increase. Compared to more natural habitat, urban areas have fewer species but more individual birds, due to large populations of introduced species like European starlings, rock doves (pigeons), and house sparrows (sometimes called English sparrows). These species are quite tolerant of human activity, and are not too particular about where they build nests or what they eat. As a result, they thrive in cities, to the point of becoming major pests. Many other species are more sensitive to disturbance by human activity, and are more selective about where they nest and what they eat, so they cannot survive in cities.

Golf can be good for birds

Golf courses have an environmental black eye. They are widely perceived as places where large amounts of toxic chemicals are dumped on water-greedy grasses to produce a pampered green desert. Because of this perception, public opposition to new course development often centers on environmental issues. From the comments of opponents, it's clear that many of them view golf courses as death traps for any animal unlucky enough to blunder onto a fairway. Highly publicized examples of birds killed by improperly applied chemicals have created lasting impressions in the minds of environmentally concerned citizens.

But a golf course is not a sterile, green desert. In recent years, pesticide use has been greatly reduced thanks to the widespread adoption of **Integrated Pest Management** practices, advances in chemical products and cultural techniques, and development of turfgrass cultivars resistant to disease and insects. Water consumption has been reduced through similar techniques. Many courses also use computer systems that link national and regional weather forecasts to local weather and evapotranspiration data, allowing more efficient timing and duration of course irrigation. Contrary to their reputation as barren wastelands, golf courses can provide significant environmental benefits, including providing habitat for healthy populations of native wildlife.

The reasons why golf courses are home to many native wildlife species are clear. A typical golf course represents about 150 acres of open space—a scarce natural resource in highly developed urban areas. Most urban land is valuable private property, subject to intense pressure to be developed for financial gain. The small amount of public land that is set aside for recreation is intensively used, often to the detriment of native plants and animals. Parks, greenways, and open space areas are crowded with people, and their activities are often high-spirited and noisy. Suburbs are filled with the bustle of cars and busy people. However, with the exception of tournaments, golf is a quiet, peaceful game, played by small groups of people without shouts or applause or whistles. For birds, a golf course is a quiet island in a sea of human activity. The vegetation on a golf course is also attractive to birds. In many urban areas, the only remaining patches of vegetation are found in parks, cemeteries, greenways, and golf courses. But golf courses are the most likely to possess the desirable combination of *large* patches of vegetation and low levels of human activity. This unique combination provides birds and other wildlife with the habitat they require.

Birds are also safer on golf courses than in other urban areas, because fewer introduced predators are found on golf courses. Domestic cats kill hundreds of millions of birds per year in the United States—they may be the major cause of bird deaths in the urban environment. Golf courses, however, are not frequented by cats, or dogs, or kids with pellet guns. Birds are free to live and raise young unmolested, and must contend only with the few natural predators that have also found a home on the golf course.

Golf courses can provide safe havens for other organisms as well. A study of the conservation value of golf courses in England found that some rare plants exist only on golf courses. The researchers felt that if the golf courses had not been built, those rare plants would have been destroyed when the natural community was replaced with housing or other developments. Similar examples of rare plants can be found in the United States, especially along coastal areas. The threatened Big Cypress fox squirrel has found the large native trees and open understory of Florida's golf courses to its liking, and in some areas the healthiest populations of this uncommon squirrel are found on golf courses. The natural vegetation retained there provides an important refuge in an area of rapid development.

In situations where the natural habitat has been extensively degraded by human activities—such as mining, agriculture, or used as a landfill—golf course development can improve the potential for the area to support plant and animal communities. However, in terms of prime habitat for native birds, nothing can replace a completely natural array of plants and water. While construction of a golf course in a healthy, natural habitat will benefit some species, it will certainly harm others. This is true not only for golf course development, but for any large-scale development. The difference is that golf courses can retain much of the natural habitat in place, undisturbed, and can therefore retain much of the natural bird community. This is not true for other types of development—not agriculture, not subdivisions, not shopping malls. Golf courses are one of the few cases where human development can coexist with the natural community.

Take the case of a natural area with plants and animals carrying out their ecological roles in a healthy, functioning ecosystem. The best thing possible for those plants and animals is for no development of any kind to take place there. The worst thing possible is for the area to be developed into a totally artificial system, such as a shopping mall, with acres and acres of concrete and asphalt, and just a few token ornamental trees and shrubs next to the buildings for aesthetics. Few birds can survive in such a sterile environment. Between these two extremes—with a totally natural environment on one end and a totally artificial one on the other—lie other possibilities. If a goal of responsible development is to conserve as many native species as possible, in numbers that reflect their natural proportions, and in an environment that resembles as much as possible the natural environment, then one of the best choices for development is a golf course. Granted, some compromises of the natural habitat will occur, but no other form of development retains as many features of the natural habitat as a golf course. A golf course can preserve patches of native habitat larger than can be found in most other types of development; a patch containing many acres of native habitat in an out-of-play area is far superior to the highly manicured nature of municipal parks or cemeteries. Few housing subdivisions leave room for such patches, and birds must make do with a few ornamental trees and shrubs planted in the corners of each yard.

Birds can be good for golf

Some birds eat fish, some eat berries, some eat seeds, and some eat animals, but many birds (including most songbirds) eat insects. Skim the feeding habits of birds listed in Appendix 5 —it may surprise you to see how many eat insects. Even some species that are not strict insect-eaters will eat them during the breeding season for the protein and calcium they provide. Young birds are often fed only insects for the same reasons. Hummingbirds, commonly thought to consume only nectar, feed insects to their young to provide them with the protein needed for growth. Adult hummingbirds also eat insects—their familiar habit of consuming nectar from flowers or sugar water from feeders provides only part of their nutritional needs.

The number of insects that a bird can eat is impressive. A biologist once found a cuckoo with 250 tent caterpillars in its stomach and intestines, a nighthawk with 500 mosquitoes, and a flicker with 5,000 ants.

A migrating warbler eats 1.5 times its weight in caterpillars each day. And birds of prey can take their toll on rodents—a large hawk or owl can eat over a thousand mice and voles per year, adding up to many thousands over the course of its lifetime. Such natural controls on insect and rodent populations are of great economic value to golf courses. Although birds usually cannot control large insect outbreaks after they have begun, under normal conditions they can suppress the numbers of insects, keeping them below the outbreak levels that require more active control by course personnel. In fact, forest managers estimate that the insect control services of birds are worth about $5000 per square mile, per year. Insect-eating birds can provide those same insect control services on golf courses, saving the courses money.

Wildlife habitat on golf courses benefits not only wildlife, but people as well. Numerous studies have found that most people find great pleasure in seeing and hearing birds and other wildlife. Other research has found that regular exposure to the natural world provides significant health benefits, both physical and mental. Playing a course with extensive natural areas and singing birds provides golfers with enjoyment from both the game and the natural beauty. Birdwatching and backyard bird feeding are two of the fastest-growing and most popular outdoor activities; in 1996, Americans spent $3.5 billion on bird food, bird baths, bird houses, and related items. For courses tied to real estate developments, the presence of wildlife and natural areas sells homes—people want to live close to nature. In fact, in some golf course developments, 80% of the homes are sold to nongolfers. They buy because of the open space and natural beauty. Presenting information on natural features of the golf course—including its wildlife—is a powerful sales tool.

Golf course developments that allow for wildlife habitat often enjoy easier approval during the planning phase. Individuals who oppose golf course development on the grounds of wildlife habitat loss may be willing to accept a proposed course if it protects and enhances existing habitat, and if the developers make clear their intentions to be good caretakers of the environment.

Which birds?

All native birds have roles to play in the ecosystem, so all native birds have equal ecological value. However, not all species have equal *conservation* value. Don't mistakenly assume that the goal of bird conservation on golf courses should be to simply maximize the number of species present. Instead, consider which species are present (and which are absent), and take steps to provide habitat for species that are uncommon or declining at the regional or national level. For golf courses to make a *significant* contribution to bird conservation—a contribution that will be applauded by the environmental community and the general public, a contribution that will help to heal the environmental black eye—the golf course industry must take steps to benefit uncommon and declining bird species. The rest of this manual outlines steps that golf course architects and superintendents can take to meet that goal.

Key Points

1. Healthy populations of birds indicate a healthy environment and a healthy golf course.
2. Golf courses can provide habitat for birds because of their large patches of vegetation and low levels of human activity.
3. Bird conservation benefits birds *and* golf courses.
4. Bird conservation should be directed toward those species most in need of conservation efforts.

CHAPTER TWO

BASIC PRINCIPLES OF
BIRD BIOLOGY

The types of birds

Over 600 species of birds live and breed in North America. They can be lumped into groups based on a combination of their physical characteristics, what they eat, and how they get their food:

- Wading birds: Medium- to large-sized birds, most with long legs, long necks, and long beaks, for wading in shallow water and capturing fish and other aquatic animals. Includes the herons, egrets, bitterns, and cranes.
- Waterfowl: Birds with webbed feet for swimming, short legs, and broad, flat bills. Most are vegetarians, eating aquatic or terrestrial plants and grains. Includes the swans, ducks, and geese.
- Shorebirds: Birds with long legs for wading in very shallow water along lake and ocean shores, although some are found far from water; they search for aquatic insects or small animals in the water, or probe for them in mud. Includes sandpipers, avocets, killdeer, and plovers.
- Gulls and terns: White and gray birds of coastal areas and inland waters, with webbed feet for swimming and long, pointed wings. Their diet reflects their homes: most eat fish or other aquatic animals.
- Pigeons and doves: These birds have short legs, short necks, and short beaks for finding seeds on the ground.

- **Raptors**: Birds with long, sharp talons (claws or nails) on their feet and hooked beaks for capturing and eating other animals. Includes eagles, kites, hawks, falcons, and owls.
- Game birds: Birds with stout bodies and short beaks for gathering seeds and vegetation on or near the ground. Includes grouse, quail, prairie chickens, and the **exotic** ring-necked pheasant.
- Hummingbirds: Very small birds with very long beaks, which they use for reaching into flowers to feed on the nectar.
- Woodpeckers: Birds with stiff tail feathers for perching on tree trunks, and strong, straight beaks for chiseling into bark to find insects. Some types of woodpeckers, such as flickers and sapsuckers, eat insects on the ground, or tree sap, or berries.
- Perching birds: Small- to medium-sized birds with three toes pointing forward and one back, for perching on branches. This is the largest group of birds, often referred to as the songbirds. It includes crows, chickadees, blue-birds, warblers, blackbirds, sparrows, finches, and many other birds. Some perching birds eat insects, some eat fruits, some eat seeds, and some eat a combination of these and other foods.

Because there are so many species of birds, and the differences be-tween them are often subtle, many books have been written to help people identify birds. These "field guides" show photographs or draw-ings of the different birds, and point out key characteristics for identify-ing each species. They also include maps that show where each species lives at different times of the year. A list of field guides can be found in Appendix 1.

Habitat needs of birds

The popularity of bird feeding and attracting birds to residential yards is reflected in the number of books devoted to the topic. How-ever, many of those books present a misleading picture. They give the impression that all that is necessary to attract a particular bird species is to put up a particular kind of feeder filled with a particular kind of bird food, then stand back while the birds come flocking in. But it's not that simple. For a site to be acceptable to a particular bird species, it needs more than just a food supply—suitable habitat is more complex. The species' habitat needs must be met on several different geographic scales.

Birds choose a particular site to live and build a nest based on habitat features not just at the site of their nest, but at larger scales as well. First, the site must be within a broad geographic area that suits the bird's physiology—a bird of hot, dry southern climates might have a difficult time adjusting to cool, rainy northern climates. Second, at a smaller geographic scale, the site must contain the proper vegetation type—a bird accustomed to finding food and nest sites in dense, mature conifer forests of the Pacific Northwest would not survive long among the sparse shrubs of California chaparral. Third, at an even smaller geographic scale, the site must contain broad habitat elements in the particular arrangement that the species needs—for example, some species require large, unbroken tracts of deciduous forest, while others require open grassy fields adjacent to forested areas. Fourth, the site must include the specific features that the species requires at a fine scale—for example, a **snag** of a particular size and stage of decomposition for a nest cavity, or a grouping of shrubs that provide fruits during critical stages of the breeding cycle.

The first two steps in the bird's decision-making process are beyond the influence of a golf course designer or superintendent: the climate and regional vegetation type of the course are set. Don't try to create habitat that isn't suited to your location by planting vegetation from some other region. Follow the example of Nature and utilize only those plants that are native to your local area. Decisions made at the third step by particular species can be influenced by the course designer, who can leave certain arrangements of natural vegetation in place. The final step is mostly under the influence of the course superintendent, whose management and maintenance decisions impact individual trees and small patches of vegetation.

A bird's habitat is the area that provides all the elements that it needs to survive and reproduce. Birds have four basic needs: *food, water, shelter,* and *nest area:*

- *Food* is an obvious need, essential for the survival of all organisms. What is not so obvious is that birds may require large areas in which to find enough food, especially if the birds are large or if their food is widely scattered, such as is the case with hawks and owls.

- *Water* is also obviously needed; birds need it not only for drinking but also for bathing. Clean feathers are essential for flight, for protection from rain, and to insulate birds from temperature extremes.
- *Shelter* refers to a place where birds can be safe from predators and inhospitable weather, such as dense evergreens in northern winters or cool streamside shrubs in desert summers.
- *Nest area* is both the actual nest site (for example, a dead tree trunk for a woodpecker) and the area around the nest site—area needed by the bird for gathering enough food to feed its growing family.

Of the basic requirements, *nest area* is the most difficult one for humans to provide. We can supplement the natural food and water supply and manipulate the vegetation to create more shelter, but we are limited by the space provided. Natural and human boundaries limit us and the birds. The only option is to create more nest area by converting developed areas into natural habitats through planting of native vegetation. This is feasible, but labor-intensive and expensive.

Each bird species has its own basic requirements, although there is overlap between species. Bird species differ in what they eat (insects, seeds, animals, etc.), where they search for food (on the ground, in shrubs, at the tops of trees, under water, etc.), and where they build their nests (on bare soil, in tree cavities, on high cliffs, etc.). Also, the geographic ranges of birds differ, as species are adapted to the particular climates and vegetation types that meet their basic requirements. The point is that each species has its own requirements, and a particular species will be found in a given area only if its basic requirements are met. A particular bird species will show up on a particular golf course only if it lies within the species' geographic range and only if suitable habitat exists there for it.

The basic requirements can be very broad and general, or they can be very narrow and specific, depending on the bird species. The American crow, for example, can eat a wide variety of foods, including insects, dead animals, bird eggs, seeds, and fruit. This is one reason why crows are found in many parts of North America. On the other hand, the snail kite (a raptor), eats almost nothing but apple snails. In the United States, this bird is restricted to the Everglades in the southern tip of Florida, where its narrow habitat needs are met. In general, species with broad habitat requirements are usually widespread, because the habitat elements they need are found in many places, while species with narrow habitat requirements are usually found in small geographic areas, where they can find the elements that meet their specialized needs. Because each species has its own unique set of habitat requirements, the only way a golf course can expect a wide variety of species is if it provides a variety of habitat elements.

Key Points

1. Birds select a particular site based on decisions made at several geographic scales, and golf course personnel can affect only the smaller scales.
2. Birds' four basic habitat requirements are food, water, shelter, and nest area.
3. Food, water, and shelter can be easily enhanced by humans, but nest area is more difficult.
4. Each bird species has its own particular set of habitat requirements.
5. Habitat diversity = bird diversity.

CHAPTER THREE

CONSERVATION EFFORTS AT LARGE SCALES

Designing a golf course that is favorable to birds involves working at a large spatial scale, known as the **landscape level.** The size of habitat elements at this scale ranges from a few acres to many thousands. Some examples of landscape-level habitat elements include rivers, lakes, and woodlots. Habitat elements at a smaller scale include things like individual trees or very small woodlots (covering less than a few acres). It is at the landscape level that bird conservation efforts are the most effective, because landscape-level factors exert greater influence over the composition of the bird community, the number of birds present, and their breeding success. Working at the landscape level requires an understanding of three basic habitat elements, the factors that determine their quality, and their arrangement in the landscape to benefit birds.

Patches

A **patch** is any area of relatively uniform habitat. Examples of habitat patches that can be used by birds include a stand of cattails, a cluster of conifers, and a grassy meadow. In general, large patches are better for breeding birds than small patches. Because the negative effects associated with habitat edges (especially increased nest predation and cowbird nest parasitism) extend far into the interior of a habitat patch, small patches are essentially all edge habitat (Figure 1). Birds have nowhere to go to escape the problems associated with edges. To counter this, *course designers should protect the largest habitat patches that can be fit into the course design. Course superintendents should plant native vegetation to*

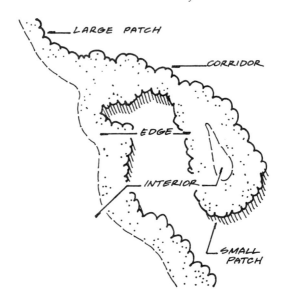

Figure 1. Landscape elements: large patch, small patch, and corridor. The solid area represents interior habitat, the stippled area is edge habitat.

enlarge existing patches, and to merge several small patches into one large one. While species with broad habitat needs can utilize patches of almost any size, many birds with more specialized habitat needs require patches greater than 20 acres, and some species require unbroken patches of hundreds or even thousands of acres. The larger the patch, the more species will use it (Figure 2). However, don't get the idea that small habitat patches have *no* value to birds. An array of small patches can serve the same function as a single large patch, by providing the same habitat components. The key is that they be close together or connected with similar habitat. Small patches are important sources of food and protective cover year round, and they should be preserved whenever possible.

The value of large patches has recently been recognized by some progressive designers of residential developments. They have adopted plans that cluster houses, streets, and utilities into small sections of the development, leaving the rest of the area as undeveloped patches. Although their primary goal is to create open-space areas for recreation, these areas also provide habitat for birds and other wildlife. Golf course architects could adopt this strategy by clustering golf course elements (fairways, buildings, roads, and parking lots), leaving large patches un-

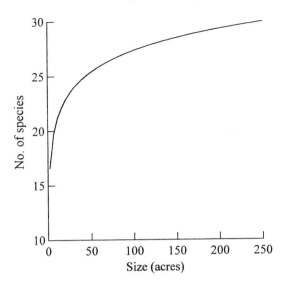

Figure 2. The relationship of patch size and number of bird species present in the patch. Notice how the number of species increases most rapidly in the lower end of the patch size range, where small increases in the size of the patch result in relatively large increases in the number of bird species present. Note: This is an example from woodlots in the Upper Midwest, and the number of species shown on the graph is valid for patches there only—other habitat types in other locations would have different numbers of species.

disturbed as bird habitat (Figure 3B). Another option would be to lay out the course in several loops, leaving patches of vegetation in the out-of-play areas framed by the fairways (Figure 3C). This doesn't create patches as large as when the fairways are clustered, but it does provide birds with some habitat and the proximity of the holes to the patches brings golfers into closer contact with natural areas.

But even if its habitat patches are too small to meet the needs of some breeding species, a golf course can still benefit birds. Many birds are far less fussy about the size of a habitat patch during migration— they just want to rest and refuel, then get on their way. The issues of increased numbers of nest predators and cowbirds in small patches don't matter to migrating birds. They often stop at a habitat patch only for a day, then continue their journey. So if it's not possible to set aside large habitat patches for breeding birds on the course, don't despair. The small patches will still be used by migrating birds.

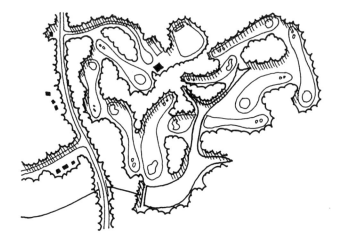

Figure 3A. Conventional golf course layout. Note that most of the land area is used, as the course is spread out over the entire property.

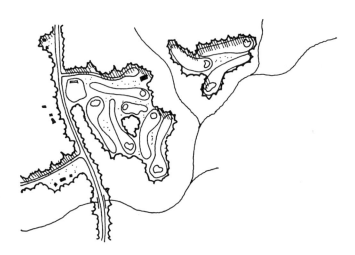

Figure 3B. Same location, but this time the golf course elements are clustered. Note the undisturbed habitat on the south side of the main stream. This could become a core conservation area on the course.

In addition to the size of a patch, its *quality and position in the landscape* must be considered. From a bird's perspective, a high-quality habitat patch is one that contains a *high proportion of native vegetation,*

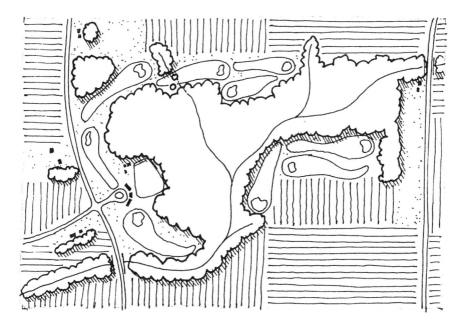

Figure 3C. Another possible layout for the same location. In this case, the holes have been laid out in several loops, to retain large habitat patches.

provides the *basic habitat needs* (food, water, shelter, and nest area), and *offers little or no disturbance from human activities*. Positioning a patch of high-quality, natural habitat next to a patch with poor habitat value lessens greatly the value of the first patch. For example, a mature woodlot is high-quality bird habitat, but not if it is adjacent to a busy warehouse with heavy truck traffic and shouting workers. The noise and commotion would disrupt routine bird activities, and most species would never settle at the site. One biologist found that the degree of nearby urban development was even more important than patch size in determining the number of birds and bird species using a forest patch: small woodlots with no adjacent development had more birds and more species than large woodlots adjacent to high levels of development. The researcher suggested several explanations, including increased disturbance by human activities, predation by house cats and squirrels, and a psychological need for some bird species to avoid human structures. Clearly, it is better for birds if high-quality habitat patches are adjacent to patches of other high-quality habitat (Figure 4). *Position the course's low-quality habitat patches and areas of disturbance (parking lots, buildings, etc.)*

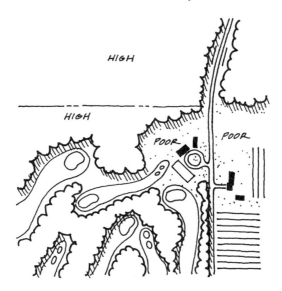

Figure 4. Examples of reduced contrast in patch quality. The parking lot and buildings have been located adjacent to the main road, across the road from buildings on the other property. In this way, low-quality habitat on the course is adjacent to low-quality habitat off the course. On the other side of the course lies high-quality habitat, a mature bottomland forest, so the architect has bordered this with similar habitat patches on the course.

alongside any patches of low-quality habitat adjacent to the course. In the same vein, *leave intact the course's high-quality habitat patches that lie adjacent to other high-quality patches off of the course.* If the course is surrounded by low-quality habitat, use the course itself to insulate the high-quality habitat patches that have been set aside. Locate such patches in the interior of the course's property. When contemplating patch quality and position, the goal is to reduce the contrast between adjacent patches.

Edges

An edge is the boundary between two distinct habitats, such as a field and a forest. For many years, biologists have recognized that more species of wildlife can be found along the edge between two habitats than in either of the habitats alone. This is because species that prefer each habitat can be found there, as well as species that favor just the edge habitat. For example, near a field/forest edge you will find forest birds, and field birds, and edge birds. And because maximizing the number of species present in an area has long been seen as desirable, maximizing the amount of edge has long been a primary goal of wildlife management. It can be found in the first book ever written on professional wildlife management, and has been echoed in almost every one since.

However, beginning in the 1980s, researchers studying songbirds in the forests of the eastern United States discovered that nests within 50 yards of edges were often less successful than nests located deeper in the woods. Eggs and young birds disappeared from nests close to edges. Closer investigation turned up the probable causes: nest predators (such as raccoons and blue jays) and a nest parasite (the brown-headed cowbird) were more common in edge areas. The clearing of forests that has taken place since settlement by Europeans has created more habitat edges, and the populations of these edge-favoring species have grown markedly as a result. Some research has suggested that forest openings as narrow as 17 yards can create conditions favorable to nest predators and cowbirds. Large populations of nest predators mean a high rate of loss of eggs and nestlings of many bird species, and large populations of the cowbird mean lower nest success for the bird species that are its victims.

Other problems with edge habitats include changes in environmental conditions and vegetation. In forested areas, for example, edge habitat receives more sun and wind than habitat found in the patch interior, so the edge habitat is drier. As a result, different plants and insects live along edges, or similar types live there but in different densities. Physical effects due to edges can extend 100 yards or more into the interior of each habitat type. These changes in the plant and insect populations are reflected in changes in the bird populations. Also, many bird species accustomed to the interior of habitat patches are unable to successfully compete for food and space with species that favor edge habitats. The interior habitat species must retreat and build their nests in the patch interiors, away from the edges. Many of these species are uncommon because of the relative shortage of such habitat. At the same time, many edge species are quite common, and their populations are increasing. While it is important to conserve all native bird species, the uncommon and declining species are a higher priority than the common ones. *Because of these detrimental effects of edges, maximizing edge habitat is no longer a goal of wildlife managers.*

The relative amount of edge is related to a patch's size and shape. Because edge effects can extend so far into the interior, a small patch is essentially all edge habitat (Figure 1). This explains why large patches are generally better than smaller ones—they contain less edge habitat. Along those same lines, a long narrow patch might also be all edge habitat, while a large patch closer to the shape of a circle will contain less. A patch with a very irregular perimeter will have more edge than one with a smoother outline. Also, edge habitats are wider on the south side of habitat blocks than on the north side (especially for wooded habitat) due to the effects of additional sunlight and heat on plants. Therefore, it is important to maintain an outline that is not highly convoluted on the south side of habitat blocks. *If an irregular edge must be created for the sake of design, save it for the north side of the patch.* Also, *place roads, buildings, fairways, cart paths, and other development on the perimeter of habitat patches, rather than the interior*, where their presence would fragment the patch into smaller patches, creating more edge habitat.

Corridors

A **corridor** is a strip of habitat connecting two patches of similar habitat. For example, a strip of trees separating two fairways can be considered a corridor if it connects wooded patches at each end. Corridors are used by many animals for traveling between patches. One of the most common corridor types is the **riparian** corridor, which consists of a stream or river and the water-loving vegetation that grows on both sides. *Riparian corridors are extremely important to birds.* The rich, moist soils produce an abundance of riparian vegetation, along with a generous supply of insects. Riparian vegetation also leafs out sooner than upland vegetation, providing a source of insects for early spring migrants. As a result, riparian corridors provide a rich source of food, water, cover, and nest sites for birds. Although riparian habitat makes up only a small percentage of the total U.S. land area, it is used by at least one-third of the bird species. Because of their value to birds, *riparian corridors should always be protected.*

While many animals, including some bird species, will use corridors only a few yards wide for moving between patches, wider corridors will be used by more species. *Ideally, corridors for birds should be at least 30 yards wide, although 30 to 100 yards is better, and greater than 100 yards is best of all.* Narrow corridors provide nesting habitat for edge species, often to the detriment of other species. Narrow corridors also make it easier for predators such as raccoons to find nests, since they can work their way efficiently along a strip of vegetation without much wandering, and can find practically every nest. Because of these negative aspects of narrow corridors, management efforts should be directed at preserving wide corridors, and widening narrow corridors with additional plantings. Where vegetation other than turf separates adjacent fairways (such as trees, shrubs, or native grasses), *keep the fairways as narrow as possible to preserve the out-of-play areas as corridors for birds and other wildlife.*

Because birds are highly mobile, most don't require corridors as protective cover while moving between habitat patches. They just fly from one patch to the next, regardless of whether there is a connecting corridor or not. However, one group of birds does need corridors. These are birds that live in dense forests or shrubs, such as thrushes, kinglets, and some warblers. Some of these birds will not cross open areas, even if the opening is only 30 yards wide. These birds are unaccustomed to being away from protective cover, and prefer to take a longer route through the woods rather than a shortcut through the open. For these species, the open habitat of a golf course fairway could represent a barrier to movement. Wooded corridors on the course would benefit these birds by providing safe travel routes, which the birds would use to find feeding areas, nesting sites, and water sources.

Roads, trails, and paths should be kept away from corridors whenever possible. It's tempting to route a cart path along a picturesque stream, but building it would require removing corridor vegetation, and the traffic flow might be enough disturbance to keep birds away forever. Also, a path down the middle of a corridor changes it from one wide corridor to two narrow ones, and narrow corridors are used by fewer birds. Instead, run the path parallel to the corridor, and outside of it. Avoid routing a path so that it cuts across a corridor, which fragments the corridor into smaller, unconnected segments. Where a path must cross a corridor, it should do so at a right angle to minimize habitat loss and human disturbance.

Nature preserve design concepts

Biologists have studied the size, composition, and arrangement of patches, edges, and corridors to determine the best designs for nature preserves (Figure 5). These design principles can be applied to golf courses, where they will contribute to bird conservation. The goals of these principles are to minimize disturbance to nesting birds from sources outside of the habitat patch, to minimize the amount of potentially detrimental edge habitat, or to facilitate movement between habitat patches.

- Principle A: Large patches are better than small patches, because they contain more interior habitat and less edge habitat relative to their size.
- Principle B: Round is better than any other patch shape; round patches contain more interior habitat and less edge habitat relative to their size.
- Principle C: One large patch is better than several small patches because the large patch contains more interior habitat and relatively less edge habitat.
- Principle D: A wide corridor is better than a narrow corridor because it has more interior habitat and less edge habitat.
- Principle E: If patches are connected with corridors, it is better to have more than one route between patches in case a corridor is blocked or cut.
- Principle F: It is better to have patches close together than far apart, to make for easier, safer travel between patches.

Which habitat patches and corridors?

How do you select which areas to protect? Look at the habitat patches in terms of *size, shape, quality, proximity to high-quality and low-quality habitat patches, and connection with patches containing similar vegetation.* Also look for areas with uncommon bird species, large numbers of birds, or large numbers of bird species. Are there areas that are unsuitable for course construction, such as steep slopes or rocky ground? Set them aside as bird habitat. Areas such as springs, seeps, creeks, streams, and wetlands are generally unsuitable for inclu-

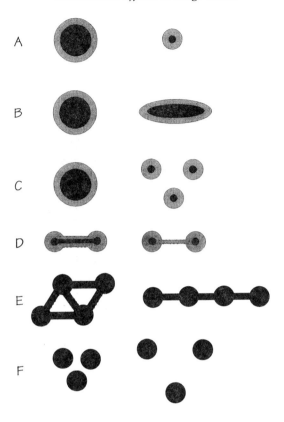

Figure 5. Design principles for habitat patches and corridors on golf courses. In A–D, the solid area represents interior habitat, the stippled area is edge habitat. In each pairing, the configuration on the left is preferable. See text for details.

sion in the golf course itself, but are of high value to birds. In out-of-play areas and zones unlikely to be played by golfers, such as below elevated tees or between the landing zone and green, leave native vegetation for birds (or replace exotic vegetation with native vegetation) (Figure 6).

How much habitat should be set aside? The best answer is "as much as possible." A bold move would be to set aside a core conservation area—a habitat patch of at least ten acres, round (or nearly round) in shape. Design the course around this natural feature. Narrow corridors and small habitat patches scattered around a typical golf course provide birds with very little nest area, but their value increases if a large habitat

Figure 6. Native or naturalized vegetation is a better choice than managed turf in out-of-play areas, like below elevated tees.

patch exists nearby. Birds will nest safely in the large area, and use all areas to search for food. The large area to be set aside should be one with high-quality habitat. If two high-quality patches are found on the property but cost or design constraints preclude protecting both, the decision as to which one to protect should be based on the regional value. In other words, the natural habitat that is uncommon in the region around the golf course should be preserved.

This is where enlisting the assistance of experts will help. Recruit dedicated amateurs—even very small towns have local birdwatching clubs or Audubon Society chapters, or people who are members of national birdwatching organizations. These people are a wealth of knowledge regarding local birdlife, and would probably be receptive to the idea of conducting bird surveys on the course, or in the area of a proposed course. Some local golfers might be knowledgeable about birds or other wildlife, or about native vegetation. Let them know that you are interested in preserving and improving bird habitat on the course, and that you are looking for assistance. Consider including a wildlife biologist on the planning team. Other sources of information include environmental consulting firms, conservation organizations, state wildlife agencies, county extension service agents, and nearby colleges and universities.

Creating habitat patches

You may be creating bird habitat where there was none, for example on farmland or a reclaimed mine or landfill. Restore the natural habitat by planting clusters of native trees and shrubs to attract birds. The birds will bring with them the seeds of fruits growing in nearby natural areas. Bird-borne seeds will germinate near the planted clusters, contributing to the number and diversity of plants growing on the restored area, at no cost. Planted clusters that include tall vegetation (trees and shrubs at least six feet tall) are more attractive to birds, so those clusters will have more bird-dispersed seedlings. Careful monitoring of which plants show up is necessary, however, and invasive, weedy plants should be aggressively controlled as soon as they appear.

If creating grasslands, use a mixture of short and tall native grasses, to provide structural diversity and create habitat for birds preferring each. Include native herbaceous plants in the tract, as most grassland species prefer low to moderate densities of them—they are used for nest cover and song perches. Germination and growth should be better if local seed sources are used.

Adjacent land use

Preserving and creating bird habitat on the golf course benefits birds on the course, but it is also possible to provide benefits off the course. A good way to extend the bird habitat beyond the course boundaries is to *coordinate habitat management with adjacent landowners*. If a neighboring business or industry can set aside a patch of habitat next to a patch that has been set aside on the course, the much larger patch that results will provide more habitat for birds. This may be the only way for some golf courses with limited natural habitat to create patches large enough to suit bird species that need large patches.

Encourage nearby homeowners to enroll in the National Wildlife Federation's Backyard Habitat Program, or Audubon International's Cooperative Sanctuary Program for Backyards. (Contact information is in Appendix 1.) Adjacent businesses can enroll in the National Wildlife Federation's Wildlife Habitat in the Workplace or Audubon International's program for corporate and business properties. Some state wildlife agencies promote similar programs. Each of these organizations can provide golf course neighbors with information on ways to improve habitat for birds and other wildlife, and the benefits of doing so.

Buffer zones

In addition to providing quality habitat, it is sometimes necessary to arrange the landscape elements in a way that protects birds from disturbance. Whenever people are nearby, birds experience stress. Even though a bird may not be bothered enough to fly away from a person, it is still stressed. Larger birds, in particular, tend to be more sensitive to human disturbance. Stressed birds sometimes eat less, or give less food to their young offspring, both of which result in lower body weight and lower survival rate. If the disturbance is intense enough, the bird may fly away, even if it is incubating eggs. In order for eggs to develop properly, they must be maintained at the proper temperature. If a disturbance causes an adult bird to leave the nest, even for a few minutes, it might be enough time for the eggs to chill (or overheat if exposed to the sun), killing the developing chicks. An unguarded nest is also in danger from predators and cowbirds. After the eggs hatch, adults protect young birds in the nest from the temperature extremes and predators. Whenever an adult is forced off the nest, the young are at risk. For these reasons, birds that are feeding or nesting should be protected from disturbance.

Buffer zones are simply a way to keep humans and birds apart. By doing so, they reduce the amount of disturbance to the birds. Reducing disturbance can be as simple as keeping people far away from nesting or feeding areas; this area that separates birds and people is one kind of buffer zone. Another type of buffer zone reduces stress in birds by blocking noise and visual disturbances with tall, dense vegetation. Given the low level of human activity on a golf course, and the fact that most golfers don't linger in one spot for more than a few minutes, *a 100-foot buffer zone should be sufficient. That distance can be further reduced if there is screening vegetation.* Human activity in the buffer zone should be limited through the use of signs or dense vegetation.

> Of course, it's not possible to protect *every* bird or nest on the golf course. Instead, use buffer zones to protect the nests of large birds (such as raptors), or to protect areas with large numbers of nests or birds. Wading birds and shorebirds often gather in large numbers for feeding (especially during migration), and some species nest together in large groups called colonies. Without buffer zones to protect such sites, disturbances can affect large

number of birds at once. Route the course so as to keep
golfers at least 100 feet away from such sites, or plant tall
vegetation (or protect existing vegetation) to act as a screen
between golfers and the birds.

Establishment of buffer zones should be site-specific. In other words,
it should take into consideration certain factors present at each site.
Factors to consider include the line of sight from the nest or feeding
area to potential disturbances, the nature of the disturbance, and the
history of the individual birds. If the view is blocked by vegetation or
topography, humans and birds can be closer together, and a narrower
buffer zone is acceptable. If the disturbance is continuous or nearly so,
such as noise from a busy parking lot, the buffer zone should be wider
than if the disturbance occurs infrequently, such as in a part of a fairway
that is not a landing zone. Some individual birds that have been in one
area for several weeks or longer can become accustomed to the human
activity that occurs there, so long as it is regular and predictable. They
will not be disturbed unless the activity changes somehow (for example,
if it becomes more frequent, louder, or begins to occur closer to them).
In general, it is better to be conservative and set up a wide buffer zone
if there is a chance that human activity will disturb the birds.

Golf courses in the landscape

The position of the golf course in the larger landscape can also affect bird conservation. Migrating birds often accumulate near the mar-
gins of unsuitable habitat, such as large urban areas, either to build up
their fat reserves for crossing the "hostile" habitat, or to rest after crossing it. Siting golf courses on the periphery of cities could help these
migrants by serving as important stopover habitat. Migrating birds lose
about 1% of their body weight per hour of flight, and need high-quality
habitat in order to quickly replenish their fat reserves. For a tired bird
flying over the concrete and asphalt of a metropolitan area, the sight of
a green golf course—with food, water, and a place to rest—must be a
welcome sight.

A golf course could also help protect natural areas by acting as a
buffer between natural and developed areas (Figure 7). The presence of
the course would block noise and the spread of exotic plants and do-

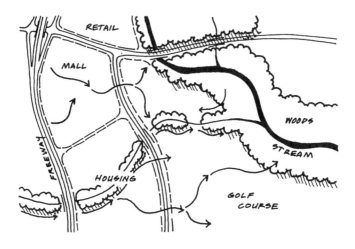

Figure 7. A golf course positioned next to a natural area can filter noise and stop the movement of exotic plants and animals from an urbanized area.

mestic animals from the developed area, and thus maintain the integrity of the natural area in a way that no other development could. This makes golf courses a good choice for development adjacent to natural areas. Of course, to be an effective buffer, a course would need to be populated by native plants, to prevent the spread of any exotics to the natural area.

Incorporate nature

Golf is the only sport where each playing field differs greatly from all others. The reason for that difference is the influence of the local environment on the course design—the constraints placed by topography, climate, vegetation, and the arrangement of landscape elements. Golf course designs should embrace and incorporate those natural constraints into unique courses, rather than accepting the artificiality of cookie-cutter course designs that have no distinguishing features regardless of their locale. Disturb as little of the existing native vegetation as possible. Route the course through existing openings. This is not only beneficial for birds; it is also more economical, since less vegetation must be cleared. By incorporating the natural environment, a course is not only made more appealing to golfers by virtue of its distinctiveness from other courses they may have played elsewhere, but it is also more attractive to birds and other wildlife by virtue of its conservation of the natural habitat unique to the area. Golf began on the windy coasts of Scotland, where it harmonized with nature, with all of its inconsistencies and irregularities. By returning to its origins, golf can benefit golfers and birds.

Key Points

1. Landscapes consist of three basic elements: patches, edges, and corridors.
2. Habitat edges may be detrimental to some bird species.
3. Large patches and corridors are better for many species, because they contain less edge habitat and more interior habitat.
4. Avoid strong contrasts in quality between adjacent patches.
5. Protect riparian areas and wetlands.
6. Coordinate habitat management with adjacent landowners.
7. Use buffer zones to protect the nests of large birds, large groups of nests, and large groups of feeding birds.

CHAPTER FOUR

CONSERVATION EFFORTS AT SMALL SCALES

If large-scale habitat manipulations are not practical or possible (as is generally the case for established courses), or if the goal is to make the course more attractive to *specific* bird species or species groups (such as hummingbirds or shorebirds), efforts should be focused on smaller scales. Here is the basic plan of action:

1. Determine which birds are potentially present on the course, based on the location of the course and the geographic ranges of North American birds (Appendix 4).
2. Use local birdwatchers or other knowledgeable people to compile a list of the birds actually present on the course.
3. Compare the two lists to see which birds could potentially be on the course but are missing, or are present but in low numbers.
4. Decide which missing or uncommon birds you want to attract to the course. (Use the guidelines in Appendix 5.)
5. Check the habitat requirements of those birds against the habitat found on the course to see where adjustments or changes can be made in order to make the course attractive to those species.
6. Integrate the habitat adjustments into the course management.
7. Evaluate the effectiveness of the habitat adjustments by periodically compiling a list of the birds present on the course (annually or every few years).

Some small-scale characteristics that can be manipulated include the internal structure of habitat patches, plant materials, snags, and water features. Protecting and enhancing natural features such as these often provides the greatest benefit to birds. On the other hand, *providing artificial features (feeders, nest boxes, and baths) probably contributes less to bird conservation than one would hope.* Such artificial enhancements benefit relatively few birds—bird feeders help only doves and songbirds that eat seeds, and nest boxes help only birds that nest in tree cavities. Also, artificial enhancements require a maintenance commitment, which should be enough to discourage any already over-burdened maintenance staff. On the plus side, birds are often easier to see when they are using artificial features. Getting a clear view of birds can create valuable educational opportunities and foster appreciation for birds among golfers and staff. With greater appreciation comes greater support for habitat protection and larger habitat enhancement projects. *A sound approach would be to provide both natural and artificial features.*

Structural diversity

Forest-dwelling birds view vegetation in their habitat as a set of vertical layers composed of the ground cover, low shrubs (0–3 feet), tall shrubs and short trees (3–10 feet), and taller trees (greater than 10 feet) (Figures 8 and 9). Birds segregate this layered habitat for nesting and searching for food, with each species using a unique combination of one or more of the layers. *If any layer is missing, the birds that use it will also be missing.* And because many birds use more than one layer, the layers must be provided together, such as tall trees above a shrub layer above a thick, leaf-litter layer. *The more layers provided in the habitat patches on the course, the more bird species will be attracted.* Accomplish this layering through a regular planting program to maintain a broad age (size) distribution of trees along with a well-developed understory of shrubs. And do not clean up leaf litter—the forest floor is one of the most important layers, as it houses many food items for birds, including seeds, insects, and small mammals.

Shrubs form an important layer in a diverse habitat. Adding this layer, especially if it includes fruit-bearing shrubs, offers benefits to many birds, such as protective cover close to the ground for ground-foraging birds, nest sites for shrub-nesting birds, and food for fruit-eating birds.

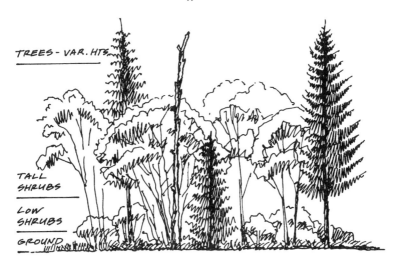

TREES - VAR. HTS.

TALL SHRUBS

LOW SHRUBS

GROUND

Figure 8. A forest contains several vegetation layers, and different birds use different layers for nesting and finding food. A wooded area that is missing layers will also be missing the birds that use them.

In addition, shrubs mature more quickly than trees, so birds can enjoy the benefits of dense, mature vegetation sooner.

Adding vertical diversity can have other benefits. Woodlots on golf courses tend to be small and isolated from larger areas of forest. One problem of isolated woodlots is their tendency to be much drier than larger woodlots because of their exposure to drying winds. One way to overcome this—and at the same time to add vertical diversity to a patch—is to plant shrubs and low trees around the outside of the patch to deflect wind over it, instead of allowing the wind to flow through. This has the added benefit of "softening" the abrupt edge between the woodlot and the open area. Bird nests often are more successful in patches with soft edges because the shrubs obstruct the view of predators that hunt by sight (such as crows).

One bonus of providing all of the vegetation layers: it can compensate somewhat for a patch's small size. A small patch of multilayered habitat will attract more species than a large patch of single-layered habitat. Also, a narrow corridor is more valuable if it contains structural diversity, which can offer more places to search for food or hide a nest.

Don't add layers that don't belong. Some areas are naturally simple habitats, and should stay that way in order to be attractive to the native

Figure 9. An example of multiple vegetation layers.

birds. Grasslands, for example, are essentially one layer, with the exception of scattered shrubs in some areas. Adding trees greatly reduces the attractiveness of the area to many grassland birds, and they will avoid it. Knowledge of the vegetation and habitat structure native to the area of the golf course is essential. Consult with local botanical or natural resource experts, and refer to the *Landscape Restoration Handbook* listed in the References section at the back of the book.

Another landscape characteristic of importance to birds is the horizontal distribution of plants. *Most birds prefer plants to be clustered rather than isolated.* Nests located within clusters of vegetation are more difficult for predators and cowbirds to find, so those nests are generally more successful. Also, birds can search for food more efficiently in clusters of plants, so they spend less time and expend less energy searching for food. One reason urban habitats are unsuitable for many bird species is that the woody vegetation is sparsely distributed. While plants in natural areas often grow in clusters, in urban areas (including golf courses) we find isolated trees and shrubs scattered over the landscape. Whenever possible, cluster plantings to increase their value to birds.

If the course doesn't already have one, *establish a planting program*. Set a goal of planting a certain number of plants each year, depending on budget constraints and the goals of the green committee. Don't just replace plants as they die, but also address long-term goals of expanding habitat patches and buffer zones, and filling gaps in corridors. A regular planting program will also ensure that habitat patches contain a diversity of tree and shrub sizes (ages), a result of plantings spread out over the years.

Planting with natives

A native plant is one that occurs naturally in a particular region, where it has been growing for thousands (or more) of its generations, without any help from humans. Every plant is a native *somewhere*. But planting with natives means using plant material that is native to your particular region. For example, even though paper birch is native to North America, it isn't native to *all* regions of North America. It is found naturally in the Great Lakes region, but not the Southwestern deserts. Someone wanting to plant native species on a golf course would

Figure 10. The unkempt, straw-colored native grasses in this picture provide an attractive visual contrast with the manicured turf.

need to know which plants are native to that particular area where the course is located. Again, consult with local experts or check the *Landscape Restoration Handbook.*

Planting with natives allows for a more natural look, as the new vegetation blends in with the existing (natural) vegetation, and the "wild" look provides a pleasing visual contrast with the manicured fairways (Figure 10). Native plants are also more attractive to birds. Researchers in urban areas have found that birds are more common where there is more native vegetation than exotic (ornamental) vegetation. This is true for many species of birds, regardless of their diets. Native plant species often harbor more insects than do exotics, and more insects means more food for insect-eating birds. Also, many exotic plants are sterile varieties, which offer no pollen or seeds or fruit for birds. Finally, native vegetation may be more appealing to birds for nesting. An example of this is the invasive Brazilian pepper—researchers in Florida found significantly fewer bird nests in stands of this exotic plant than in stands of native vegetation. The lesson here is that more birds are attracted to native plants than to exotics.

Occasionally, an exotic species is dangerous—even deadly—to birds. The most common eucalyptus in California, the blue gum (*Eucalyptus globulus*), was imported from Australia in the 1800s. Its flowers produce a sticky black resin that attracts insects, which in turn attract insect-eating birds. North American birds that forage for insects on the blue gum are smaller than their Australian counterparts, with shorter beaks. Australian birds can avoid the resin, but North American birds cannot, so it coats their feathers and beaks. The resin buildup can be so thick that it can clog the birds' nostrils, causing death by suffocation. In Australia, this is not a problem because the birds that use this tree are adapted to its characteristics. The case of the blue gum illustrates the importance of avoiding exotic plant materials, since the native birds are not adapted to them.

The low grasses of manicured fairways and greens do not provide suitable protective cover or nesting area for any bird species, although some species will search the grasses for food. In general, manicured turf offers little to meet the basic needs of birds. Native grasses and other vegetation are generally taller, and provide more food and places for birds to hide or build nests. Besides, using native plants should eliminate the need for mowing, irrigating, fertilizing, and applying pesticides in that area, since the native plants are adapted to the region's soil type, nutrient and precipitation levels, and insects. This saves time, materials, labor, and money.

If native plants are chosen, keep in mind their water requirements when laying out irrigation systems. Natives should thrive with natural precipitation, and supplemental watering is not only wasteful, it could also kill them. Instead of installing turfgrass in areas with native trees and shrubs, consider allowing natural ground cover to grow, and direct irrigation water away from the area.

Native plants that bear fruit are an excellent choice for birds. Some plants produce fruit that ripens during the summer months, such as elderberry and serviceberry. These fruits are generally high in fluids and sugar. Other plants, such as hackberry and dogwood, bear fruit that ripens during late summer and fall. These fruits are drier, with a higher fat content, and give fruit-eating birds an opportunity to pack on more fat to fuel their long migration. Even some birds that are insect-eaters during the breeding season switch to fruits during migration because of the energy boost they provide. Birds that do not migrate but remain in an area over the winter benefit from the energy provided by these fruits on cold winter days. Consider planting a variety of fruiting plants, with different maturity dates, to provide birds with a high-energy food source for summer breeding, fall migration, and winter survival. A list of native plants of value to birds is provided in Appendix 2. Whatever fruit-bearing trees or shrubs are planted, do not place them so that they overhang walkways, patios, or parking places because of the mess and staining caused by fallen fruit and by birds passing fruit.

Finally, golf courses have an environmental responsibility to use native plant materials. Exotic plant species often become invasive pests that replace native vegetation, without offering birds the food and nesting sites to which they are adapted. Exotic plants on a golf course can easily spread to nearby natural areas: seeds can be carried by wind, water, or animals, or the plants can spread by sprouting from the roots. Golf course personnel should be concerned about environmental effects beyond the borders of their golf course, and should avoid using exotic plant materials.

Snags

A snag is a dead, standing tree. To many people, snags are eyesores. But to many birds, snags are places to find food, watch for prey, build homes, and attract mates. Snags are used by at least 85 North American bird species, including many owls, woodpeckers, chickadees, swallows, and other songbirds. *Snags are so valuable to birds and other wildlife that their protection is an integral part of public forest management plans.* Snags should be protected on golf courses, too. Birds need large snags, at least six inches in diameter—the larger the snag the more opportunities for nesting and foraging. Snags can be made more aesthetically pleasing to golfers and homeowners by trimming back the branches. Trimming also reduces the chances that dead limbs will fall onto the course, which could be hazardous to golfers or course personnel. Leave 1 to 3 feet of each limb so birds can perch. Removing the top of the tree, where it narrows to about 5 inches in diameter, will also provide a margin of safety—these skinny treetops often snap off in high winds.

Recommended snag densities to benefit cavity-nesting birds range from 3 to 16 per acre of forest. Where snag density is lower, they can be created by killing live trees. Several methods have been tested, including girdling, injecting with herbicides, and even blasting the upper half of the tree with explosives. However, the most cost-effective method is to cut off the leaf- or needle-bearing portions of all limbs. (An easier but less effective method is to simply cut off the top one-third of the tree.) The tree will die because it has lost its leaves (or needles), which are necessary for photosynthesis. Insects will attack the dead tree and begin the decomposition process. Woodpeckers and other birds will feed on the insects. As the heartwood rots, woodpeckers and chickadees will excavate cavities. The tree you select for sacrifice should be in a group of other trees, rather than isolated or out in the open. Snags are even more beneficial in clusters of three or more, within a 10- or 15-yard radius, as this makes searching for food and nest sites easier.

Eventually, a snag will rot to the point that it will fall. Let fallen logs lie. A log on the ground still provides feeding and nesting sites for many species, and as it decomposes, it returns valuable nutrients to the soil.

Nest structures

When natural cavities are lacking, nest boxes are valuable for forest-dwelling species, such as woodpeckers and cavity-nesting songbirds. As a rule of thumb, add boxes where snag density is less than three per acre of forest. Plans for basic nest structures and information for specific species can be found in Appendix 3.

Below is some general information about artificial nest structures:

- Wood is the best building material for birdhouses, although commercial structures sometimes use plastic, ceramic, or even metal (e.g., for purple martin condominiums).
- The front panel should be rough on the inside of the box, to help birds climb up to the opening; cut shallow grooves across the panel if the wood is smooth.
- Do not paint or apply wood preservative to the insides of nest boxes.
- Nests may become infested with parasites (small insects, such as fleas and lice, that consume the blood, feather parts, and bits of skin of young birds). *Do not apply insecticides to nest structures to control parasites, flies, or any other insects.*
- Do not attach perches on the front of the boxes. They are not necessary and make the boxes more attractive to undesirable house sparrows.
- Avoid mounting boxes on posts that have vines growing up them, or other vegetation at the base of the post. Such vegetation provides a hiding place for predators, and aids them in climbing up to the nest box.
- Don't mount boxes near bird feeders, or the nesting pair will monopolize the feeder (and expend a lot of energy chasing away intruders).
- Position the box so that the opening is not obscured by branches or other objects, so as to leave the birds a clear flight path to and from the box.
- Most birds prefer to nest well away from human activity, so do not mount boxes near parking lots, building entrances, tee boxes, or other areas frequently used by humans (Figure 11).
- Do not open a box during the nesting season. Unnecessary disturbance at the wrong time could cause the birds to abandon the nest. The only exceptions to this are if it is necessary as part of a research project on nesting suc-

Figure 11. An area with high levels of human activity—this would *not* be a good place for a bird house, feeder, or bath.

cess, or for evicting wasps, squirrels, house sparrows, or starlings.

- Check all nest boxes for damage each fall or winter, and make repairs as necessary. Birds will not use leaky, drafty nest boxes.
- Nesting platforms should have drainage holes, or should be built of 2-by-4s with gaps between the boards. Build a crude "nest" of sticks on the platform to attract birds and get them started on nest building (Figure 12).

Some people suggest removing old nest material to eliminate parasites (such as mites, fleas, and blowflies) that can overwinter in a nest box. If abundant, these parasites can severely weaken young birds. Whether or not you should clean out the old nests depends on which bird species used the box. Purple martin houses, for example, should be cleaned out each year, but not wren boxes, since they will do the job anyway in the spring. Bluebirds, on the other hand, seem to prefer nest boxes with the old material still in them. If it's not clear what kind of bird is using a box, it's better to play it safe and clean it out.

Unfortunately, native birds sometimes don't get a chance to use nest boxes or natural cavities. European starlings aggressively acquire

Figure 12. An unfinished osprey nesting platform. Before ospreys will use this structure, it needs boards across the top to make it a true platform.

and defend such nest sites. This species has been extraordinarily successful, spreading across the continent from an initial introduction of 60 individuals in 1890 in New York City, increasing to an estimated 200 million today. Their enormous success is attributed to their broad diet, their aggressiveness, and their ability to exclude other cavity-nesters from nest sites all season. House sparrows also aggressively displace native cavity-nesters, often destroying their eggs and young birds, and squirrels will sometimes take over the larger nest boxes (screech owl or flicker size). These species can be discouraged by building nest boxes with the proper dimensions and placing them in the appropriate locations. (See Appendix 3.)

Wood duck nest boxes are traditionally placed on poles in the shallow water of a pond, or along the shoreline. While this highly visible placement is good for public relations, allowing the nest box to be seen by golfers and visitors to the course, it is not necessarily the best place as far as the ducks are concerned. A better alternative is to attach the nest box directly to a deciduous tree that is in or near water. A box could also be placed on a 6- to 8-foot post in shallow water, so long as there is a lot of woody vegetation around it to make it less obvious. Making wood duck nest boxes less conspicuous in this way improves their nesting success, because it reduces the incidence of "egg dumping." Egg dumping occurs when a female wood duck lays extra eggs in the nests of other wood ducks. This makes it harder for the other ducks to successfully incubate their own eggs, and so fewer eggs hatch. Egg dumping occurs far more often in areas with very visible nest boxes.

Besides nest boxes, other artificial nest structures can be provided. Nest boxes with open fronts are sometimes used by robins, phoebes, and barn swallows. Simple wooden platforms on top of utility poles are readily accepted by ospreys and other large birds (Figure 12). Local power companies are often willing to donate a pole and the labor to erect it.

Feeders

In general, artificial feeding with bird feeders does not contribute much to bird conservation. Birds clearly prefer natural food sources, as research in urban areas has shown that feeders provide less than 25% of their food, and only serve to supplement natural food sources. So why bother with feeders? Birds at a feeder are valuable educational tools. Feeders are a visible example of your efforts to improve conditions for birds on the course and a clear demonstration that birds actually use the course. Also, the noise and activity of birds at a feeder will often attract other birds, even birds that do not visit feeders. The presence of the feeder birds indicates to other birds that the area is safe and that food is available. Finally, birds with access to a feeder during winter have higher survival rates than those that have to rely entirely on natural food sources, because of the constant supply of food in the feeder.

In general, more birds will use feeders in the winter than during the summer. Natural sources of food are more plentiful during summer than winter, and birds do not need to supplement their diet. Also, many species of birds defend the **territory** around their nest during summer. If that territory happens to include the bird feeder, probably only one pair will be able to use it. On the other hand, most birds do not defend territories in winter, and even travel together in flocks containing different species, looking for food. During spring and fall, migrating birds may visit the feeder to help them fuel up for their long flights. This is a chance to assist species that breed farther north, which you would not otherwise encounter.

Feeder types: Many, many types of bird feeders are available. Each is designed to meet the needs of a particular group of birds, so selecting a feeder will depend on the birds that use the course and the species you want to encourage. The simplest type is a platform feeder, which is simply a flat surface, usually with a lip around the perimeter to retain seed. This type of feeder is for birds that forage on the ground, so it should be placed directly on the ground or mounted on legs or a short pole no more than a foot high. Two other standard feeder designs are available. The first is the hopper type. The advantages of this feeder are that it is popular with many different bird species, it keeps the seed dry, and it has a large capacity (so it doesn't have to be refilled as often). The other standard design is the tube feeder. This feeder is generally for smaller birds, such as goldfinches, and smaller seed, such as niger (thistle). Basic bird feeders are available at many retail stores, but a broader selection and helpful information are available from stores that specialize in bird feeding supplies.

Feed: Don't put a lot of effort into selecting a feeder and then put the wrong seed in it. Inexpensive seed mixes usually contain seeds that few birds eat, and much of the seed ends up wasted on the ground, where it can attract pests such as mice and rats. A premium mix will contain seed proven to be attractive to a variety of birds. The cost of premium seed is higher, but less of it is wasted. You may have to do some experimentation to determine the best seed for birds in your area. Some common bird feeder seeds:

- *Black oil sunflower.* By far the favorite bird seed, this small seed is easier to open than the larger striped sunflower seed, has a high oil content for energy, and is preferred by many birds, including finches and chickadees. If you can provide only one type of seed, it should be this small sunflower.
- *Striped sunflower.* This seed is difficult for some small birds to crack open, but attractive to jays, chickadees, grosbeaks, finches, cardinals, and some sparrows.

- *Niger.* Commonly known as thistle (don't worry—this is not the invasive Canada thistle, but the seed of an African plant, and has been heat-treated to prevent germination), this very small seed is popular with finches and goldfinches.
- *Millet.* This seed is preferred by many ground-feeding birds, including sparrows and doves.
- *Safflower.* This seed is preferred by cardinals, and is also attractive to sparrows and doves.
- *Peanut hearts, kernels, or chips.* These are attractive to jays, finches, sparrows. They are also highly prized by squirrels, so peanuts should not be offered if squirrels are a problem.

Insect-eating birds like woodpeckers and chickadees will be attracted to a suet feeder. Suet is rendered beef fat—often the thick, waxy fat from around the kidneys—which can serve as an energy source for birds. This is especially important during cold winter months, when insects may be harder to find. Suet cakes are commercially available—many include a blend of seed or dried fruit or even dried insects. Commercially rendered suet can be offered any time of year, regardless of temperature, but it is far more important to offer it during the winter.

Don't feed birds popcorn, bread, donuts, or other baked goods. These foods attract the nuisance species—starlings and house sparrows—when you should be doing all you can to discourage them. Also, such artificial foods are alien to birds, do not provide the nutrients they need, and spoil quickly; moldy foods can sicken or even kill birds.

Feeder placement: Because different bird species search for food at different heights, food should be offered at different heights. Platform feeders should be just a foot or two above the ground, while other feeders can be mounted on posts or hung from trees at a height of 6 to 10 feet. Suet feeders and thistle feeders can be placed even higher, although it is not necessary. Place several feeders in the same area, at different heights, and with different types of food. This will attract a more interesting variety of birds, in greater numbers, than if only one feeder was available.

Feeders should be placed near trees and shrubs, to give birds a safe place to land before coming to a feeder (but not too close; see the information on squirrels, below). Birds like to land in the safety of the branches of the trees or shrubs and check the area for predators before flying to the feeder. Also, some birds, such as chickadees, need a branch against which they can hold a seed while they hammer away at the hull with their bill. Place feeders where the birds will be easily seen by golfers and other visitors, as this will demonstrate your commitment to providing a safe home for birds on the course.

Feeder problems: Spilled seed can cause management problems. Ground-feeding birds and squirrels will damage the grass under the feeder as they search for spilled seed. Sunflower seed hulls can accumulate and kill grass. Spilled seed can germinate, resulting in a small forest of sunflowers or other plants. Herbicide application below a feeder is not recommended. Instead, mount a seed tray under the feeder to catch hulls and spilled seed, and clean it out as necessary. Clear the sod away from under the feeder and leave it as bare ground, then periodically remove unwanted plants, seeds, and hulls manually.

Squirrels can wreak havoc on bird feeding efforts. They will keep birds away from the feeders and eat large quantities of seed and suet, sometimes damaging the feeders in the process. Squirrels are very determined, and their ability to get around squirrel-proofing efforts has inspired numerous magazine articles and books. Some feeders are specifically designed to exclude them, and baffles, funnels, and disks are available to keep them from climbing up poles or along wires to reach feeders. For additional protection, do not hang feeders from tree limbs or position them within leaping distance of a branch, rooftop, or other elevated surface—no closer than 8 or 10 feet.

One drawback to artificially concentrating birds at feeders is the increased likelihood of transmitting disease throughout the local bird population. Several different diseases can afflict birds at feeders, and they affect birds differently. Watch the feeders for birds that seem less alert, or have unusual growths around their eyes or beaks. Any type of feeder can spread disease, but the worst are improperly maintained platform feeders. The problem comes from allowing bird droppings or rotting seed to remain in the feeder. Wet or moldy seed should be discarded immediately. All feeders should be cleaned at least once a month with a solution of 1 part bleach to 9 parts water. Allow the feeder to dry thoroughly before refilling with seed. If dead or diseased birds are found at the feeder, take it down, dispose of the seed, thoroughly clean the feeder, wait at least 10 days before putting it back up, and put it in a new location. If you're unable to commit the time and effort needed to maintain feeders, perhaps you can recruit homeowners to "adopt" a feeder on the course near their home, or near a path they use frequently, volunteering to clean and fill the feeder as needed.

Some people are concerned that concentrating birds around feeders makes them more susceptible to predators. Cooper's hawks and other raptors commonly visit suburban feeders during the winter months, hunting for songbirds. Such predation should not be viewed negatively, but accepted as part of the natural order. Each species has an ecological role to play; birds can be both predator and prey, and each role is equally important.

Baths

Birds need to bathe regularly to remove dirt and oils that accumulate in their feathers. If they do not bathe, their feathers become matted, and matted feathers are no good for insulation or flying. Birds usually bathe in water, but they will also use fine dirt or even snow. Bathing is so important that birds will bathe even when temperatures are well below freezing. If natural sources of water are scarce on the course, or you want to attract birds to a particular area (near the clubhouse, for example), provide an artificial bird bath. A bath will be used by many different songbird species. A wide variety of bird baths are available—some quite decorative and others plain but functional. Look for one that is no deeper than 3 inches, with gradually sloping sides to accommodate small birds. Bird baths should be placed near trees or shrubs so that birds have perching sites while waiting their turn at the bath and for preening their feathers and drying off after their bath. Do not place a bath closer than about 10 feet to an area with dense, low vegetation (0 to 2 feet tall), which could provide a hiding place for cats or other predators. As with feeders, baths require regular cleaning to reduce the likelihood of disease transmission. A thorough scrubbing weekly with household bleach (1 part bleach to 9 parts water) should be sufficient. Rinse thoroughly before refilling with fresh water; adding one or two drops of bleach per gallon of water will help control disease organisms without harming the birds.

Most bird baths will crack if the water is allowed to freeze. *Never use additives such as anitfreeze or salt to keep baths from freezing, as they can kill birds.* Instead, drain the water before freezing weather, and cover the basin or tip the bath on its side to prevent accumulation of liquid. The best solution is to install one of the small heating units that are designed specifically for keeping bird baths ice-free. They cost little to operate, and allow birds access to water during winter, when water is much needed and often harder to find than food.

Brush piles

The limbs removed from trimming snags and maintaining trees on the course can be heaped up to create a brush pile. Many songbirds, especially ground-dwelling species, will use the safety of the tangled branches for foraging, resting, and hiding from predators. Criss-cross large logs and branches to form a 12- to 15-foot-diameter base for the pile, then heap smaller branches on top to a height of about 5 feet. Replenish the pile as it settles.

Water features

More than half the country's original wetlands have been lost— filled in for agriculture or other development. But golf courses generally embrace wetlands as a feature, and course developers sometimes build them when they are absent. One of the most important conservation roles for golf courses is wetlands protection. Wetlands can filter sediment, phosphorous, nitrogen, pesticides, and heavy metals, and provide aesthetic amenities. They can also serve as important habitat for many kinds of birds, especially wading birds and shorebirds, but also many songbirds and raptors.

As with other habitat patches, a pond or wetland should be as large as possible to offer the greatest benefit to birds. A good starting size is 2.5 acres, although birds will certainly use smaller ones. Irregular shorelines on ponds will reduce erosion due to wave action, and allow more birds to use the pond (fewer territorial squabbles will occur, since the birds won't be able to see each other well). Ponds with gently sloping bottoms (1 foot of drop in every 10 feet of run) or littoral shelves (shallow water areas adjacent to deeper water) will provide habitat for more species of wading birds and shorebirds, and will create proper conditions for the growth of emergent vegetation. Up to half the water surface area should be 2 feet deep or less.

Structure: A snag or log in the shallow water or along the shoreline will provide a popular place for perching and resting by a number of bird species. Overhanging vegetation or nearby trees will provide perching locations. If there are few perches, place an artificial perch of wood or metal in shallow water—this should be a post extending about 6 feet above the water, topped by a crossbar 2 feet long and 1 to 2 inches in diameter. Islands in ponds will provide safe homes for animals such as turtles, but they're also popular nesting sites for ducks and geese. Few other bird species will benefit from islands. If waterfowl are not overly abundant on the course, consider creating small islands. If waterfowl are already a problem, don't create any new islands, and remove existing islands or make them less attractive to waterfowl by planting dense shrubs or tall wetland vegetation.

Vegetation: Adding floating and submerged plants will help reduce algal blooms by regulating oxygen levels in the pond. Adding shoreline and emergent plants to a pond will help filter debris and nitrates from runoff, while creating protective cover for many birds and their prey. A 50:50 ratio of emergent vegetation to open water provides good habitat for many bird species. Fluctuating water levels are problematic, as the plants are alternately exposed and flooded. However, some shoreline plants— such as spike rush and arrowhead—can tolerate fluctuation and should be considered for ponds with unstable water levels. Most wetland plants are easily transplanted from other areas by harvesting rhizomes and tubers in the spring and burying them in the mud in shallow water. Some seeds and plants are available commercially from firms specializing in habitat restoration. If golfers insist on having turf right down to the shoreline of fairway ponds, add wetland plants along the pond's edge in out-of-play areas, where they won't interfere with play (Figure 13).

Additional ideas

Some courses have hired naturalists to guide environmentally sensitive course management, conduct wildlife surveys, monitor water quality, conduct training workshops for staff, lead tours for club members, school groups, or other interested parties, and produce educational materials such as signs and pamphlets describing the natural resources of the course. Some courses allow birdwatchers to visit the course. This produces public relations benefits, as word spreads about the numbers

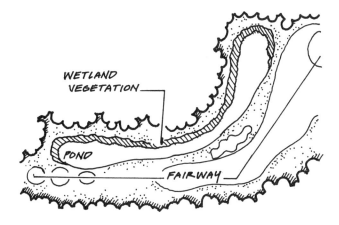

Figure 13. Wetland plants added to the out-of-play side of a water hazard, to provide bird habitat without interfering with play.

and types of birds that have found a home on the course, and the environmentally responsible management activities occurring on the course. To avoid conflicts with golfers, birders can be restricted to the back nine in the early morning, and the front nine in the late afternoon.

> *Key Points*
> 1. Work with natural habitat features first, then artificial features.
> 2. Provide each vertical layer of habitat: ground, low, medium, and tall vegetation.
> 3. Don't add vegetation layers that don't belong.
> 4. Plant in clusters, rather than isolated plants.
> 5. Establish a regular planting program.
> 6. Plant species native to your area.
> 7. Leave large snags standing.
> 8. Provide artificial nest structures for specific species by meeting their requirements for size and location.
> 9. Place bird feeders and bird baths 8 to 10 feet from trees, and clean them regularly.
> 10. Provide a variety of water depths, perching sites, and vegetation with water features.

CHAPTER FIVE

COURSE MAINTENANCE

Pesticide use

Insecticides are usually applied during periods when insect levels are highest, which tend to coincide with the bird breeding period. This is when birds are most active in hunting for insects. As a result, breeding birds are at a particularly high risk of exposure to these chemicals. Birds can be contaminated by direct contact with the product, by eating insects that have been treated, or by eating granular products (mistaking the granules for seeds or grit). Acute effects of contamination by organophosphorus or carbamate insecticides include convulsions, paralysis, and death. Sublethal effects include weight loss, decreased cold tolerance, lethargy, reduced care of young, and decreased growth rates of young. A loss of insect prey can also force birds to change their diet or their foraging territory, even to the point of shifting their home several miles to someplace where insects are plentiful (i.e., where no insecticides are applied). Making the course safer and more attractive for birds might require using fewer insecticides, and accepting some insect damage.

A number of courses around the country do not use pesticides. Reaching a pesticide-free state requires an even higher commitment to maintenance than is found on courses maintained conventionally. Hand-pulling weeds is time-consuming, but it can be done, even in areas where it might seem impossible. At one course in Florida, each member of the maintenance staff has a daily quota of weeds, a manageable number from 10 to 30. That may not seem like much, but over the course of a year it adds up to over 14,000 weeds pulled by hand rather than treated with herbicides.

If a course decides to reduce pesticide use, the toughest obstacle to overcome is acceptance by golfers of conditions that are less than picture-perfect. Educate golfers through signs and brochures, and promote tolerance of mosquitoes and other insects and the occasional brown spot and renegade weed. Remind them that golf is a sport that has always been coupled with the natural world, and that many of the historic courses of Europe are "wilder" than American courses.

For many courses, however, complete elimination of pesticides is not practical. But any reduction in pesticide use will benefit birds. Integrated Pest Management (IPM) is a strategy for reducing pesticide use by establishing tolerable levels of turf and plant damage, and treating problems only when they exceed those levels. The first step in treatment is altering cultivation practices (such as irrigation or mowing, or by replacing the affected plants with a different variety), then by physical treatment of the problems (such as hand-pulling weeds or setting traps), next by biological treatment (employing natural predators such as ladybugs, or applying organic-based control products such as the bacterium *Bacillus thuringiensis*). Chemical treatments are used only as a last resort. If chemicals are eventually used, they are only applied in the damaged areas (as opposed to a blanket application over large areas), and at the lowest effective application rate. Golf industry sources are able to help you set up an IPM program, so that won't be covered here. For more information, contact the Golf Course Superintendents Association of America. (Their address is in Appendix 1.)

An IPM program benefits birds directly. Reduced pesticide use means fewer opportunities for birds to come in contact with the chemicals, thereby eliminating the problems of contamination. Also, golf courses that implement IPM programs retain more diverse insect populations, which means more prey available for birds. Conventional pest management, on the other hand, utilizes broadcast application of insecticides, eliminating target and nontarget insects, many of which are important food sources for birds. If insect populations are allowed to peak and wane naturally, birds will generally keep the populations in check, preventing them from reaching outbreak levels. Birds are so effective at consuming insects that they should be considered an integral part of the IPM program. And although birds cannot control a large outbreak once it occurs, allowing the infestation to run its course benefits birds, since insect outbreaks provide a superabundant food supply, allowing breeding birds to raise more young. Migrating birds benefit, too. In fact, researchers have concluded that some migrating bird species *must* find areas with insect outbreaks in order to eat enough to provide the energy necessary for their long-distance flights.

Managing habitat patches

The simplest start to naturalizing a habitat patch is to simply stop managing it. Without regular mowing, fertilizing, or irrigating, cultivated grass species will often be replaced with native species (some situations may require sowing or planting native species). The native vegetation will be taller, with more insects and more kinds of insects to feed birds. If desired, these areas can be mowed seasonally or annually to keep down woody vegetation, although it would be preferable to rotate the mowing among patches rather than cut them all at once, so that at any given time there are patches of tall vegetation and patches of short vegetation. If possible, native grasslands should not be mown. If they must be cut, it should occur in the late winter or early spring, which will allow them a season of growth before winter, when they can provide cover and food for birds. Mowing in late spring will interfere with nesting, so hold off on mowing until after young birds have left their nests, usually after late July or early August. If possible, native grasslands should be cut only every second or third year, with different patches cut on a rotating basis. Cut no more than 50 to 60% of any large patch (greater than 25 acres) at a time, or mow entire small patches on a rotating basis, mowing about 20% of the patches each year (so that each patch is mowed once every 5 years). This should be sufficient to eliminate woody vegetation and maintain diverse grassland habitat.

Although mowing is the easiest method of keeping down woody vegetation in grasslands, controlled burning is often the preferred method. Burning has the added advantage of removing excess plant material and recycling nutrients faster than through simple decomposition. Burn grassland tracts very early in spring (March to early April) or late fall/early winter (October and November). Allow the fire to burn part way into adjacent woods, rather than creating a sharp fire break or edge. This "feathering" of the burned area should reduce nest predation. The complexities of planning and executing a controlled burn— air temperature, wind speed, humidity level, fuel conditions, personnel safety, suppression plans, etc.—are beyond the scope of this manual. Consult with local fire officials and your state wildlife agency for guidance and any necessary permits before starting a burning program. Keep in mind that such large management activities may attract the attention not only of golfers, but the local community as well. Use such events to promote the golf course and the environmentally friendly management techniques used.

Other types of habitat patches require their own management regimes. Wetlands and some shrublands require periodic burning to rejuvenate the vegetation. Check with local botanical experts to determine if the course contains any such fire-dependent vegetation. Forested patches and patches with desert vegetation need little attention. Just make sure they do not receive unnaturally high levels of fertilizer or irrigation.

Complaints from golfers about the unkempt appearance of habitat patches can be addressed through education. Explain the benefits of these areas to wildlife, and the benefits to the golf industry of providing wildlife habitat. Speak with golfers on the course, put up signs, or create pamphlets or information sheets to distribute. Golfers can be kept out of protected areas through the use of signs (Figure 14), or natural barriers such as large logs or thorny vegetation like wild roses or blackberries. Some courses even impose fines or revoke privileges when golfers ignore signs and enter environmentally sensitive areas.

Other maintenance issues

Although removing ground vegetation or the lower limbs of trees greatly simplifies finding golf balls in the rough, birds need that vegetation as protective cover from predators and humans (Figure 15). A golf course without that sort of protective cover is far less attractive to birds, and they will find other places to make their homes. If golfers insist on it, lower tree limbs can be removed from trees that stand alone or form part of a narrow corridor; isolated trees and narrow corridors provide little bird habitat anyway. However, avoid removing lower limbs from trees that are in clusters or form part of a habitat patch.

Food scraps and other garbage make an attractive and easy meal for many birds and mammals. Some of those species, such as jays, crows, and raccoons, might finish off their meal with a dessert of bird eggs or young birds. Don't encourage or artificially support these predators by

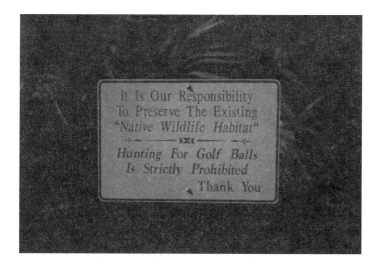

Figure 14. Signs can be used effectively to educate golfers about wildlife habitat.

leaving garbage readily accessible. They can find enough natural foods to live on, so keep trash containers securely covered.

European starlings and house sparrows take over nest boxes and natural cavities that should be homes for native birds. But they also like to nest on buildings. Any small crevice or opening is attractive to these species, including drain spouts, open eaves, ventilation louvers, gaps between architectural elements, and openings formed by decorative features. Even though they are not taking these artificial nest sites away from native species, if the nests are successful, some of the surplus birds might move into other areas of the course, where they will displace native birds. Whenever possible, cover or screen openings on structures that might be used as nest cavities. In early spring, watch for signs of nest construction on course buildings (starlings or house sparrows carrying grass, twigs, or other nesting material into openings), and take steps to restrict the birds' access.

Cats are used on some golf courses for controlling rodents in buildings. However, in addition to killing rodents, free-roaming cats kill many other wildlife species, including birds. For example, researchers have estimated that cats kill 26 million birds in Virginia and 39 million birds in Wisconsin *each year*. Such proficient hunting is contributing to the declines of rare bird species in several states. One reason cats are so

Figure 15. Trees with manicured turf underneath. While this is suitable habitat for some species, including the bluebirds using this nest box, more species could be attracted to the area in the background if at least part of it contained dense shrubs and a thick leaf layer.

devastating to bird populations has to do with their innate *need* to hunt, even if they are well fed by their owners. Whereas some predators will stop hunting for a time after eating, a full stomach does nothing to dull a cat's desire to hunt. Rather than rely on cats, golf courses should use mouse traps and chemical controls, which are safer for birds and often more effective at controlling undesirable rodents.

Because insects are important in the diets of so many bird species, no insects should be killed unless absolutely necessary. A good place to start is by eliminating any electric "bug zappers" on the course. Rather than killing mosquitoes or other biting insects, these devices kill mostly moths and beetles, two important food items for birds. While they may look and sound impressive as they "zap" bugs, they are actually destroying food essential for the survival of birds on the golf course.

Key Points

1. Insecticides can kill or incapacitate birds, or reduce the populations of insects on which they depend for food.
2. Reduce insecticide use through an Integrated Pest Management program.
3. Maintain grassland patches by mowing or burning to control woody vegetation.
4. Educate golfers about the value of habitat patches.
5. Keep garbage securely covered.
6. Close off openings on buildings that could be used as nest cavities by undesirable birds.
7. Remove cats from the course.
8. Remove electric bug zappers.

CHAPTER SIX

PROBLEMS WITH BIRDS

Wild, native birds are protected by federal and state statutes, and harming them is a punishable offense. The only birds that are not protected by federal law are rock doves (pigeons), European starlings, and house sparrows, all nonnative species. However, because of the difficulties of identifying bird species accurately, no problem birds should be physically harmed. Persistent problems with birds should be brought to the attention of your state wildlife agency.

Waterfowl

Many people find ducks and geese beautiful to watch, in flight and on ponds. But these birds can cause significant problems when they gather in large numbers. Waterfowl populations are often high in urban areas, especially in winter, due to warmer temperatures found in cities (which allows for more open water during the winter), hunting restrictions, supplemental feeding by humans, and the presence of numerous ponds surrounded by open, grassy areas. Golf courses provide very attractive, almost ideal, habitat for waterfowl. However, ducks and geese damage turf by pulling out grass plants while feeding, and leave behind droppings that offer lots of mess with little fertilizer value. Canada Geese, in particular, cause problems—they are the number one maintenance problem on many courses.

Numerous strategies have been used to discourage ducks and geese, such as spraying turf with bad-tasting chemicals. But most techniques have proven costly and only temporarily effective. Long-term solutions involve habitat manipulation. Waterfowl favor ponds with less than 50% of the shoreline occupied by emergent vegetation, since they prefer an unobstructed view as they move from pond to upland. It might be possible to discourage them by letting vegetation grow up around the pond to a height that is over their heads, blocking their view. Don't mow these areas, or plant shoreline vegetation or a low hedge. Also, remove islands from water bodies, which the birds use for nesting or resting.

A drastic solution sometimes tried by wildlife agencies is capturing and relocating flocks of nonmigratory geese. Within flocks, geese are organized into subflocks—small groups of birds that forage and rest together. Control by capturing and relocating can be directed at the subflock level, rather than attempting to remove all birds. In other words, it is possible to remove just the problem birds—those birds that habitually use an area where they are not wanted. However, translocating is expensive, not always highly successful (many of the birds will return), and is often accompanied by media coverage and controversy. Also, it is becoming increasingly difficult to find someplace that will accept the birds. Another drastic solution is the scheduling of special hunts, where allowable by law. Again, these are often controversial.

Overabundant geese and ducks grazing on turf can be driven from a course by repeated harassment. Chasing them with golf carts or maintenance equipment until they fly off can be effective, as can the use of cracker shells, available from your state wildlife agency. But the most promising technique found so far is harassment by a dog. A fast, persistent dog that chases the birds until they take off can be extremely effective. Even birds that have grown oblivious to humans will still flee from a dog, which they recognize as a predator. A number of courses around the country have used this technique successfully. Herding breeds such as border collies seem to be the most effective—since they have a strong instinct to herd the birds—but probably any breed can be trained to pursue them. The key to making this work is persistence—the birds must be harassed each time they land on the course, and the harassment must continue until all the birds in a flock take flight. The idea is to disrupt the birds' roosting and grazing routines, to keep them from developing a pattern based on habit, which would be difficult to break. Be sure to check first with local wildlife officials regarding the legality of any type of harassment.

Nest defenders

Another bird problem that golf courses sometimes experience is when aggressive birds defend their nests against humans. Kingbirds, mockingbirds, and many raptors are known to dive at humans that come too close to their nests. Perhaps the most notorious example is the Mississippi kite. These raptors are fiercely protective of their nests, and will defend them against humans, particularly small humans (women and children). Kites will defend their nests even when the humans have no intention of causing harm. To the birds, their very presence is a threat. Nest defense involves one or two (sometimes more) birds diving and occasionally striking the person. Injuries are usually limited to lacerations, which sometimes require stitches, although more serious injuries can occur as people try to avoid the diving birds. Your management response should start with posting signs to inform golfers about the birds and their behavior. If possible, restrict human access in at least a 20- to 30-yard buffer zone around the nest tree—kites generally ignore people, provided they do not come very close to the nest. After the young have left the nest, the signs can come down. In the case of a nest tree that is problematic each year, a very effective strategy is to place life-size models of kites in the nest trees, and 20 to 30 yards on either side, before the kites arrive in the spring. The kites think the nest site is already occupied by another pair, and will look for a new nest site, hopefully farther away from golfers. Contact your local wildlife agency to inquire about the availability of kite models. In extreme cases, wildlife officials may transplant eggs and nestlings into the nests of kites in more rural areas, and the offending pair will stop defending its nest.

Woodpeckers

Woodpeckers drum up numerous complaints from property owners each spring. In the mind of a woodpecker, a wooden-sided building is just a big stump. They hammer on it for the same reasons they hammer on tree trunks—to proclaim their territory and attract a mate, to get at insects under the surface of the wood, or to excavate a nest cavity. The first reason is the most common, the third one the least. The good news is that the drumming usually causes little or no damage, and usually ends once the breeding season is over (by early summer). The bad news is that they can cause quite a bit of aggravation in the meantime. Because the birds' instincts are so strong, no completely effective methods have been found for deterring this behavior. The best solution may be repeatedly (and harmlessly) harassing the birds, such as spraying them with a garden hose whenever they land on the building. Hanging aluminum pie plates or shiny metal strips in the favored area may help for a while. Windsocks or pennants will also work, and should draw fewer complaints about their appearance. Birds hammering rapidly on the roof or other high points, or on metal objects, are probably proclaiming their territory. If possible, cover drumming sites with a soft material, to deaden the sound and thus reduce their attractiveness. Birds hammering slowly on the side of a building are probably either searching for food or creating a nest cavity. Fill in or cover with metal any holes the birds create. Finally, protecting snags on the course may provide woodpeckers with a natural outlet for their instincts so they have no reason to drum on buildings.

Perching flocks

Birds sometimes gather in large numbers to perch on buildings or in trees. Besides noise, the mess from their droppings is annoying and a potential human health hazard. One popular method of discouraging such perching is by making the birds think the area is under the watchful eye of a predator. However, plastic owls, snakes, or other devices are only effective if they are moved to a new location every two or three days. Birds learn quickly that the stationary figure is not a threat. Once a few bold birds land near it, others will quickly figure out that there is nothing to fear, and soon birds will be perching on your plastic owl's head. The same is true of other repellants, such as balloons with a giant "eye," aluminum pie plates, or metal strips that move in the wind. Birds are very adaptable, and get accustomed to the presence of such deterrents unless they are relocated regularly. Physical barriers can prevent birds from perching on ledges, windowsills, or other narrow perch sites. These barriers generally consist of metal or plastic spikes that harmlessly block birds from landing where they are not wanted. An undesirable option is the use of adhesive strips or chemical barriers, as these products can injure or even kill birds.

Collisions with windows

An estimated 100 million birds are killed in the United States each year in collisions with windows, and the actual number may be considerably higher. Window strikes rank second behind hunting in total number of human-caused bird deaths. Windows are responsible for more deaths than bird damage control efforts, scientific research, pollution, vehicle collisions, and collisions with towers and other tall structures. The problem is the birds cannot always see the glass, and sometimes see instead an inviting reflection of sky and vegetation. Large panes (at least 2 square yards) near ground level are particularly lethal. Some people tape paper hawk silhouettes to windows as a deterrent, but they probably don't fool any birds, since birds can easily tell the difference between a hungry falcon diving at 60 mph and a flat, motionless, paper falcon. However, silhouettes do serve to make the surface of the glass more obvious. A falcon silhouette is not necessary—any shape should suffice. However, under certain lighting conditions, any silhouette taped to the *inside* of the window will be invisible to birds on the outside, due to reflections in the glass. Also, birds sometimes attempt to fly around a silhouette. Even if many silhouettes were put on a window, birds might still try to fly through any gaps if they can see vegetation or sky on the other side, or a reflection of them. For these reasons, collisions with windows cannot be significantly reduced with silhouettes. An effective (but potentially unsightly) option is placing fine netting (available from garden supply centers) or streamers of cloth or metal in front of the window, to act as physical barriers. Also, a window angled slightly toward the ground will present birds with reflections of the ground, instead of the sky and trees, so they will be less likely to fly into it. Finally, be aware of the potential for window collisions when positioning bird-attracting features. Fruiting trees and shrubs, bird feeders, and birdbaths should be positioned either well away from windows (at least 15 feet) or very close to windows (within a few feet).

Key Points

1. Use a trained dog to chase overabundant waterfowl from the course.
2. Establish temporary buffer zones around the nests of aggressive birds.
3. Discourage unwanted woodpeckers and other birds with repeated hazing or physical barriers.
4. Reduce collisions with windows by blocking the glass, or by careful positioning of bird-attracting features.

CHAPTER SEVEN

HIGHLIGHTED BIRDS

Some birds are more likely than others to turn up on a golf course. The birds presented here are good candidates for management activities, because they will probably use golf courses, they are in need of conservation efforts, and they respond well to specific management actions.

Loggerhead shrike

The loggerhead shrike got its name because its head seems too large for its body ("loggerhead" is another way of saying "blockhead," and is indeed descriptive of this bird). Another name for this bird is "butcherbird," for it is a bird of prey. It lives in open country, where it hunts primarily large insects, such as grasshoppers, but also amphibians, reptiles, and small birds and mammals. Its fondness for large insects should make it a popular visitor to golf courses. However, unlike hawks and owls—which have strong talons on their feet for holding prey securely while it is torn apart with their hooked beak—the loggerhead shrike has relatively weak feet. It makes up for this shortcoming by skewering its prey on thorns or barbed wire, which hold the prey securely so the shrike can feed on it easily. Impaling its prey is also a way of storing extra food, either to demonstrate hunting abilities to potential mates, or simply to stock up on food while it is available. This may be especially important during winter, when prey is harder to find. This habit of stockpiling extra food earned the shrike its reputation as a "butcher." That reputation is undeserved, however, as the loggerhead does not kill wantonly, but kills only what it needs to survive.

Although the loggerhead shrike is classified as a *songbird*, its musical repertoire is mostly limited to clicks, peeps, whistles, and rattles. When a male "sings," he produces a series of trills and single notes—hardly melodic to human ears, but it serves its purpose of attracting a mate. Some biologists believe the sounds may also lure insects and grasshoppers close enough to be captured.

Unfortunately, this species is in trouble. Its populations are declining in 37 of the 43 states where it breeds; few other North American birds are declining as quickly or over such a widespread area. No one is certain of the reasons for these declines, although the probable causes are increased predation (from edge species), direct contamination and loss of prey due to insecticide use, and habitat loss (roadside mowing and herbicide application, and loss of farmland in the East, shrublands in the Midwest and West, and hedgerows everywhere).

Shrikes like to perch on roadside utility lines and fences, and often swoop low across the road to capture prey. It's not surprising, then, that the second most common cause of death (after predation) is collision with automobiles. Golf courses should provide something of a safe haven for shrikes, given the limited probability of collision with slow-moving golf carts and maintenance equipment.

Shrikes' preferred habitat is composed of short vegetation (less than 9 inches high) with scattered trees or shrubs to provide perches for hunting—especially trees and shrubs with thorns. Young birds, still honing their hunting skills, prefer hunting over bare ground. Also important is the availability of a variety of perch heights, from nearly ground level up to 15 or 20 feet, although 6 feet seems to be the preferred height. Fences provide important perch sites, and barbed-wire fences provide a place to impale prey. Besides open country, this species is attracted to habitat edges between fields and forests.

Given its tolerance for human activity, and fondness for open habitat with scattered perch sites, this species should be able to find a home on golf courses. Encouraging shrikes to nest on the course may be as simple as avoiding insecticide applications in nonplay areas, especially where shrubs grow among medium and tall grasses. If possible, barbed-wire fences should not be removed. Nest sites and feeding perches can be provided by planting trees and shrubs with thorns such as hawthorns (*Crataegus* species), honey locust (*Gleditsia triacanthos*), and osage orange (*Maclura pomifera*); shrikes are also fond of red cedar for nesting. Plant in open grassy areas, where grasshoppers, lizards, and small rodents are abundant. Since shrikes usually limit their hunting to an area about 10 yards around each perch, space the plantings at least 20 yards apart.

Purple martin

Purple martin condominiums are a familiar sight around homes in the East and Midwest. They should become a familiar sight on golf courses as well, since martins prefer open areas with water nearby, they readily take to artificial nest structures, and they are a species in need of conservation efforts. Although they will not clear the course of mosquitoes, a colony will eat a large number of other flying insects, including beetles, grasshoppers, and flies. The Purple Martin Conservation Association is a good source of information on meeting the needs of martins, and they have several programs in which golf courses can participate. (Their address is in Appendix 1.)

Purple martins in the Rocky Mountains and Southwest nest in natural cavities, such as saguaro cactus and large deciduous trees, while martins in the Northwest use either natural cavities or clusters of single nest boxes. Martins east of the Rockies are dependent on human-provided nest sites. Historically, these martins nested in tree cavities excavated by woodpeckers, or in rock crevices. But due to competition for nest sites with starlings and house sparrows, and a long association with humans (Native Americans hung hollow gourds around their homes for martins to nest in), the eastern birds now use only artificial nest structures. Martins are colonial nesters, which means a large number of them will nest close to each other. Their need to have close neighbors is met by providing a nest structure such as a martin condominium, which typically houses up to 24 nesting pairs.

In areas where natural cavities might be used, management activity should focus on preserving those sources of natural cavities. Protect snags, live trees with heart rot, and giant saguaros. Where artificial structures are used, they should be checked regularly to confront problems of unwanted species (wasps, squirrels, house sparrows, and starlings), parasites and other insects, and predator activities (snakes, raccoons, crows, and owls). Martins are quite tolerant of humans, and checking their nests will not cause the birds to abandon them. Purple martin house plans and finished houses are available commercially, along with mounting poles and predator guards. The traditional artificial nest structures—hollow gourds—are a good (and inexpensive) option because they sway in the wind, making them less attractive to other species and more difficult for predators to attack. The outside surfaces of any nest structure should be painted white to keep the inside cool.

Before choosing to provide a nest structure, remember to consider maintenance. A large martin house looks impressive, but it also represents a considerable amount of work, both to maintain the house in good repair, and to manage it correctly for martins. Putting up housing for martins may require daily attention at first, to keep other birds from claiming the housing. The biggest problem will probably be house sparrows; this species is not protected by law, so its nests can be removed (a house sparrow nest is a bulky, messy mass of grass and small twigs, while a purple martin nest is a small, shallow cup of grasses, with fresh green leaves from trees or shrubs). Once martins are settled in, the housing should be lowered and checked once a week, to make sure the nests are dry and parasites are not a problem. Wet or parasite-infested nests can be replaced with wood shavings or pine straw with a shallow cup to hold the eggs or young birds. After martins have left for the winter, the housing should be cleaned. Remove the old nests and wash the compartments with a bleach solution (1 part bleach to 9 parts water).

Pulley-and-winch systems are available to simplify raising and lowering the housing for maintenance tasks. A word of caution: if you lower the housing to check its contents, it is very important when you raise it that you keep the same orientation that it had before. In other words, make sure that the side facing north when you lower it is again facing north when you raise it back up. That is the only way the martins will find their own nests and young. Numbering compartments or gourds will make it easy to maintain the correct orientation.

Even the most attractive nest structure will be ignored by martins if it is not mounted in the right place. Martins need wide open spaces to hunt for food, including the area around their nests; they will not nest in wooded areas. Mount the structure at least 40 feet from any tree, shrub, or building. Martins seem to prefer areas close to humans, so place the structure within 100 feet of a building, if possible. Martins also prefer areas close to water, but it is not a necessity. Keep the structure at least 10 feet away from utility wires—martins like to perch on the wires, but they will avoid nest sites that could be invaded by leaping squirrels.

Put up the nest structure by early spring. In the first year, leave most (but not all) of the openings closed for about four weeks after the first martins arrive in your area. (Plugs designed for this purpose are available commercially.) These so-called "scouts" are older, experienced males, returning to their favorite nest sites. The next wave of migrating martins arrives about a month later, and will include the younger males—the ones looking for their first apartments. These birds are the ones that will be interested in colonizing the new nest structure. In subsequent years, after the colony is established, keep the openings plugged only until the first wave of martins arrives (this prevents other bird species from taking over the housing). Refer to Figure 16 to find the proper date for opening the housing in your area.

Wait until the first part of September to remove old nests and plug the openings. Young birds may not decide on next year's nest site until late summer or even fall, while migrating, and they need to inspect the nest sites. Store the structure where it will be protected from the elements, but don't store it in an occupied building, because parasites and other insects hidden in the crevices of the structure may invade the building.

Like many songbirds, nesting martins will eat crushed eggshells (from chicken eggs) in the spring to supplement natural sources of calcium, which is essential for producing their own eggs. Simply rinse and dry the eggshells thoroughly, then crush them in a paper bag until the pieces are all less than 1/4 inch in diameter. Place them on a platform feeder near the martin houses. Keep them dry, and replace them if they get wet.

Bluebirds

There are three bluebird species: eastern, western, and mountain. They are members of the insect-eating thrush family, which includes the familiar American robin and the European blackbird (which looks like an all-black robin)—the bird immortalized in the nursery rhyme about "four and twenty blackbirds." Bluebirds are found only in the Western hemisphere; at least one of the three species breeds in every state but Hawaii. Eastern bluebirds were once common suburban nesters, with territories encompassing suburban yards. However, their populations have been reduced by 90% in the last 50 years—largely due to habitat loss, but also due to intense competition for nest sites with non-native starlings and house sparrows.

Because bluebirds have been losing the competition for natural nest sites, humans have stepped in to help. Bluebird boxes have been put up in many parts of the country, and have helped to stop the population

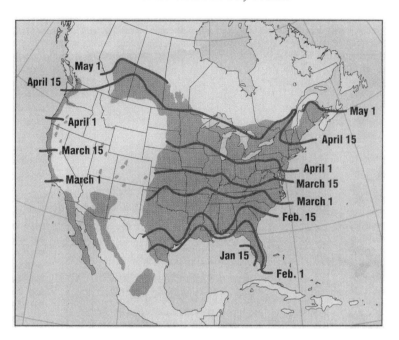

Figure 16. Breeding range and spring arrival dates of older, adult Purple Martins, as they return to the sites where they bred the previous year. The younger, subadult martins, do not arrive until 4–6 weeks later. The subadults are looking for someplace to establish their first nest sites. If no birds used your site during the previous year, do not open the housing until 4–6 weeks *after* these dates. Any sooner, and the housing will probably be colonized by unwanted species. If the housing *was* used by birds the previous year, open it on about the date shown here. (This map provided courtesy of the Purple Martin Conservation Association.)

free fall. Bluebird nest boxes are available commercially, or they can be easily constructed using the plans in Appendix 3.

Bluebirds are extremely tolerant of human activity, even watching calmly as humans check their nest boxes. However, they will not tolerate other bluebirds nesting nearby. For that reason, bluebird boxes should be about 100 yards apart—more if the habitat is very open—with few trees, hills, or buildings to obscure their view. House wrens and house sparrows will destroy bluebird eggs, and sometimes also the young bluebirds and even the adults. For this reason, care should be taken to place the bluebird boxes at least 100 yards away from buildings and wooded areas, where these nest competitors are found.

Bluebirds require open habitat with very low vegetation, which allows them to see flying and crawling insects, and provides them with the room they need for aerial pursuit of their prey. They will readily utilize any exposed perch site, such as utility posts or wires, or a fence. The openness of golf courses makes them an obvious choice for bluebird habitat.

The boxes must be checked at least once a year, preferably more often. If only once, it should be in late winter. Bluebird nests (loosely woven, dried grasses) can be left, but nests of any other birds or rodents should be removed, along with wasp nests, ants, and any other uninvited guests.

Other desirable, native, insect-eating birds will sometimes use bluebird boxes. They may take over the boxes, leaving the bluebirds homeless. But they will live close together peacefully if given the proper arrangement of nest boxes. In areas with tree swallows, two boxes should be put up, no more than 5 feet apart. They can even be mounted on the same pole. The swallows will take one box, bluebirds the other. If they are farther apart, swallows will take them both. In western areas with both tree and violet-green swallows, boxes can be put out in sets of three. Each species will defend its territory only against members of its own species, but will accept members of the other species. In this case, each species will take a box. This arrangement helps all three species, and increases the number of birds clearing insects off of the golf course.

In winter, bluebirds move to areas of mild weather, traveling only a few hundred miles at most. They spend nights in nest boxes or other cavities for warmth, so leave bluebird boxes up all year in southern states. Since insects are not as abundant during winter, bluebirds will also eat small fruits, so plant some shrubs with fruits that persist into winter.

If your staff doesn't have time to maintain bluebird boxes, there may be other people who can do it. Local birdwatching groups enthusiastically set up and maintain bluebird boxes, and might be interested in encouraging bluebirds on the golf course. Start by checking with the local Audubon Society chapter.

Hummingbirds

Hummingbirds seem to be universally appreciated by humans. Their remarkable flying abilities, their small size, and their jewel-like coloration make them fascinating additions to the golf course bird community. Hummingbirds are found nowhere in the world except the Americas. Over 300 hummingbird species exist, but only ten have breeding ranges that extend well into the United States. Of those, only the ruby-throated hummingbird breeds in the eastern United States. The ruby-throat also has the most amazing annual migration. Many fly south across the Gulf of Mexico to spend the winter, then return the same way in the spring to their breeding grounds.

Contrary to what many people believe, hummingbirds have a varied diet. They capture insects they find in flowers, spiders in their webs, and flying insects in midair. They even feed on tree sap. However, hummingbirds are best known for their habit of hovering in front of flowers, sipping nectar. They extract the nectar with their long, forked tongues. The fork allows the tongue to be shaped into a channel, through which the nectar is drawn back into the beak and swallowed. In the process of extracting the nutritious nectar from flowers, a hummingbird returns the favor by carrying pollen from one plant to another on the feathers of its head.

In natural areas, hummingbirds prefer open meadows and forest openings with wildflowers or flowering shrubs. You can attract hummingbirds to your course by mimicking this layout. Plant wildflowers native to your region in open areas and along the edges of open areas, such as fairways. Commercial wildflower seed mixes are available for most regions of the country. For smaller areas, plant dense beds of wildflowers, especially tubular flowers in shades of red. Position this "hummingbird garden" where golfers can see and appreciate the birds. Select plant varieties that bloom at different times of the year, to ensure a continuous supply of nectar. A list of suitable flowering plants can be found in Appendix 2. Avoid spraying insecticides in the flower meadow or garden, so that hummers can find spiders and insects to eat and to feed their growing young.

Hummingbird feeders require special care. These feeders come in a variety of shapes and sizes, but each is basically a container for the liquid nectar solution, with tubes or access holes colored red to mimic flowers. The nectar solution is 1 part sugar to 4 parts water, made by boiling the solution to kill bacteria and dissolve the sugar. Let it cool before filling the feeders, and refrigerate any extra solution. *Do not use honey instead of sugar;* honey promotes the growth of a fungus harmful to hummingbirds. There is no need to add vitamin supplements or red food coloring, which can be harmful to the birds. The birds don't need vitamins, because they get enough nutrients from insects, and the sugar solution doesn't need to be red to attract the birds since the feeder parts are already red. Clean the feeder with hot water and replace the solution daily when temperatures are above 85°F, and every two or three days in cooler weather. If mold or other deposits accumulate in the feeder, clean it with a bottle brush or fill it with vinegar and uncooked rice and shake vigorously. Clean sugar solution off the outside of the feeder to discourage bees. If one bird keeps chasing others away from the feeder, it may be necessary to hang a second feeder out of sight of the first. In spite of some people's worries, leaving a feeder up late into the fall will not cause hummingbirds to linger too long and get caught in winter weather. Hummingbirds know when to migrate (based on day length), and they won't stay any longer than they need to in order to build up energy reserves for migration. So don't rely on the calendar to decide when to take the feeders down; wait until you no longer see hummingbirds in the area.

Shorebirds

This group of birds includes the various species of plovers, sandpipers, avocets, and other birds that breed or forage along the shores of lakes, oceans, and wetlands. (Herons and egrets are in a different group, usually referred to as wading birds.) Most shorebirds nest in the Arctic or subarctic regions, and migrate long distances. Some species fly as far as the southern tip of South America to spend the winter. Along the way, they make regular stops to rest and build up fat reserves to fuel their journey. Some birds eat enough to double their weight during a stay at a stopover site. Shorebirds have narrower habitat requirements than songbirds, and so have fewer available migratory stopover points because relatively few sites meet their requirements. Golf courses can serve as important stopover points for migrating shorebirds, and as breeding habitat for some species. *Golf courses are in a unique position of being able to protect shorebird habitat while still allowing human use of the area,* in part because of the relatively low level of human activity on a course in comparison with public beaches and lake shores that are heavily used by anglers, off-road vehicle enthusiasts, and other recreationists.

During migration, shorebirds search for food in areas of shallow water (less than about 7 inches deep), especially where there are exposed mudflats. They will forage where vegetation is present, provided it is less than about half the birds' height and total coverage does not exceed about 25%. For most birds, this means vegetation no more than a few inches tall. Shorebirds search the mud and water for invertebrates, including snails, shrimp, midges, flies, mosquitoes, dragonflies, and beetles. The methods used to find food vary by species, but in general they either sweep their bills through the water, pick invertebrates off the water surface, or probe in mud with their bills.

Conservation strategies for shorebirds include reducing disturbance, and protecting and enhancing existing habitat. Shorebirds are sensitive to disturbance, and migrating shorebirds cannot afford to expend energy avoiding humans—they need to invest their time in building up energy reserves for their long journeys. Areas on the course with large concentrations of breeding or migrating shorebirds should be placed off limits to people and equipment by seasonal signing and/or fencing. The goal of shorebird habitat management should be to increase the number and availability of invertebrates for shorebird food. This can be done by keeping ponds flooded during winter, drawing down the water level slowly in the spring, flooding them again in summer after shallowly working any vegetation into the soil, and slowly drawing them down again in late summer and fall. Drawdowns should be timed to coincide with periods of migration, which in spring is roughly late March through early June, while the fall migration is spread out between July and November. Winter flooding protects invertebrate eggs and larvae; slow drawdowns maintain soil moisture and encourage establishment of vegetation; working vegetation into the soil releases nutrients for invertebrates. Gradually drawing down the water level continually exposes new areas of saturated soil and keeps a steady supply of invertebrates available to birds. The combination of exposed mudflats and shallow water will be a powerful draw for many shorebird species.

If more than one water body is managed, the drawdowns should be staggered to provide a diversity of water depths and to extend the period of availability. To maximize production of wetland plants and invertebrates, each pond should be drawn down only once every 3 to 10 years. If salinity is a problem in ponds that have been drawn down, they should be flushed with fresh water as necessary. Undesirable vegetation can be eliminated by keeping an area flooded for 1 to 3 years. The water level can still be drawn down slowly during the nongrowing season to provide foraging opportunities for wintering shorebirds (in coastal areas).

A potentially serious disease problem can occur in ponds with fluctuating water levels during warm weather: avian botulism. Outbreaks generally kill waterfowl, but shorebirds can also be affected. It causes paralysis, so that the birds cannot fly or even walk. Death is by drowning or respiratory failure. If you see large numbers of dead birds or birds that appear uncoordinated or disoriented, contact local wildlife officials immediately. The problem can be corrected by either draining the pond completely or flooding it deeply.

CHAPTER EIGHT

OTHER GOLF COURSE RESIDENTS

Bats

Bats have been persecuted for centuries. Only recently has their important role in ecosystem function been appreciated, along with their value to humans. A single little brown bat can eat more than 1000 insects *per hour,* making bats an effective biological control tool. Bats consume many insects considered pests, including mosquitoes and many types of beetles and moths. Bats benefit from many of the same management actions that benefit birds, especially retaining snags, reducing pesticide use, and providing artificial housing.

If bats are already using a golf course, they can be encouraged to continue by putting up artificial bat houses for daytime roosting. Bat boxes are a relatively new management tool, and results have been mixed. Some boxes have been accepted by bats right away, while others that have been in place for several years have been ignored. Boxes may be more useful in areas with a shortage of "natural" roost sites (including hollow trees, under loose slabs of bark, in the foliage of trees, and in abandoned buildings). Bats are creatures of habit, and prefer roosting in places that are familiar to them, where they have roosted for a long time. Getting them to change to an unfamiliar place, like a bat box, may be very difficult. Also, bats are very sensitive to temperature, and temperatures inside a bat box must stay within a particular range. The success rate for bat boxes should increase as knowledge grows about such aspects as box design, materials, color, and location. Golf course personnel can contribute to that body of knowledge by passing along information about successful (or even unsuccessful) bat boxes to bat researchers. Bat Conservation International has a bat house research project to which golf courses can contribute valuable information. (See Appendix 1 for the address.)

Bats like it hot: If the average high temperature in July is less than 80°F, mount the bat boxes where they will receive at least 10 hours of direct sunlight each day; if temperatures average 80 to 100°F, the boxes should receive at least 6 hours of sun daily. Mount boxes 15 to 30 feet high, on a building or pole (not on a tree), preferably within a quarter of a mile of fresh water. Avoid mounting on buildings with metal siding, or locations that receive nighttime illumination. Finally, bats need room to fly in the area of the box: there should not be any obstacles (trees, buildings, etc.) within 20 feet. Commercially made boxes and box kits are available, as are detailed construction plans. (See Tuttle and Hensley 1993 in the References section.)

Some people have concerns about encouraging bats, but those concerns are based on outdated beliefs and inaccurate information. Putting up bat boxes will not result in bats entering nearby buildings to roost. Fear of rabies is unfounded, as less than one-half of one percent of all bats contract rabies. Those that do become rabid die quickly, without becoming aggressive. They won't get tangled in your hair, and they won't drink your blood. And no, they're not blind.

Butterflies

Butterflies can add flashes of color to the golf course to please golfers, while providing a source of food for many birds. And they do this without causing harm—butterfly caterpillars are rarely responsible for the kind of plant damage caused by moth caterpillars. Butterflies will thrive naturally on the course if provided with out-of-play areas where wildflowers or flowering shrubs grow, and where insecticides are not used. As with birds, set aside the largest such natural areas possible. Smaller areas can be created specifically for butterflies. A butterfly garden planted where golfers and visitors can see it will generate interest and demonstrate your commitment to integrating the course with nature. A butterfly garden should receive at least half a day's sunlight in summer, especially early morning sun. Include large rocks where they will be heated by the early morning sun, to provide a place for butterflies to warm up before taking off for the day. If wet soil is available, it will provide moisture and minerals (if water soaks into the ground quickly, provide a shallow pan or tray filled with moist soil). The garden should be protected from the wind, because butterflies cannot fly well in wind.

Many of the same flowering plants that attract hummingbirds will also attract butterflies. In particular, butterflies are attracted to sun-loving flowers that are fragrant, single- rather than double-flowered, with purple, pink, yellow, or white blossoms, and are flattened or have short tubes, which make it easier for butterflies to reach the nectar. Flowers planted in large clusters will attract more butterflies than scattered plants. Consult with local botanical experts to determine which of these butterfly-attracting plant species are appropriate for your area:

yarrow (*Achillea* spp.)
milkweed (*Asclepias* spp.)
aster (*Aster* spp.)
butterfly bush (*Buddleia davidii*)
coneflower (*Echinacea* spp.)
daisy (*Erigeron* spp.)
gayfeather/blazing star (*Liatris* spp.)
privet (*Ligustrum* spp.)
lupine (*Lupinus* spp.)
spearmint (*Mentha spicata*)
monarda/bergamot/bee balm (*Monarda* spp.)
penstemon/beard tongue (*Penstemon* spp.)
phlox (*Phlox* spp.)
black-eyed susan (*Rudbeckia* spp.)
sage (*Salvia* spp.)
sedum/stonecrop (*Sedum* spp.)
goldenrod (*Solidago* spp.)
verbena (*Verbena* spp.)
ironweed (*Veronia* spp.)

GLOSSARY

corridor—A relatively narrow area consisting of a particular vegetation type that connects two or more **patches** of similar vegetation.

edge—The area where two distinct habitat types meet, such as a field and a forest.

exotic—A plant or animal species that is living in an area where it is not **native**.

forb—Any nonwoody, herbaceous plant, other than grass.

habitat—In the strictest sense, this is an area that provides all of the features needed for survival by a plant or animal. However, the word is often broadly applied to any area that provides at least some of a species' requirements, hence "riparian habitat" or "urban habitat."

home range—An area of habitat that is used regularly by an individual animal or a breeding pair—generally larger than a **territory**.

Integrated Pest Management—A plan of action for dealing with insects, weeds, and plant diseases that relies on first setting an acceptable level of infestation or damage, with treatment only after that level has been exceeded. Treatment utilizes cultural practices and biological controls, with chemical controls used only as a last resort.

native—A plant or animal species that has occurred naturally in a particular area for a long time (perhaps thousands of its generations) without the help of humans.

naturalized—An **exotic** plant species or community of exotic plant species that have adapted to the local weather and soil conditions, and continue to grow without the help of humans (i.e., without additional irrigation, fertilizer, or pesticides).

nest parasite—A bird that lays its eggs in the nests of other birds, usually of another species, to be raised by the other birds. The brown-headed cowbird is a nest parasite.

patch—An area consisting of a particular type of vegetation, adjacent to areas with other types of vegetation—for example, a patch of forest next to grassland and shrubland.

raptor—A bird that preys on other animals; examples include hawks, owls, and eagles.

riparian—Refers to the area adjacent to water sources (such as lakes, streams, or marshes), and the vegetation growing there.

snag—A dead, standing tree.

territory—An area of habitat that is used exclusively by an individual animal or breeding pair; the territory is defended against intrusions by other animals. A territory is generally smaller than a **home range**.

urban—Refers to an area that has been built up by humans, including suburban neighborhoods, municipal parks, and city centers.

REFERENCES

Arendt, R.G. 1996. *Conservation Design for Subdivisions: A Practical Guide to Creating Open Space Networks.* Island Press, Washington, DC.

Balogh, J.C. and W.J. Walker, Eds. 1992. *Golf Course Management and Construction: Environmental Issues.* Lewis Publishers, Boca Raton, FL.

Burton, R. 1995. *National Audubon Society North American Birdfeeder Handbook.* Dorling Kindersley Publishing, New York.

Dennis, J.V. and M. Tekulsky. 1991. *How to Attract Hummingbirds and Butterflies.* Ortho Books, San Ramon, CA.

Ehrlich, P.R., D.S. Dobkin, and D. Wheye. 1988. *The Birder's Handbook: A Field Guide to the Natural History of North American Birds.* Simon and Schuster, Inc. New York.

Harker, D., S. Evans, M. Evans, and K. Harker. 1993. *Landscape Restoration Handbook.* Lewis Publishers, Boca Raton, FL.

Helmers, D.L. 1992. *Shorebird Management Manual.* Western Hemisphere Shorebird Reserve Network, Manomet, MA.

Kaufman, K. 1996. *Lives of North American Birds.* Houghton Mifflin Company, Boston.

Kress, S.W. 1995. *The Bird Garden.* Dorling Kindersley Publishing, New York.

Love, W.R. 1992. *An Environmental Approach to Golf Course Development.* American Society of Golf Course Architects, Chicago, IL.

Mackay, J. 1996. *A Guide to Environmental Stewardship on the Golf Course.* Audubon International, Selkirk, New York.

Martin, A.C., H.S. Zim, and A.L. Nelson. 1951. *American Wildlife & Plants: A Guide to Wildlife Food Habits.* McGraw-Hill Co., Inc. New York.

Terborgh, J. 1989. *Where Have All the Birds Gone?* Princeton University Press, NJ.

Tuttle, M.D. and D.L. Hensley. 1993. *The Bat House Builder's Handbook.* University of Texas Press, Austin, TX.

SOURCES OF
ADDITIONAL INFORMATION

General References

Many of these magazines and books are available at public libraries. The magazines and recent books can be obtained through any bookstore.

Magazines with bird-related content, including articles with suggestions for attracting birds:

Bird Watcher's Digest
Birder's World
Wild Bird

Field guides: these are books that help you to identify bird species by pointing out key characteristics unique to each species. With about 650 species breeding in North America, a good field guide is essential for correct identification. A number of such guides are on the market, and titles of the most popular ones are listed below.

American Bird Conservancy: All the Birds of North America
Audubon Society Field Guide to North American Birds: Eastern Region and *Western Region* (two volumes)
Golden Field Guide: Birds of North America
National Geographic Society Field Guide to the Birds of North America

Peterson Field Guides: Eastern Birds and *Western Birds* (two volumes)

Stokes Field Guide to Birds: Eastern Region and *Western Region* (two volumes)

Organizations

American Society of Golf Course Architects
221 N. LaSalle St.
Chicago, IL 60601-1520
312-372-7090
312-372-6160 (fax)
http://www.golfdesign.org

Audubon Cooperative Sanctuary System
Audubon International
46 Rarick Road
Selkirk, NY 12158
518-767-9051
518-767-9076 (fax)
http://www.audubonintl.org

Bat Conservation International, Inc.
P.O. Box 162603
Austin, TX 78716-2603
512-327-9721
512-327-9724 (fax)
http://www.batcon.org

Colorado Bird Observatory
13401 Piccadilly Road
Brighton, CO 80601
303-659-4348
303-659-5489 (fax)
http://www.cbobirds.org

Cornell Lab of Ornithology (Project Feeder Watch)
159 Sapsucker Woods Road
Ithaca, NY 14850
607-254-2442
607-254-2415 (fax)
http://www.ornith.cornell.edu

Golf Course Superintendents Association of America
1421 Research Park Drive
Lawrence, KS 66049
800-472-7878
http://www.gcsaa.org

National Audubon Society
700 Broadway
New York, NY 10003-9501
212-979-3000
212-353-0377 (fax)
http://www.audubon.org

National Wildlife Federation
(Backyard Wildlife Habitat *and* Wildlife Habitat
    in the Workplace Programs)
8925 Leesburg Pike
Vienna, VA 22184-0001
http://www.nwf.org

North American Bluebird Society
P.O. Box 6295
Silver Spring, MD 20906-0295
301-384-2798
http://www.nabluebirdsociety.org

Purple Martin Conservation Association
Edinboro University of Pennsylvania
Edinboro, PA 16444
814-734-4420
814-734-5803 (fax)
http://www.purplemartin.org

Wildlife Habitat Council
(Corporate Wildlife Habitat Certification, Backyard
    Conservation, and Nest Box Monitoring Programs)
1010 Wayne Avenue, Suite 920
Silver Spring, MD 20910
http://www.wildlifehc.org

APPENDIX TWO

PLANTS FOR BIRDS

When the time comes to add trees or shrubs to the course, either as replacement for dead plants or to enhance wildlife habitat, it's important to know that some plants are more valuable to birds than others. Below is a list of trees, shrubs, and wetland plants that are particularly valuable to birds by virtue of their structure (which provides opportunities for nesting or protective cover) or the food value of their seeds, buds, or fruits. Some plants, such as oaks and willows, are also attractive to insects, which in turn makes them attractive to insect-eating birds. Plants that produce berries may provide food in summer, fall, or winter, depending on the date of ripening. The winter foods are often persistent fruits that may not be appealing to birds during fall or early winter, but become more attractive after they have undergone several freeze-thaw cycles, and as supplies of preferred fruits are exhausted.

These plants are native to North America, however they are not native to all regions. Plant only species that are native to the region, because these are the plants to which the native birds are adapted. Consult with local horticultural experts to determine which species are native to your region. An outstanding source of information on native plant species is the *Landscape Restoration Handbook*. (The full citation can be found in References.)

The list of birds attracted to each of these plants is by no means complete. An exhaustive list has never been compiled—there is much that biologists don't know about the feeding and nesting habits of birds. So use this list as a starting point, to get some idea of the relative value of each plant. Through your own observations and trials with different plants, you will discover which plants are most attractive to birds on your golf course.

Trees	Value	Birds Attracted
firs *Abies* spp.	nesting, seeds	mourning dove, chickadees, nuthatches, American robin, purple finch, grosbeaks, crossbills
boxelder *Acer negundo*	seeds	evening grosbeak, purple finch
maples *Acer* spp.	nesting, seeds, buds, insects	yellow-bellied sapsucker, white-breasted nuthatch, house wren, American robin, vireos, warblers, northern cardinal, grosbeaks, song sparrow, orioles, American goldfinch, pine siskin, purple finch
birches *Betula* spp.	seeds, buds, insects	yellow-bellied sapsucker, chickadees, tufted titmouse, red-breasted nuthatch, Baltimore oriole, grosbeaks, purple finch, common redpoll, pine siskin, American goldfinch, crossbills, fox sparrow, dark-eyed junco
hickories *Carya* spp.	nuts	red-bellied woodpecker, Carolina chickadee, tufted titmouse, white-breasted nuthatch, yellow-rumped warbler, pine warbler, northern cardinal, eastern towhee, field sparrow
hackberries *Celtis* spp.	nesting, fall and winter fruits	greater roadrunner, woodpeckers, eastern phoebe, tufted titmouse, cactus wren, northern mockingbird, gray catbird, brown thrasher, American robin, thrushes, eastern bluebird, cedar waxwing, orioles, northern cardinal, pyrrhuloxia, evening grosbeak, eastern towhee

dogwoods *Cornus* spp.	fruit	woodpeckers, northern mockingbird, brown thrasher, American robin, thrushes, bluebirds, cedar waxwing, yellow-rumped warbler, summer tanager, northern cardinal, grosbeaks
common persimmon *Diospyros virginiana*	fruit	eastern phoebe, northern mockingbird, gray catbird, American robin, cedar waxwing
American beech *Fagus grandifolia*	nuts, flowers	woodpeckers, blue jay, American crow, chickadees, tufted titmouse, white-breasted nuthatch, rose-breasted grosbeak, common grackle, white-throated sparrow
ashes *Fraxinus* spp.	nesting, seeds	cedar waxwing, red-winged blackbird, northern cardinal, grosbeaks, purple finch
American holly *Ilex opaca*	nesting, fall and winter fruit	northern mockingbird, gray catbird, eastern bluebird, cedar waxwing, northern cardinal
butternut *Juglans cinerea*	nuts	red-bellied woodpecker, chickadees, tufted titmouse, nuthatches, Carolina wren, yellow-rumped warbler, pine warbler, purple finch, field sparrow
black walnut *Juglans nigra*	nesting, nuts	woodpeckers, blue jay, American crow, Carolina chickadee, tufted titmouse, brown-headed nuthatch, Carolina wren, gray catbird, ruby-crowned kinglet, yellow-rumped warbler, pine warbler, northern cardinal, dark-eyed junco, white-crowned sparrow, song sparrow

Trees	Value	Birds Attracted
eastern red cedar *Juniperus virginiana*	nesting, winter fruit	yellow-bellied sapsucker, northern mockingbird, brown thrasher, American robin, eastern bluebird, cedar waxwing, loggerhead shrike, yellow-rumped warbler, northern cardinal, grosbeaks, purple finch, chipping sparrow, fox sparrow
American sweetgum *Liquidambar styraciflua*	seeds	mourning dove, black-capped chickadee, northern cardinal, evening grosbeak, purple finch, common redpoll, pine siskin, American goldfinch, dark-eyed junco, white-throated sparrow
tuliptree (yellow poplar, tulip poplar) *Liriodendron tulipifera*	nesting, sap, seeds, nectar	ruby-throated hummingbird, northern cardinal, purple finch
apples, crabapples *Malus* spp.	nesting, flowers, buds, fall and winter fruit, nectar	hummingbirds, woodpeckers, eastern kingbird, jays, chickadees, tufted titmouse, northern mockingbird, gray catbird, American robin, cedar waxwing, red-eyed vireo, orioles, yellow-rumped warbler, northern cardinal, grosbeaks, eastern towhee, American goldfinch, finches, white-throated sparrow
red mulberry *Morus rubra* Texas mulberry *Morus microphylla*	fruit	cuckoos, woodpeckers, eastern kingbird, great crested flycatcher, blue jay, American crow, tufted titmouse, northern mockingbird, gray catbird, brown thrasher, American robin, thrushes, veery, eastern bluebird, cedar waxwing, vireos, bay-breasted warbler, yellow warbler, red-winged blackbird, orioles, tanagers, northern cardinal, rose-breasted grosbeak, indigo bunting, eastern towhee, purple finch, American goldfinch, white-throated sparrow, song sparrow

sourgum (black tupelo, blackgum) *Nyssa sylvatica*	fruit	woodpeckers, eastern kingbird, northern mockingbird, gray catbird, brown thrasher, American robin, thrushes, eastern bluebird, cedar waxwing, scarlet tanager
spruces *Picea* spp.	cover, nesting, seeds	woodpeckers, chickadees, jays, nuthatches, brown creeper, American robin, cedar waxwing, kinglets, warblers, grosbeaks, purple finch, pine siskin, crossbills, white-throated sparrow, chipping sparrow, American goldfinch
pines *Pinus* spp.	cover, nesting, seeds	band-tailed pigeon, woodpeckers, chickadees, jays, nuthatches, titmice, brown creeper, thrushes, kinglets, warblers, northern cardinal, grosbeaks, finches, pine siskin, crossbills, dark-eyed junco, white-crowned sparrow, white-throated sparrow, chipping sparrow
aspens and cottonwoods *Populus* spp.	nesting, buds, insects	woodpeckers, chickadees, house wren, plumbeous vireo, yellow warbler, Abert's towhee, orioles, evening grosbeak, finches
mesquites *Prosopis* spp.	nesting, seeds	greater roadrunner, common raven, cactus wren, curve-billed thrasher
cherries *Prunus* spp.	nesting, fruit	band-tailed pigeon, woodpeckers, eastern kingbird, great crested flycatcher, jays, chickadees, titmice, northern mockingbird, American crow, gray catbird, brown thrasher, American robin, thrushes, veery, bluebirds, cedar waxwing, vireos, orioles, tanagers, grosbeaks, white-throated sparrow

Trees	Value	Birds Attracted
oaks *Quercus* spp.	nesting, nuts, insects	band-tailed pigeon, mourning dove, woodpeckers, jays, chickadees, titmice, white-breasted nuthatch, Carolina wren, blue-gray gnatcatcher, brown thrasher, vireos, warblers, scarlet tanager, northern cardinal, Baltimore oriole, common grackle, towhees, rose-breasted grosbeak
sassafras *Sassafras albidum*	fruit	woodpeckers, eastern phoebe, eastern kingbird, great crested flycatcher, northern mocking-bird, gray catbird, brown thrasher, American robin, eastern bluebird, hermit thrush, wood thrush, vireos, eastern towhee
American mountain ash *Sorbus americana*	fall and winter fruit	downy woodpecker, red-headed woodpecker, gray catbird, brown thrasher, American robin, eastern bluebird, cedar waxwing, common grackle, orioles, grosbeaks
hemlocks *Tsuga* spp.	cover, nesting, seeds	eastern phoebe, blue jay, chickadees, American robin, wood thrush, dark-eyed junco, pine siskin, American goldfinch, crossbills
American elm *Ulmus americana*	nesting, seeds, buds, insects	woodpeckers, black-capped chickadee, vireos, warblers, Baltimore oriole, yellow-rumped warbler, northern cardinal, grosbeaks, purple finch, American goldfinch, pine siskin

Shrubs	Value	Birds Attracted
alders *Alnus* spp.	seeds	mourning dove, chickadees, rose-breasted grosbeak, redpolls, pine siskin, American goldfinch, purple finch
juneberries (serviceberries) *Amelanchier* spp.	fruit	woodpeckers, chickadees, tufted titmouse, eastern phoebe, eastern kingbird, gray catbird, northern mockingbird, brown thrasher, American robin, thrushes, bluebirds, veery, cedar waxwing, red-eyed vireo, Baltimore oriole, tanagers, towhees, northern cardinal, grosbeaks, American goldfinch, finches
chokeberries *Aronia* spp.	fruit	brown thrasher, cedar waxwing, eastern meadowlark
dogwoods *Cornus* spp.	nesting, fruit, buds	woodpeckers, eastern kingbird, American crow, violet-green swallow, gray catbird, brown thrasher, American robin, thrushes, bluebirds, cedar waxwing, vireos, pine warbler, summer tanager, northern cardinal, grosbeaks, purple finch, American goldfinch
hawthorns *Crataegus* spp.	nesting, fall and winter fruit, nectar	hummingbirds, northern flicker, blue jay, willow flycatcher, gray catbird, northern mockingbird, brown thrasher, California thrasher, American robin, hermit thrush, cedar waxwing, loggerhead shrike, orioles, northern cardinal, grosbeaks, fox sparrow, purple finch

Shrubs	Value	Birds Attracted
hollies, winterberry *Ilex* spp.	cover, nesting, fall and winter fruit	woodpeckers, blue jay, chickadees, northern mockingbird, gray catbird, brown thrasher, American robin, thrushes, veery, eastern bluebird, cedar waxwing, yellow-rumped warbler, purple finch
common juniper *Juniperus communis*	cover, nesting, fall and winter fruit	American robin, eastern bluebird, cedar waxwing, grosbeaks, purple finch, chipping sparrow
bayberries, waxmyrtles *Myrica* spp.	cover, nesting, fall and winter fruit	woodpeckers, chickadees, jays, tufted titmouse, wrentit, Carolina wren, tree swallow, violet-green swallow, towhees, gray catbird, brown thrasher, eastern bluebird, thrushes, red-winged blackbird, eastern meadowlark, white-eyed vireo, yellow-rumped warbler
buckthorns *Rhamnus* spp.	fruit	band-tailed pigeon, pileated woodpecker, jays, gray catbird, brown thrasher, American robin, northern mockingbird, phainopepla, thrushes, grosbeaks, tanagers, finches
sumacs *Rhus* spp.	fall and winter fruit	greater roadrunner, eastern phoebe, American crow, chickadees, wrentit, northern mockingbird, gray catbird, brown thrasher, American robin, thrushes, eastern bluebird, red-eyed vireo, yellow-rumped warbler, northern cardinal

Plant	Uses	Birds
gooseberries, currants *Ribes* spp.	cover, nesting, fruit, nectar	hummingbirds, magpies, jays, woodpeckers, northern mockingbird, gray catbird, brown thrasher, American robin, Townsend's solitaire, bluebirds, thrushes, cedar waxwing, fox sparrow, song sparrow
brambles (blackberries, raspberries, thimbleberries) *Rubus* spp.	cover, nesting, fruit	band-tailed pigeon, woodpeckers, willow flycatcher, alder flycatcher, jays, fish crow, wrentit, chickadees, tufted titmouse, northern mockingbird, gray catbird, brown thrasher, American robin, thrushes, bluebirds, veery, cedar waxwing, vireos, yellow-breasted chat, common grackle, orioles, tanagers, northern cardinal, grosbeaks, indigo bunting, towhees, field sparrow, fox sparrow, song sparrow
willows *Salix* spp.	nesting, buds, insects, nectar	hummingbirds, sapsuckers, willow flycatcher, yellow warbler, MacGillivray's warbler, Wilson's warbler, grosbeaks, American goldfinch, Abert's towhee, Lincoln's sparrow
elderberries *Sambucus* spp.	cover, nesting, fruit	band-tailed pigeon, woodpeckers, western kingbird, alder flycatcher, jays, wrentit, chickadees, tufted titmouse, bushtit, nuthatches, cactus wren, northern mockingbird, gray catbird, brown thrasher, American robin, bluebirds, thrushes, veery, bluebirds, cedar waxwing, phainopepla, yellow warbler, yellow-rumped warbler, yellow-breasted chat, orioles, northern cardinal, grosbeaks, American goldfinch, towhees, fox sparrow, white-throated sparrow, song sparrow

Shrubs	Value	Birds Attracted
buffaloberries *Shepherdia* spp.	fruit	gray catbird, brown thrasher, American robin
snowberries *Symphoricarpos* spp.	cover, fall and winter fruit, nectar	hummingbirds, American robin, thrushes, grosbeaks
blueberries *Vaccinium* spp.	nesting, fruit	woodpeckers, blue jay, eastern kingbird, tufted chickadees, titmouse, gray catbird, brown thrasher, American robin, thrushes, veery, eastern bluebird, cedar waxwing, yellow-breasted chat, orioles, scarlet tanager, eastern towhee, fox sparrow, white-throated sparrow, song sparrow

Wetland Plants	Value	Birds Attracted
sedges *Carex* spp.	nesting, seeds	sora, rails, horned lark, sedge wren, towhees, Lincoln's sparrow, savannah sparrow, song sparrow, swamp sparrow
spikerushes *Eleocharis* spp.	seeds	purple gallinule, sora, rails
rice cutgrass *Leersia oryzoides*	seeds	sora, swamp sparrow
duckweeds *Lemna* spp.	food (birds eat the entire plant)	purple gallinule, sora
smartweeds *Polygonum* spp.	seeds	sora, rails, red-winged blackbird, northern cardinal, rose-breasted grosbeak, brown towhee, fox sparrow, song sparrow, swamp sparrow, vesper sparrow, white-crowned sparrow, white-throated sparrow
arrowheads *Sagittaria* spp.	seeds, roots	king rail, sandhill crane
bulrushes *Scirpus* spp.	nesting, seeds, roots	grebes, bitterns, sora, Virginia rail, marsh wren, blackbirds, song sparrow
cattails *Typha* spp.	nesting	sora, rails, marsh wren, red-winged blackbird, yellow-headed blackbird

Native perennial plants for hummingbirds:

red buckeye (*Aesculus pavia*)
yellow giant hyssop (*Agastache nepetoides*)
century plant/American aloe (*Agave americana*)
columbine (*Aquilegia canadensis*)
butterfly milkweed (*Asclepius tuberosa*)
Canada milk vetch (*Astragalus canadensis*)
bouvardia (*Bouvardia* spp.)
butterfly bush (*Buddleia* spp.)
red basil (*Calamintha coccinea*)
trumpet creeper (*Campsis radicans*)
partridge pea (*Cassia fasciculata*)
wild senna (*Cassia hebecarpa*)
Maryland senna (*Cassia marilandica*)
paintbrush (*Castilleja* spp.)
turtlehead (*Chelone glabra*)
Rocky Mountain bee plant (*Cleome serrulata*)
scarlet larkspur (*Delphinium cardinale*)
coneflower (*Echinacea* spp.)
fireweed (*Epilobium angustifolium*)
coral bean (*Erythrina herbacea*)
ocotillo (*Fouquieria splendens*)
gilia (*Gilia* spp.)
firebush (*Hamelia patens*)
red star hibiscus (*Hibiscus coccineus*)
impatiens/jewelweed/touch-me-not (*Impatiens* spp.)
red morning glory (*Ipomoea coccinea*)
scarlet gilia (*Ipomopsis aggregata*)
lantana (*Lantana camara*)
blazing stars (*Liatris* spp.)
cardinal flower (*Lobelia cardinalis*)
honeysuckle (*Lonicera* spp.)
lupine (*Lupinus* spp.)
crimson monkeyflower (*Mimulus cardinalis*)
beebalm (*Monarda didyma* or *M. fistulosa*)
prairie lousewort (*Pedicularis canadensis*)
penstemon/beardtongue (*Penstemon* spp.)
phlox (*Phlox* spp.)

false dragonhead/obedient plant (*Physostegia* spp.)
large solomon's seal (*Polygonatum canaliculatum*)
small solomon's seal (*Polygonatum pubescens*)
red-flowering currant (*Ribes sanguineum*)
Texas sage (*Salvia coccinea*)
red sage (*Salvia greggii*)
figwort (*Scrophularia coccinea*)
snowberry (*Symphoricarpos* spp.)
early horse gentian (*Triosteum aurantiacum*)
late horse gentian (*Triosteum perfoliatum*)
California fuschia (*Zauschneria californica*)

ARTIFICIAL NEST STRUCTURES

Basic nest box design. (See illustration on following page.) Holes (1/4″) drilled at the top of each side are for ventilation. Holes drilled in the back are for mounting screws. The corners of the floor are cut off to provide drainage. The exact angle of the pitched roof is not critical; 60° is satisfactory. The floor should be square, with the width of the sides matching the size of the floor. Cleaning out the box is easiest with a hinged front or side (not the roof) held shut with a hook and eye. For species that prefer an open-fronted box, omit the front piece, ventilation holes, and drainage openings. Use the dimensions given in the following tables to create boxes suitable for particular bird species.

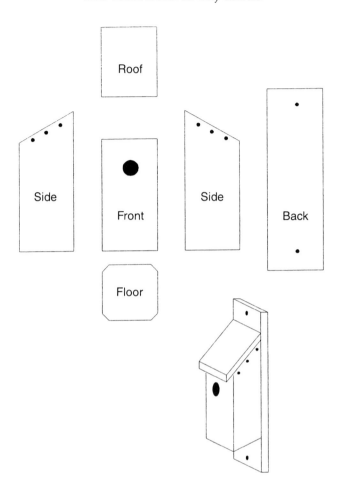

Species	Floor	Front	Opening	Mounting	Notes
osprey	48" × 48"			At least 10 ft high on post or tree that has been topped	Platform.
red-tailed hawk	24" × 24"			At least 10 ft high on post, or tree that has been topped	Platform.
American kestrel	10" × 10"	14–16"	3" diameter, 9–12" above floor	10–30 ft high on post, tree, or building, with box opening facing east or southeast	Should be mounted in a clearing, >20 yd from woods (>150 yd is better). Boxes should be ≥500 yd apart (200 yd if food is abundant). Box should not be hidden by vegetation.
barn owl	10" × 18"	15–18"	6" diameter, 4" above floor	12–18 ft high, attached to tree trunk or side of building if seldom used by humans	Prefer open areas, with few trees.
eastern and western screech-owls	8" × 8"	12–15"	3" diameter, 9–12" above floor	10–30 ft high on post or tree trunk	Prefer shaded spot at the edge of an open area. Put 2" of small wood chips or coarse sawdust in the bottom.
great horned owl and great gray owl	24" × 24"			20–50 ft high on post or tree that has been topped	Platform. For great gray owls, platform should be in forested area.
boreal owl	8" × 8"	18–20"	3-1/2" diameter	15–30 ft high on post or tree trunk	

Species	Floor	Front	Opening	Mounting	Notes
northern saw-whet owl	7" × 7"	16–18"	3" diameter	15–30 ft high on post or tree trunk	
downy woodpecker	4" × 4"	8–10"	1-1/4" diameter, 6–8" above floor	5–20 ft high on post, tree trunk, or tree limb	Put several inches of small wood chips or coarse sawdust in the bottom. Boxes covered with natural bark are more likely to attract woodpeckers.
hairy woodpecker	6" × 6"	12–15"	1-1/2" diameter, 9–12" above floor	8–20 ft high on post, tree trunk, or tree limb	Put several inches of small wood chips or coarse sawdust in the bottom. Boxes covered with natural bark are more likely to attract woodpeckers.
Lewis's woodpecker	7" × 7"	16–18"	2-1/2" diameter, 14–16" above floor	12–20 ft high on post, tree trunk, or tree limb	Put several inches of small wood chips or coarse sawdust in the bottom.
northern flicker	7" × 7"	16–18"	2-1/2" diameter, 14–16" above floor	8–10 ft high on post, tree trunk, or tree limb	Fill box completely with small wood chips or coarse sawdust, so birds can "excavate" the cavity.
pileated woodpecker	8" × 8"	16–24"	oblong: 3" high × 4" wide, 12–20" above floor	15–25 ft high on post, tree trunk, or tree limb	Put several inches of small wood chips or coarse sawdust in the bottom.

Species	Floor	Depth	Entrance	Placement	Comments
red-headed woodpecker	6″ × 6″	12–15″	2″ diameter, 9–12″ above floor	10–20 ft high on post, tree trunk, or tree limb, in the open but near large deciduous trees	Put several inches of small wood chips or coarse sawdust in the bottom. Generally will not use a nest box, preferring natural cavities in snags or dead limbs.
red-bellied woodpecker	6″ × 6″	12–15″	2-1/2″ diameter, 9–12″ above floor	12–20 ft high on post, tree trunk, or tree limb	Put several inches of small wood chips or coarse sawdust in the bottom.
yellow-bellied sapsucker	5″ × 5″	12–15″	1-1/2″ diameter, 9–12″ above floor	10–20 ft high on post, tree trunk, or tree limb	Put several inches of small wood chips or coarse sawdust in the bottom.
ash-throated flycatcher	6″ × 6″	8–12″	1-1/2″ diameter, 6–10″ above floor	5–15 ft high on post, tree trunk, or tree limb	Place in a wooded area.
great crested flycatcher	6″ × 6″	8–12″	1-3/4″ diameter, 6–10″ above floor	5–15 ft high on post, tree trunk, or tree limb, preferably in shady spot	Place in a wooded area. Boxes covered with natural bark are more likely to attract this species.
eastern phoebe	6″ × 6″	6″		8–12 ft high on side of building	Use a three-sided, open-faced box with narrow sides.

Species	Floor	Front	Opening	Mounting	Notes
purple martin	7" wide × 12" long	7"	2-1/8" diameter, with the bottom of the opening 1" above floor, or oblong 1-3/16" high × 3" wide	10–15 ft high within 100 ft of a building, but with at least 40–50 ft of open space around the martin house.	Dimensions given are for a single unit of a multiple-unit apartment house. Natural gourds can also be used; hang them so that they sway but do not swivel in the wind.
purple martin (Pacific Northwest only)	6" wide × 11" long	7"	2-1/8" diameter, or oblong 1-3/16" high × 3" wide	Mount in groups of 5 on pilings or posts 5–15 ft high over water	
barn swallow	6" × 6"	6"		8–12 ft high on the side of a building, up under the eaves	Three-sided, open-faced box with narrow sides and no roof. Alternatively, attach two-by-fours horizontally to the side of a building; the swallows will build their nests on the top surface, using it as a narrow supporting shelf.
tree and violet-green swallows	6" × 6"	5–7"	1-1/2" diameter, 4–6" above floor	5–15 ft high on post or attached to trunk of snag	Place several boxes 10 ft apart, near open area, close to open water or wetlands but away from dense woods.

Species	Floor	Height	Entrance	Placement	Notes
chickadees	4" × 4"	8–10"	1-1/8" diameter, 6–8" above floor	5–15 ft high, hanging from tree branch or attached to post, trunk, or limb	Place near trees or shrubs; partially fill with coarse sawdust or fine wood chips.
titmice	4" × 4"	10–12"	1-1/4" diameter, 6–10" above floor	5–15 ft high on post, tree trunk, or tree limb	Place near trees or shrubs.
brown-headed, pygmy, and red-breasted nuthatches	4" × 4"	8–10"	1-1/4" diameter, 6–8" above floor	5–15 ft high on post, hanging from tree branch, or attached to post, trunk, or limb	Place near trees; boxes covered with natural bark are more likely to attract nuthatches.
white-breasted nuthatch	4" × 4"	8–10"	1-3/8" diameter, 6–8" above floor	5–15 ft high on post, hanging from tree branch, or attached to post, trunk, or limb	Boxes covered with natural bark are more likely to attract nuthatches.
Bewick's, house, and winter wrens	4" × 4"	6–8"	1" diameter, or slot 1" high × 2" across, 4–6" above floor	5–10 ft high on post, hanging from tree branch, or attached to post, trunk, or limb	Place several boxes within 10 ft of each other (males often build several nests), near trees or shrubs.
Carolina wren	4" × 4"	6–8"	1-1/2" diameter, or slot 1-1/2" high × 2-1/2" across, 4–6" above floor	5–10 ft high, hanging from tree branch or attached to post, trunk, or limb	May prefer the slot opening.
American robin	7" × 8"	8"		6–15 ft high on tree trunk or side of building	Three-sided, open-faced box with narrow sides.

Species	Floor	Front	Opening	Mounting	Notes
bluebirds	5" × 5"	8–12"	1-1/2" (eastern or western bluebird) or 1-5/8" (mountain bluebird) diameter, 5–6" above floor; alternatively, leave a 1-1/8"-high opening across the top of the box face for a slot-type opening	4–15 ft high, on fence or post (not a tree)	Prefer open areas, well away from trees and shrubs. Mount 100 yd apart. Outside can be painted a light color.
prothonotary warbler	5" × 5"	6"	1-1/8" diameter, 4–5" above floor	4–8 ft high, on post, tree trunk, or tree limb	Prefers areas next to water, with dense canopy of trees.
song sparrow	6" × 6"	6"		1–4 ft high on post in marshy or streamside area with shrubs or tall emergent vegetation	Three-sided, open-faced box with narrow sides.
house finch	6" × 6"	6"	2" diameter, 4" above floor	8–12 ft high on post or side of building	

BREEDING BIRD LISTS

What follows is a series of lists of birds that have been known to nest (or are probably nesting) in different regions of the United States. The country is divided into 61 regions, based on vegetation (Figure 17). Find the region where the golf course is located, and use the corresponding bird list (organized in taxonomic order) as a starting point for bird management activities. If the course is located near the boundary between two regions, you may need to look at both bird lists to get an accurate list of birds in the area of the course. Select birds that occur on the course in low numbers, or birds that should occur but are absent. Then compare the habitat needs for those species (Appendix 5) with the habitats found on the course to determine what habitat needs are not being met. In particular, select species that have high conservation values. Plan habitat enhancement and management activities accordingly.

For example, if the course is near the North Carolina coast, it would be in Region 3. Suppose that local bird experts tell you there are no white-eyed vireos on the course, even though they appear in the list for that region. Checking the White-eyed Vireo habitat requirements in Appendix 5 reveals that this species needs dense shrubby areas, perhaps several acres of such habitat. It also eats insects. Encouraging this species to take up residence on the course might require implementing a program of planting clusters of native shrubs, with the goal of creating patches of several acres of shrubby habitat. Within those patches, you would restrict or eliminate insecticide applications to ensure an adequate supply of insects for food.

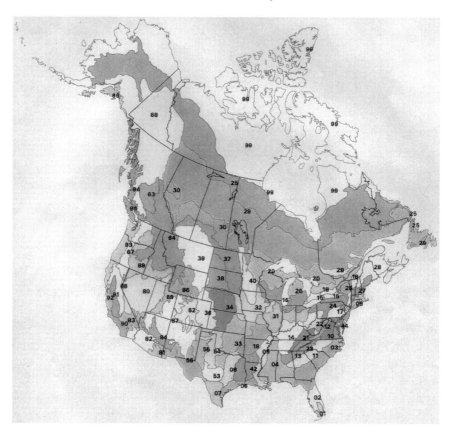

Figure 17. Vegetation regions of North America; these regions correspond with the lists of breeding birds that follow. (This map provided courtesy of Partners in Flight.)

However, don't expect the birds to show up right away. It may take years for the vegetation to mature to the point where it is attractive to the birds. If the species is not already using the course, it may be several more years before individuals even find the habitat. In the meantime, you'll be providing additional habitat for a number of bird species already using the course.

Occasionally, the habitat needs of two species are mutually exclusive. In that case, the habitat enhancement activities should address the needs of the species with the greater conservation priority. Let's suppose that loggerhead shrikes and yellow warblers have been seen on the course, and you would like to encourage more nesting by these species. However, shrikes like open habitat with only scattered shrubs, while yellow warblers prefer dense shrub cover. You have two options: set aside different parts of the course for each species, or manage all habitat on the course for one species. If you opt for picking one species, in this case it should be the shrike, which has a conservation score of 17, while the warbler has a conservation score of only 8.

Be realistic in your expectations. Some bird species will never use a golf course. Many species need large areas—areas that are much larger than a golf course can provide. Other species are too sensitive to disturbance by human activities, and will live only in very remote locations. Information on some of these species is included in Appendix 5 anyway, to answer the "why aren't there any such-and-such birds on the course?" questions.

The region information and bird lists are based on work done by Partners in Flight, a coalition of government agencies, nonprofit organizations, and industry representatives who collaborate on bird conservation efforts in North America.

Region 1

pied-billed grebe
brown pelican
double-crested cormorant
anhinga
least bittern
great blue heron
great egret
snowy egret
little blue heron
tricolored heron
cattle egret
green heron
black-crowned night-heron
yellow-crowned night-heron
white ibis
glossy ibis
roseate spoonbill
wood stork
black vulture
turkey vulture
osprey
swallow-tailed kite
white-tailed kite
snail kite
bald eagle
red-shouldered hawk
short-tailed hawk
red-tailed hawk
crested caracara
American kestrel
king rail
purple gallinule
common moorhen
American coot
limpkin
sandhill crane
killdeer
black-necked stilt
white-winged dove
mourning dove
common ground-dove
yellow-billed cuckoo
mangrove cuckoo
smooth-billed ani
barn owl

eastern screech-owl
great horned owl
burrowing owl
barred owl
short-eared owl
common nighthawk
Chuck-Will's-widow
ruby-throated hummingbird
red-bellied woodpecker
downy woodpecker
red-cockaded woodpecker
northern flicker
pileated woodpecker
great crested flycatcher
eastern kingbird
purple martin
cave swallow
barn swallow
blue jay
Florida scrub-jay
American crow
fish crow
tufted titmouse
Carolina wren
marsh wren
blue-gray gnatcatcher
eastern bluebird
northern mockingbird
brown thrasher
loggerhead shrike
white-eyed vireo
black-whiskered vireo
yellow warbler
pine warbler
prairie warbler
common yellowthroat
northern cardinal
eastern towhee
grasshopper sparrow
seaside sparrow
red-winged blackbird
eastern meadowlark
boat-tailed grackle
common grackle
shiny cowbird
brown-headed cowbird

Region 2

pied-billed grebe
brown pelican
double-crested cormorant
anhinga
least bittern
great blue heron
great egret
snowy egret
little blue heron
tricolored heron
reddish egret
cattle egret
green heron
black-crowned night-heron
yellow-crowned night-heron
white ibis
glossy ibis
roseate spoonbill
wood stork
black vulture
turkey vulture
osprey
swallow-tailed kite
white-tailed kite
snail kite
Mississippi kite
bald eagle
Cooper's hawk
red-shouldered hawk
broad-winged hawk
short-tailed hawk
red-tailed hawk
crested caracara
American kestrel
clapper rail
king rail
common moorhen
American coot
limpkin
killdeer
black-necked stilt
willet
white-winged dove
mourning dove
common ground-dove

yellow-billed cuckoo
mangrove cuckoo
smooth-billed ani
barn owl
eastern screech-owl
great horned owl
burrowing owl
barred owl
common nighthawk
Chuck-Will's-widow
chimney swift
ruby-throated hummingbird
belted kingfisher
red-headed woodpecker
red-bellied woodpecker
downy woodpecker
hairy woodpecker
red-cockaded woodpecker
northern flicker
pileated woodpecker
eastern wood-pewee
acadian flycatcher
great crested flycatcher
eastern kingbird
purple martin
northern rough-winged swallow
barn swallow
blue jay
Florida scrub-jay
American crow
fish crow
Carolina chickadee
tufted titmouse
white-breasted nuthatch
brown-headed nuthatch
Carolina wren
marsh wren
blue-gray gnatcatcher
eastern bluebird
American robin
gray catbird
northern mockingbird
brown thrasher
loggerhead shrike
white-eyed vireo
yellow-throated vireo

red-eyed vireo
black-whiskered vireo
northern parula
yellow-throated warbler
pine warbler
prairie warbler
prothonotary warbler
common yellowthroat
hooded warbler
summer tanager
northern cardinal
blue grosbeak
indigo bunting
painted bunting
eastern towhee
Bachman's sparrow
field sparrow
grasshopper sparrow
seaside sparrow
red-winged blackbird
eastern meadowlark
boat-tailed grackle
common grackle
shiny cowbird
brown-headed cowbird
orchard oriole

Region 3

pied-billed grebe
brown pelican
double-crested cormorant
anhinga
great blue heron
great egret
snowy egret
little blue heron
tricolored heron
cattle egret
green heron
black-crowned night-heron
yellow-crowned night-heron
white ibis
glossy ibis
wood stork

black vulture
turkey vulture
osprey
swallow-tailed kite
Mississippi kite
bald eagle
sharp-shinned hawk
Cooper's hawk
red-shouldered hawk
short-tailed hawk
red-tailed hawk
American kestrel
clapper rail
king rail
purple gallinule
common moorhen
limpkin
sandhill crane
killdeer
willet
American woodcock
mourning dove
common ground-dove
black-billed cuckoo
yellow-billed cuckoo
barn owl
eastern screech-owl
great horned owl
burrowing owl
barred owl
common nighthawk
Chuck-Will's-widow
whip-poor-will
chimney swift
ruby-throated hummingbird
belted kingfisher
red-headed woodpecker
red-bellied woodpecker
downy woodpecker
hairy woodpecker
red-cockaded woodpecker
northern flicker
pileated woodpecker
eastern wood-pewee
willow flycatcher
eastern phoebe

great crested flycatcher
eastern kingbird
horned lark
purple martin
tree swallow
northern rough-winged swallow
barn swallow
blue jay
Florida scrub-jay
American crow
fish crow
Carolina chickadee
bridled titmouse
tufted titmouse
white-breasted nuthatch
brown-headed nuthatch
Carolina wren
house wren
marsh wren
blue-gray gnatcatcher
eastern bluebird
American robin
gray catbird
northern mockingbird
brown thrasher
cedar waxwing
loggerhead shrike
white-eyed vireo
yellow-throated vireo
warbling vireo
red-eyed vireo
Bachman's warbler
northern parula
yellow warbler
black-throated green warbler
yellow-throated warbler
pine warbler
prairie warbler
cerulean warbler
black-and-white warbler
American redstart
prothonotary warbler
worm-eating warbler
Swainson's warbler
ovenbird
Louisiana waterthrush

Kentucky warbler
common yellowthroat
hooded warbler
yellow-breasted chat
summer tanager
scarlet tanager
northern cardinal
blue grosbeak
indigo bunting
painted bunting
dickcissel
eastern towhee
Bachman's sparrow
chipping sparrow
field sparrow
grasshopper sparrow
Henslow's sparrow
saltmarsh sharp-tailed sparrow
seaside sparrow
song sparrow
red-winged blackbird
eastern meadowlark
boat-tailed grackle
common grackle
brown-headed cowbird
orchard oriole
Baltimore oriole
house finch
American goldfinch

Region 4

pied-billed grebe
brown pelican
double-crested cormorant
anhinga
American bittern
least bittern
great blue heron
great egret
snowy egret
little blue heron
tricolored heron
reddish egret
cattle egret

green heron
black-crowned night-heron
yellow-crowned night-heron
white ibis
black vulture
turkey vulture
osprey
swallow-tailed kite
Mississippi kite
bald eagle
sharp-shinned hawk
Cooper's hawk
red-shouldered hawk
broad-winged hawk
red-tailed hawk
American kestrel
clapper rail
king rail
purple gallinule
common moorhen
American coot
limpkin
sandhill crane
Wilson's plover
killdeer
American oystercatcher
willet
American woodcock
mourning dove
black-billed cuckoo
yellow-billed cuckoo
barn owl
eastern screech-owl
great horned owl
barred owl
common nighthawk
Chuck-Will's-widow
whip-poor-will
chimney swift
ruby-throated hummingbird
belted kingfisher
red-headed woodpecker
red-bellied woodpecker
downy woodpecker
hairy woodpecker
red-cockaded woodpecker

northern flicker
pileated woodpecker
eastern wood-pewee
acadian flycatcher
willow flycatcher
eastern phoebe
great crested flycatcher
eastern kingbird
horned lark
purple martin
tree swallow
northern rough-winged swallow
bank swallow
cliff swallow
barn swallow
blue jay
American crow
fish crow
Carolina chickadee
tufted titmouse
white-breasted nuthatch
brown-headed nuthatch
Carolina wren
Bewick's wren
house wren
marsh wren
blue-gray gnatcatcher
eastern bluebird
American robin
gray catbird
northern mockingbird
brown thrasher
cedar waxwing
loggerhead shrike
white-eyed vireo
Bell's vireo
yellow-throated vireo
warbling vireo
red-eyed vireo
Bachman's warbler
blue-winged warbler
northern parula
yellow warbler
black-throated blue warbler
yellow-throated warbler
pine warbler

prairie warbler
cerulean warbler
black-and-white warbler
American redstart
prothonotary warbler
worm-eating warbler
Swainson's warbler
ovenbird
Louisiana waterthrush
Kentucky warbler
common yellowthroat
hooded warbler
yellow-breasted chat
summer tanager
scarlet tanager
northern cardinal
blue grosbeak
indigo bunting
painted bunting
dickcissel
eastern towhee
Bachman's sparrow
chipping sparrow
field sparrow
lark sparrow
savannah sparrow
grasshopper sparrow
seaside sparrow
song sparrow
red-winged blackbird
eastern meadowlark
boat-tailed grackle
common grackle
brown-headed cowbird
orchard oriole
Baltimore oriole
house finch
American goldfinch

Region 5

pied-billed grebe
double-crested cormorant
anhinga
American bittern

least bittern
great blue heron
great egret
snowy egret
little blue heron
tricolored heron
cattle egret
green heron
black-crowned night-heron
yellow-crowned night-heron
white ibis
black vulture
turkey vulture
osprey
swallow-tailed kite
Mississippi kite
bald eagle
sharp-shinned hawk
Cooper's hawk
red-shouldered hawk
broad-winged hawk
red-tailed hawk
American kestrel
black rail
king rail
sora
common moorhen
American coot
killdeer
black-necked stilt
spotted sandpiper
American woodcock
mourning dove
yellow-billed cuckoo
barn owl
eastern screech-owl
great horned owl
barred owl
long-eared owl
common nighthawk
Chuck-Will's-widow
whip-poor-will
chimney swift
ruby-throated hummingbird
belted kingfisher
red-headed woodpecker

red-bellied woodpecker
downy woodpecker
hairy woodpecker
northern flicker
pileated woodpecker
eastern wood-pewee
acadian flycatcher
willow flycatcher
eastern phoebe
great crested flycatcher
western kingbird
eastern kingbird
scissor-tailed flycatcher
horned lark
purple martin
tree swallow
northern rough-winged swallow
bank swallow
cliff swallow
barn swallow
blue jay
American crow
fish crow
Carolina chickadee
tufted titmouse
white-breasted nuthatch
brown-headed nuthatch
brown creeper
Carolina wren
Bewick's wren
house wren
sedge wren
marsh wren
blue-gray gnatcatcher
eastern bluebird
American robin
gray catbird
northern mockingbird
brown thrasher
cedar waxwing
loggerhead shrike
white-eyed vireo
Bell's vireo
yellow-throated vireo
warbling vireo
red-eyed vireo

Bachman's warbler
blue-winged warbler
northern parula
yellow warbler
black-throated blue warbler
yellow-throated warbler
pine warbler
prairie warbler
cerulean warbler
black-and-white warbler
American redstart
prothonotary warbler
worm-eating warbler
Swainson's warbler
ovenbird
Louisiana waterthrush
Kentucky warbler
common yellowthroat
hooded warbler
yellow-breasted chat
summer tanager
scarlet tanager
northern cardinal
rose-breasted grosbeak
blue grosbeak
indigo bunting
painted bunting
dickcissel
eastern towhee
Bachman's sparrow
chipping sparrow
field sparrow
lark sparrow
savannah sparrow
grasshopper sparrow
song sparrow
red-winged blackbird
eastern meadowlark
boat-tailed grackle
common grackle
bronzed cowbird
brown-headed cowbird
orchard oriole
Baltimore oriole
house finch
American goldfinch

Region 6

pied-billed grebe
double-crested cormorant
anhinga
least bittern
great blue heron
great egret
snowy egret
little blue heron
tricolored heron
cattle egret
green heron
black-crowned night-heron
yellow-crowned night-heron
white ibis
white-faced ibis
roseate spoonbill
black vulture
turkey vulture
osprey
swallow-tailed kite
white-tailed kite
Mississippi kite
bald eagle
northern harrier
Harris's hawk
red-shouldered hawk
broad-winged hawk
Swainson's hawk
white-tailed hawk
red-tailed hawk
crested caracara
American kestrel
clapper rail
king rail
purple gallinule
common moorhen
American coot
Wilson's plover
killdeer
black-necked stilt
willet
white-winged dove
mourning dove
inca dove
common ground-dove

yellow-billed cuckoo
greater roadrunner
groove-billed ani
barn owl
eastern screech-owl
great horned owl
burrowing owl
barred owl
lesser nighthawk
common nighthawk
Chuck-Will's-widow
chimney swift
ruby-throated hummingbird
black-chinned hummingbird
belted kingfisher
green kingfisher
red-headed woodpecker
golden-fronted woodpecker
red-bellied woodpecker
ladder-backed woodpecker
downy woodpecker
hairy woodpecker
northern flicker
pileated woodpecker
eastern wood-pewee
acadian flycatcher
eastern phoebe
vermilion flycatcher
ash-throated flycatcher
great crested flycatcher
western kingbird
eastern kingbird
scissor-tailed flycatcher
horned lark
purple martin
tree swallow
northern rough-winged swallow
bank swallow
cliff swallow
cave swallow
barn swallow
blue jay
American crow
fish crow
Carolina chickadee
tufted titmouse

Carolina wren
Bewick's wren
marsh wren
blue-gray gnatcatcher
eastern bluebird
American robin
gray catbird
northern mockingbird
brown thrasher
long-billed thrasher
loggerhead shrike
white-eyed vireo
Bell's vireo
yellow-throated vireo
red-eyed vireo
northern parula
yellow-throated warbler
pine warbler
black-and-white warbler
prothonotary warbler
Swainson's warbler
Kentucky warbler
common yellowthroat
hooded warbler
yellow-breasted chat
summer tanager
northern cardinal
pyrrhuloxia
blue grosbeak
indigo bunting
painted bunting
dickcissel
eastern towhee
Bachman's sparrow
Cassin's sparrow
chipping sparrow
field sparrow
lark sparrow
grasshopper sparrow
Henslow's sparrow
seaside sparrow
red-winged blackbird
eastern meadowlark
yellow-headed blackbird
great-tailed grackle
boat-tailed grackle

common grackle
bronzed cowbird
brown-headed cowbird
orchard oriole
hooded oriole
Audubon's oriole
Baltimore oriole
Bullock's oriole

Region 7

pied-billed grebe
great blue heron
great egret
snowy egret
little blue heron
cattle egret
green heron
white-faced ibis
black vulture
turkey vulture
white-tailed kite
northern harrier
Cooper's hawk
common black-hawk
Harris's hawk
red-shouldered hawk
Swainson's hawk
white-tailed hawk
red-tailed hawk
crested caracara
American kestrel
common moorhen
American coot
Wilson's plover
killdeer
black-necked stilt
willet
white-winged dove
mourning dove
inca dove
common ground-dove
yellow-billed cuckoo
greater roadrunner
groove-billed ani

barn owl
eastern screech-owl
great horned owl
ferruginous pygmy-owl
elf owl
burrowing owl
barred owl
lesser nighthawk
common nighthawk
common poorwill
Chuck-Will's-widow
chimney swift
ruby-throated hummingbird
black-chinned hummingbird
belted kingfisher
green kingfisher
red-headed woodpecker
golden-fronted woodpecker
red-bellied woodpecker
ladder-backed woodpecker
downy woodpecker
northern beardless-tyrannulet
western wood-pewee
black phoebe
eastern phoebe
vermilion flycatcher
ash-throated flycatcher
great crested flycatcher
western kingbird
eastern kingbird
scissor-tailed flycatcher
horned lark
purple martin
northern rough-winged swallow
bank swallow
cliff swallow
cave swallow
barn swallow
American crow
chihuahuan raven
Carolina chickadee
tufted titmouse
verdin
cactus wren
rock wren
canyon wren

Carolina wren
Bewick's wren
marsh wren
blue-gray gnatcatcher
black-tailed gnatcatcher
eastern bluebird
American robin
northern mockingbird
long-billed thrasher
curve-billed thrasher
loggerhead shrike
white-eyed vireo
Bell's vireo
red-eyed vireo
common yellowthroat
yellow-breasted chat
summer tanager
northern cardinal
pyrrhuloxia
blue grosbeak
indigo bunting
varied bunting
painted bunting
dickcissel
Cassin's sparrow
rufous-crowned sparrow
chipping sparrow
field sparrow
lark sparrow
black-throated sparrow
grasshopper sparrow
seaside sparrow
red-winged blackbird
eastern meadowlark
western meadowlark
yellow-headed blackbird
great-tailed grackle
common grackle
bronzed cowbird
brown-headed cowbird
orchard oriole
hooded oriole
Audubon's oriole
Bullock's oriole
house finch
lesser goldfinch

Region 8

great blue heron
great egret
snowy egret
little blue heron
cattle egret
green heron
yellow-crowned night-heron
black vulture
turkey vulture
swallow-tailed kite
white-tailed kite
Mississippi kite
northern harrier
Cooper's hawk
Harris's hawk
red-shouldered hawk
broad-winged hawk
Swainson's hawk
red-tailed hawk
crested caracara
American kestrel
killdeer
American woodcock
white-winged dove
mourning dove
inca dove
common ground-dove
black-billed cuckoo
yellow-billed cuckoo
greater roadrunner
barn owl
eastern screech-owl
great horned owl
burrowing owl
barred owl
common nighthawk
common poorwill
Chuck-Will's-widow
whip-poor-will
chimney swift
ruby-throated hummingbird
black-chinned hummingbird
belted kingfisher
red-headed woodpecker
golden-fronted woodpecker

red-bellied woodpecker
ladder-backed woodpecker
downy woodpecker
hairy woodpecker
northern flicker
pileated woodpecker
eastern wood-pewee
acadian flycatcher
eastern phoebe
vermilion flycatcher
ash-throated flycatcher
great crested flycatcher
western kingbird
eastern kingbird
scissor-tailed flycatcher
horned lark
purple martin
northern rough-winged swallow
bank swallow
cliff swallow
cave swallow
barn swallow
blue jay
American crow
fish crow
Carolina chickadee
tufted titmouse
white-breasted nuthatch
cactus wren
canyon wren
Carolina wren
Bewick's wren
house wren
marsh wren
blue-gray gnatcatcher
eastern bluebird
American robin
gray catbird
northern mockingbird
brown thrasher
curve-billed thrasher
loggerhead shrike
white-eyed vireo
Bell's vireo
yellow-throated vireo
warbling vireo

red-eyed vireo
northern parula
yellow warbler
yellow-throated warbler
pine warbler
prairie warbler
black-and-white warbler
American redstart
prothonotary warbler
worm-eating warbler
Swainson's warbler
Louisiana waterthrush
Kentucky warbler
common yellowthroat
hooded warbler
yellow-breasted chat
summer tanager
northern cardinal
pyrrhuloxia
blue grosbeak
indigo bunting
painted bunting
dickcissel
Cassin's sparrow
rufous-winged sparrow
chipping sparrow
field sparrow
lark sparrow
grasshopper sparrow
red-winged blackbird
eastern meadowlark
western meadowlark
great-tailed grackle
common grackle
bronzed cowbird
brown-headed cowbird
orchard oriole
Baltimore oriole
Bullock's oriole
house finch
American goldfinch

Region 9

common loon
pied-billed grebe

double-crested cormorant
American bittern
least bittern
great blue heron
great egret
snowy egret
little blue heron
tricolored heron
cattle egret
green heron
black-crowned night-heron
yellow-crowned night-heron
glossy ibis
turkey vulture
osprey
northern harrier
sharp-shinned hawk
Cooper's hawk
northern goshawk
red-shouldered hawk
broad-winged hawk
red-tailed hawk
American kestrel
peregrine falcon
black rail
clapper rail
king rail
Virginia rail
sora
common moorhen
American coot
piping plover
killdeer
American oystercatcher
willet
spotted sandpiper
upland sandpiper
common snipe
American woodcock
Wilson's phalarope
mourning dove
black-billed cuckoo
yellow-billed cuckoo
barn owl
eastern screech-owl
great horned owl

barred owl
long-eared owl
short-eared owl
northern saw-whet owl
common nighthawk
Chuck-Will's-widow
whip-poor-will
chimney swift
ruby-throated hummingbird
belted kingfisher
red-headed woodpecker
red-bellied woodpecker
yellow-bellied sapsucker
downy woodpecker
hairy woodpecker
northern flicker
pileated woodpecker
olive-sided flycatcher
eastern wood-pewee
acadian flycatcher
alder flycatcher
willow flycatcher
least flycatcher
eastern phoebe
great crested flycatcher
eastern kingbird
horned lark
purple martin
tree swallow
northern rough-winged swallow
bank swallow
cliff swallow
barn swallow
blue jay
American crow
fish crow
common raven
black-capped chickadee
tufted titmouse
red-breasted nuthatch
white-breasted nuthatch
brown creeper
Carolina wren
house wren
winter wren
sedge wren

marsh wren
golden-crowned kinglet
blue-gray gnatcatcher
eastern bluebird
veery
hermit thrush
American robin
gray catbird
northern mockingbird
brown thrasher
cedar waxwing
white-eyed vireo
blue-headed vireo
yellow-throated vireo
warbling vireo
red-eyed vireo
blue-winged warbler
golden-winged warbler
Nashville warbler
northern parula
yellow warbler
chestnut-sided warbler
magnolia warbler
black-throated blue warbler
yellow-rumped warbler
black-throated green warbler
blackburnian warbler
pine warbler
prairie warbler
cerulean warbler
black-and-white warbler
American redstart
prothonotary warbler
worm-eating warbler
ovenbird
northern waterthrush
Louisiana waterthrush
Kentucky warbler
common yellowthroat
hooded warbler
Canada warbler
yellow-breasted chat
scarlet tanager
northern cardinal
rose-breasted grosbeak
blue grosbeak

indigo bunting
eastern towhee
chipping sparrow
field sparrow
vesper sparrow
savannah sparrow
grasshopper sparrow
Henslow's sparrow
saltmarsh sharp-tailed sparrow
seaside sparrow
song sparrow
swamp sparrow
white-throated sparrow
dark-eyed junco
bobolink
red-winged blackbird
eastern meadowlark
boat-tailed grackle
common grackle
brown-headed cowbird
orchard oriole
Baltimore oriole
purple finch
house finch
red crossbill
pine siskin
American goldfinch
evening grosbeak

Region 10

great blue heron
green heron
black vulture
turkey vulture
osprey
bald eagle
northern harrier
sharp-shinned hawk
Cooper's hawk
red-shouldered hawk
broad-winged hawk
red-tailed hawk
American kestrel
killdeer

upland sandpiper
American woodcock
mourning dove
black-billed cuckoo
yellow-billed cuckoo
barn owl
eastern screech-owl
great horned owl
barred owl
long-eared owl
short-eared owl
common nighthawk
Chuck-Will's-widow
whip-poor-will
chimney swift
ruby-throated hummingbird
belted kingfisher
red-headed woodpecker
red-bellied woodpecker
downy woodpecker
hairy woodpecker
northern flicker
pileated woodpecker
eastern wood-pewee
acadian flycatcher
willow flycatcher
least flycatcher
eastern phoebe
great crested flycatcher
eastern kingbird
horned lark
purple martin
tree swallow
northern rough-winged swallow
bank swallow
cliff swallow
barn swallow
blue jay
American crow
fish crow
common raven
black-capped chickadee
Carolina chickadee
tufted titmouse
white-breasted nuthatch
brown-headed nuthatch

brown creeper
Carolina wren
house wren
sedge wren
marsh wren
blue-gray gnatcatcher
eastern bluebird
veery
American robin
gray catbird
northern mockingbird
brown thrasher
cedar waxwing
loggerhead shrike
white-eyed vireo
blue-headed vireo
yellow-throated vireo
warbling vireo
red-eyed vireo
blue-winged warbler
northern parula
yellow warbler
chestnut-sided warbler
black-throated green warbler
yellow-throated warbler
pine warbler
prairie warbler
cerulean warbler
black-and-white warbler
American redstart
prothonotary warbler
worm-eating warbler
ovenbird
Louisiana waterthrush
Kentucky warbler
common yellowthroat
hooded warbler
Canada warbler
yellow-breasted chat
summer tanager
scarlet tanager
northern cardinal
rose-breasted grosbeak
blue grosbeak
indigo bunting
dickcissel

eastern towhee
Bachman's sparrow
chipping sparrow
field sparrow
vesper sparrow
savannah sparrow
grasshopper sparrow
Henslow's sparrow
song sparrow
swamp sparrow
dark-eyed junco
bobolink
red-winged blackbird
eastern meadowlark
common grackle
brown-headed cowbird
orchard oriole
Baltimore oriole
house finch
red crossbill
American goldfinch

Region 11

great blue heron
great egret
little blue heron
cattle egret
green heron
black vulture
turkey vulture
osprey
bald eagle
sharp-shinned hawk
Cooper's hawk
red-shouldered hawk
broad-winged hawk
red-tailed hawk
American kestrel
killdeer
American woodcock
mourning dove
common ground-dove
black-billed cuckoo
yellow-billed cuckoo

barn owl
eastern screech-owl
great horned owl
barred owl
common nighthawk
Chuck-Will's-widow
whip-poor-will
chimney swift
ruby-throated hummingbird
belted kingfisher
red-headed woodpecker
red-bellied woodpecker
downy woodpecker
hairy woodpecker
red-cockaded woodpecker
northern flicker
pileated woodpecker
eastern wood-pewee
acadian flycatcher
willow flycatcher
eastern phoebe
great crested flycatcher
eastern kingbird
horned lark
purple martin
tree swallow
northern rough-winged swallow
bank swallow
cliff swallow
barn swallow
blue jay
American crow
fish crow
Carolina chickadee
tufted titmouse
white-breasted nuthatch
brown-headed nuthatch
Carolina wren
house wren
blue-gray gnatcatcher
eastern bluebird
American robin
gray catbird
northern mockingbird
brown thrasher
cedar waxwing

loggerhead shrike
white-eyed vireo
blue-headed vireo
yellow-throated vireo
warbling vireo
red-eyed vireo
blue-winged warbler
northern parula
yellow warbler
chestnut-sided warbler
black-throated blue warbler
black-throated green warbler
yellow-throated warbler
pine warbler
prairie warbler
cerulean warbler
black-and-white warbler
American redstart
prothonotary warbler
worm-eating warbler
Swainson's warbler
ovenbird
Louisiana waterthrush
Kentucky warbler
common yellowthroat
hooded warbler
yellow-breasted chat
summer tanager
scarlet tanager
northern cardinal
rose-breasted grosbeak
blue grosbeak
indigo bunting
painted bunting
dickcissel
eastern towhee
Bachman's sparrow
chipping sparrow
field sparrow
grasshopper sparrow
song sparrow
red-winged blackbird
eastern meadowlark
common grackle
brown-headed cowbird
orchard oriole

Baltimore oriole
house finch
red crossbill
American goldfinch

Region 12

American bittern
great blue heron
green heron
black vulture
turkey vulture
osprey
bald eagle
northern harrier
sharp-shinned hawk
Cooper's hawk
northern goshawk
red-shouldered hawk
broad-winged hawk
red-tailed hawk
American kestrel
peregrine falcon
Virginia rail
sora
killdeer
spotted sandpiper
upland sandpiper
common snipe
American woodcock
mourning dove
black-billed cuckoo
yellow-billed cuckoo
barn owl
eastern screech-owl
great horned owl
barred owl
long-eared owl
northern saw-whet owl
common nighthawk
Chuck-Will's-widow
whip-poor-will
chimney swift
ruby-throated hummingbird
belted kingfisher

red-headed woodpecker
red-bellied woodpecker
yellow-bellied sapsucker
downy woodpecker
hairy woodpecker
northern flicker
pileated woodpecker
olive-sided flycatcher
eastern wood-pewee
yellow-bellied flycatcher
acadian flycatcher
alder flycatcher
willow flycatcher
least flycatcher
eastern phoebe
great crested flycatcher
eastern kingbird
horned lark
purple martin
tree swallow
northern rough-winged swallow
bank swallow
cliff swallow
barn swallow
blue jay
American crow
fish crow
common raven
black-capped chickadee
Carolina chickadee
tufted titmouse
red-breasted nuthatch
white-breasted nuthatch
brown creeper
Carolina wren
Bewick's wren
house wren
winter wren
sedge wren
golden-crowned kinglet
blue-gray gnatcatcher
eastern bluebird
veery
Swainson's thrush
hermit thrush
American robin

gray catbird
northern mockingbird
brown thrasher
cedar waxwing
loggerhead shrike
white-eyed vireo
blue-headed vireo
yellow-throated vireo
warbling vireo
red-eyed vireo
blue-winged warbler
golden-winged warbler
Nashville warbler
northern parula
yellow warbler
chestnut-sided warbler
magnolia warbler
black-throated blue warbler
yellow-rumped warbler
black-throated green warbler
blackburnian warbler
yellow-throated warbler
pine warbler
prairie warbler
cerulean warbler
black-and-white warbler
American redstart
prothonotary warbler
worm-eating warbler
Swainson's warbler
ovenbird
northern waterthrush
Louisiana waterthrush
Kentucky warbler
mourning warbler
common yellowthroat
hooded warbler
Canada warbler
yellow-breasted chat
summer tanager
scarlet tanager
northern cardinal
rose-breasted grosbeak
blue grosbeak
indigo bunting
dickcissel

eastern towhee
chipping sparrow
field sparrow
vesper sparrow
savannah sparrow
grasshopper sparrow
Henslow's sparrow
song sparrow
swamp sparrow
white-throated sparrow
dark-eyed junco
bobolink
red-winged blackbird
eastern meadowlark
common grackle
brown-headed cowbird
orchard oriole
Baltimore oriole
purple finch
house finch
red crossbill
pine siskin
American goldfinch

Region 13

pied-billed grebe
American bittern
least bittern
great blue heron
great egret
cattle egret
green heron
black-crowned night-heron
yellow-crowned night-heron
black vulture
turkey vulture
sharp-shinned hawk
Cooper's hawk
red-shouldered hawk
broad-winged hawk
red-tailed hawk
American kestrel
king rail
common moorhen

killdeer
American woodcock
mourning dove
black-billed cuckoo
yellow-billed cuckoo
barn owl
eastern screech-owl
great horned owl
barred owl
common nighthawk
Chuck-Will's-widow
whip-poor-will
chimney swift
ruby-throated hummingbird
belted kingfisher
red-headed woodpecker
red-bellied woodpecker
downy woodpecker
hairy woodpecker
red-cockaded woodpecker
northern flicker
pileated woodpecker
eastern wood-pewee
acadian flycatcher
willow flycatcher
eastern phoebe
great crested flycatcher
eastern kingbird
horned lark
purple martin
northern rough-winged swallow
bank swallow
cliff swallow
barn swallow
blue jay
American crow
fish crow
Carolina chickadee
tufted titmouse
white-breasted nuthatch
brown-headed nuthatch
Carolina wren
Bewick's wren
house wren
blue-gray gnatcatcher
eastern bluebird

American robin
gray catbird
northern mockingbird
brown thrasher
cedar waxwing
loggerhead shrike
white-eyed vireo
blue-headed vireo
yellow-throated vireo
warbling vireo
red-eyed vireo
blue-winged warbler
golden-winged warbler
northern parula
yellow warbler
black-throated blue warbler
black-throated green warbler
yellow-throated warbler
pine warbler
prairie warbler
cerulean warbler
black-and-white warbler
American redstart
prothonotary warbler
worm-eating warbler
Swainson's warbler
ovenbird
Louisiana waterthrush
Kentucky warbler
common yellowthroat
hooded warbler
yellow-breasted chat
summer tanager
scarlet tanager
northern cardinal
blue grosbeak
indigo bunting
dickcissel
eastern towhee
Bachman's sparrow
chipping sparrow
field sparrow
savannah sparrow
grasshopper sparrow
song sparrow
red-winged blackbird

eastern meadowlark
common grackle
brown-headed cowbird
orchard oriole
Baltimore oriole
house finch
red crossbill
American goldfinch

Region 14

pied-billed grebe
American bittern
least bittern
great blue heron
great egret
snowy egret
little blue heron
tricolored heron
cattle egret
green heron
black-crowned night-heron
yellow-crowned night-heron
black vulture
turkey vulture
osprey
Mississippi kite
bald eagle
northern harrier
sharp-shinned hawk
Cooper's hawk
red-shouldered hawk
broad-winged hawk
red-tailed hawk
American kestrel
peregrine falcon
king rail
Virginia rail
sora
common moorhen
American coot
killdeer
spotted sandpiper
common snipe
American woodcock

mourning dove
black-billed cuckoo
yellow-billed cuckoo
barn owl
eastern screech-owl
great horned owl
barred owl
short-eared owl
northern saw-whet owl
common nighthawk
Chuck-Will's-widow
whip-poor-will
chimney swift
ruby-throated hummingbird
belted kingfisher
red-headed woodpecker
red-bellied woodpecker
downy woodpecker
hairy woodpecker
northern flicker
pileated woodpecker
eastern wood-pewee
acadian flycatcher
willow flycatcher
least flycatcher
eastern phoebe
great crested flycatcher
eastern kingbird
horned lark
purple martin
tree swallow
northern rough-winged swallow
bank swallow
cliff swallow
barn swallow
blue jay
American crow
fish crow
Carolina chickadee
tufted titmouse
red-breasted nuthatch
white-breasted nuthatch
brown creeper
Carolina wren
Bewick's wren
house wren

sedge wren
marsh wren
blue-gray gnatcatcher
eastern bluebird
American robin
gray catbird
northern mockingbird
brown thrasher
cedar waxwing
loggerhead shrike
white-eyed vireo
Bell's vireo
blue-headed vireo
yellow-throated vireo
warbling vireo
red-eyed vireo
blue-winged warbler
northern parula
yellow warbler
chestnut-sided warbler
black-throated green warbler
yellow-throated warbler
pine warbler
prairie warbler
cerulean warbler
black-and-white warbler
American redstart
prothonotary warbler
worm-eating warbler
Swainson's warbler
ovenbird
Louisiana waterthrush
Kentucky warbler
common yellowthroat
hooded warbler
yellow-breasted chat
summer tanager
scarlet tanager
northern cardinal
rose-breasted grosbeak
blue grosbeak
indigo bunting
dickcissel
eastern towhee
Bachman's sparrow
chipping sparrow

field sparrow
vesper sparrow
lark sparrow
savannah sparrow
grasshopper sparrow
Henslow's sparrow
song sparrow
bobolink
red-winged blackbird
eastern meadowlark
western meadowlark
common grackle
brown-headed cowbird
orchard oriole
Baltimore oriole
house finch
American goldfinch

Region 15

pied-billed grebe
double-crested cormorant
American bittern
least bittern
great blue heron
green heron
black-crowned night-heron
turkey vulture
osprey
bald eagle
northern harrier
sharp-shinned hawk
Cooper's hawk
northern goshawk
red-shouldered hawk
broad-winged hawk
red-tailed hawk
American kestrel
king rail
Virginia rail
sora
common moorhen
American coot
killdeer
spotted sandpiper

upland sandpiper
common snipe
American woodcock
mourning dove
black-billed cuckoo
yellow-billed cuckoo
barn owl
eastern screech-owl
great horned owl
barred owl
long-eared owl
short-eared owl
northern saw-whet owl
common nighthawk
whip-poor-will
chimney swift
ruby-throated hummingbird
belted kingfisher
red-headed woodpecker
red-bellied woodpecker
yellow-bellied sapsucker
downy woodpecker
hairy woodpecker
northern flicker
pileated woodpecker
eastern wood-pewee
acadian flycatcher
alder flycatcher
willow flycatcher
least flycatcher
eastern phoebe
great crested flycatcher
eastern kingbird
horned lark
purple martin
tree swallow
northern rough-winged swallow
bank swallow
cliff swallow
barn swallow
blue jay
American crow
fish crow
black-capped chickadee
tufted titmouse
red-breasted nuthatch

white-breasted nuthatch
brown creeper
Carolina wren
house wren
winter wren
sedge wren
marsh wren
golden-crowned kinglet
blue-gray gnatcatcher
eastern bluebird
veery
hermit thrush
American robin
gray catbird
northern mockingbird
brown thrasher
cedar waxwing
loggerhead shrike
white-eyed vireo
blue-headed vireo
yellow-throated vireo
warbling vireo
red-eyed vireo
blue-winged warbler
golden-winged warbler
Nashville warbler
yellow warbler
chestnut-sided warbler
magnolia warbler
black-throated blue warbler
yellow-rumped warbler
black-throated green warbler
blackburnian warbler
pine warbler
prairie warbler
cerulean warbler
black-and-white warbler
American redstart
prothonotary warbler
ovenbird
northern waterthrush
Louisiana waterthrush
Kentucky warbler
mourning warbler
common yellowthroat
hooded warbler

Canada warbler
yellow-breasted chat
scarlet tanager
northern cardinal
rose-breasted grosbeak
indigo bunting
dickcissel
eastern towhee
chipping sparrow
clay-colored sparrow
field sparrow
vesper sparrow
savannah sparrow
grasshopper sparrow
Henslow's sparrow
song sparrow
swamp sparrow
white-throated sparrow
dark-eyed junco
bobolink
red-winged blackbird
eastern meadowlark
western meadowlark
Brewer's blackbird
common grackle
brown-headed cowbird
orchard oriole
Baltimore oriole
purple finch
house finch
pine siskin
American goldfinch
evening grosbeak

Region 16

pied-billed grebe
red-necked grebe
western grebe
American white pelican
double-crested cormorant
American bittern
least bittern
great blue heron
great egret

snowy egret
cattle egret
green heron
black-crowned night-heron
yellow-crowned night-heron
turkey vulture
osprey
bald eagle
northern harrier
sharp-shinned hawk
Cooper's hawk
northern goshawk
red-shouldered hawk
broad-winged hawk
Swainson's hawk
red-tailed hawk
American kestrel
peregrine falcon
black rail
king rail
Virginia rail
sora
common moorhen
American coot
sandhill crane
killdeer
spotted sandpiper
upland sandpiper
common snipe
American woodcock
Wilson's phalarope
mourning dove
black-billed cuckoo
yellow-billed cuckoo
barn owl
eastern screech-owl
great horned owl
barred owl
long-eared owl
short-eared owl
northern saw-whet owl
common nighthawk
Chuck-Will's-widow
whip-poor-will
chimney swift
ruby-throated hummingbird

belted kingfisher
red-headed woodpecker
red-bellied woodpecker
yellow-bellied sapsucker
downy woodpecker
hairy woodpecker
northern flicker
pileated woodpecker
eastern wood-pewee
acadian flycatcher
alder flycatcher
willow flycatcher
least flycatcher
eastern phoebe
great crested flycatcher
western kingbird
eastern kingbird
horned lark
purple martin
tree swallow
northern rough-winged swallow
bank swallow
cliff swallow
barn swallow
blue jay
American crow
black-capped chickadee
Carolina chickadee
tufted titmouse
red-breasted nuthatch
white-breasted nuthatch
brown creeper
Carolina wren
Bewick's wren
house wren
winter wren
sedge wren
marsh wren
blue-gray gnatcatcher
eastern bluebird
veery
American robin
gray catbird
northern mockingbird
brown thrasher
cedar waxwing

loggerhead shrike
white-eyed vireo
Bell's vireo
blue-headed vireo
yellow-throated vireo
warbling vireo
red-eyed vireo
blue-winged warbler
golden-winged warbler
Nashville warbler
northern parula
yellow warbler
chestnut-sided warbler
black-throated green warbler
blackburnian warbler
yellow-throated warbler
pine warbler
prairie warbler
cerulean warbler
black-and-white warbler
American redstart
prothonotary warbler
worm-eating warbler
ovenbird
northern waterthrush
Louisiana waterthrush
Kentucky warbler
mourning warbler
common yellowthroat
hooded warbler
Canada warbler
yellow-breasted chat
summer tanager
scarlet tanager
northern cardinal
rose-breasted grosbeak
blue grosbeak
indigo bunting
dickcissel
eastern towhee
chipping sparrow
clay-colored sparrow
field sparrow
vesper sparrow
lark sparrow
savannah sparrow

grasshopper sparrow
Henslow's sparrow
song sparrow
swamp sparrow
white-throated sparrow
bobolink
red-winged blackbird
eastern meadowlark
western meadowlark
yellow-headed blackbird
Brewer's blackbird
common grackle
brown-headed cowbird
orchard oriole
Baltimore oriole
purple finch
house finch
pine siskin
American goldfinch

Region 17

pied-billed grebe
American bittern
least bittern
great blue heron
great egret
snowy egret
cattle egret
green heron
black-crowned night-heron
yellow-crowned night-heron
black vulture
turkey vulture
osprey
bald eagle
northern harrier
sharp-shinned hawk
Cooper's hawk
northern goshawk
red-shouldered hawk
broad-winged hawk
red-tailed hawk
American kestrel
peregrine falcon

king rail
Virginia rail
sora
common moorhen
American coot
killdeer
spotted sandpiper
upland sandpiper
common snipe
American woodcock
mourning dove
black-billed cuckoo
yellow-billed cuckoo
barn owl
eastern screech-owl
great horned owl
barred owl
long-eared owl
northern saw-whet owl
common nighthawk
whip-poor-will
chimney swift
ruby-throated hummingbird
belted kingfisher
red-headed woodpecker
red-bellied woodpecker
yellow-bellied sapsucker
downy woodpecker
hairy woodpecker
northern flicker
pileated woodpecker
olive-sided flycatcher
eastern wood-pewee
yellow-bellied flycatcher
acadian flycatcher
alder flycatcher
willow flycatcher
least flycatcher
eastern phoebe
great crested flycatcher
eastern kingbird
horned lark
purple martin
tree swallow
northern rough-winged
    swallow

bank swallow
cliff swallow
barn swallow
blue jay
American crow
fish crow
common raven
black-capped chickadee
Carolina chickadee
tufted titmouse
red-breasted nuthatch
white-breasted nuthatch
brown creeper
Carolina wren
house wren
winter wren
sedge wren
marsh wren
golden-crowned kinglet
blue-gray gnatcatcher
eastern bluebird
veery
Bicknell's thrush
Swainson's thrush
hermit thrush
American robin
gray catbird
northern mockingbird
brown thrasher
cedar waxwing
loggerhead shrike
white-eyed vireo
blue-headed vireo
yellow-throated vireo
warbling vireo
red-eyed vireo
blue-winged warbler
golden-winged warbler
Nashville warbler
northern parula
yellow warbler
chestnut-sided warbler
magnolia warbler
black-throated blue warbler
yellow-rumped warbler
black-throated green warbler

blackburnian warbler
yellow-throated warbler
pine warbler
prairie warbler
cerulean warbler
black-and-white warbler
American redstart
prothonotary warbler
worm-eating warbler
ovenbird
northern waterthrush
Louisiana waterthrush
Kentucky warbler
mourning warbler
common yellowthroat
hooded warbler
Canada warbler
yellow-breasted chat
scarlet tanager
northern cardinal
rose-breasted grosbeak
blue grosbeak
indigo bunting
dickcissel
eastern towhee
chipping sparrow
field sparrow
vesper sparrow
savannah sparrow
grasshopper sparrow
Henslow's sparrow
song sparrow
swamp sparrow
white-throated sparrow
dark-eyed junco
bobolink
red-winged blackbird
eastern meadowlark
common grackle
brown-headed cowbird
orchard oriole
Baltimore oriole
purple finch
house finch
pine siskin
American goldfinch

Region 18

common loon
pied-billed grebe
double-crested cormorant
American bittern
least bittern
great blue heron
green heron
black-crowned night-heron
turkey vulture
osprey
bald eagle
northern harrier
sharp-shinned hawk
Cooper's hawk
northern goshawk
red-shouldered hawk
broad-winged hawk
red-tailed hawk
American kestrel
Virginia rail
sora
common moorhen
American coot
piping plover
killdeer
spotted sandpiper
upland sandpiper
common snipe
American woodcock
mourning dove
black-billed cuckoo
yellow-billed cuckoo
barn owl
eastern screech-owl
great horned owl
barred owl
long-eared owl
short-eared owl
northern saw-whet owl
common nighthawk
whip-poor-will
chimney swift
ruby-throated hummingbird
belted kingfisher
red-headed woodpecker

red-bellied woodpecker
yellow-bellied sapsucker
downy woodpecker
hairy woodpecker
northern flicker
pileated woodpecker
olive-sided flycatcher
eastern wood-pewee
alder flycatcher
willow flycatcher
least flycatcher
eastern phoebe
great crested flycatcher
eastern kingbird
horned lark
purple martin
tree swallow
northern rough-winged swallow
bank swallow
cliff swallow
barn swallow
blue jay
American crow
common raven
black-capped chickadee
tufted titmouse
red-breasted nuthatch
white-breasted nuthatch
brown creeper
Carolina wren
house wren
winter wren
sedge wren
marsh wren
golden-crowned kinglet
ruby-crowned kinglet
blue-gray gnatcatcher
eastern bluebird
veery
Swainson's thrush
hermit thrush
American robin
gray catbird
northern mockingbird
brown thrasher
cedar waxwing

loggerhead shrike
blue-headed vireo
yellow-throated vireo
warbling vireo
Philadelphia vireo
red-eyed vireo
blue-winged warbler
golden-winged warbler
Tennessee warbler
Nashville warbler
yellow warbler
chestnut-sided warbler
magnolia warbler
black-throated blue warbler
yellow-rumped warbler
black-throated green warbler
blackburnian warbler
pine warbler
prairie warbler
bay-breasted warbler
cerulean warbler
black-and-white warbler
American redstart
ovenbird
northern waterthrush
Louisiana waterthrush
mourning warbler
common yellowthroat
hooded warbler
Wilson's warbler
Canada warbler
scarlet tanager
northern cardinal
rose-breasted grosbeak
indigo bunting
eastern towhee
chipping sparrow
clay-colored sparrow
field sparrow
vesper sparrow
savannah sparrow
grasshopper sparrow
Henslow's sparrow
song sparrow
Lincoln's sparrow
swamp sparrow

white-throated sparrow
dark-eyed junco
bobolink
red-winged blackbird
eastern meadowlark
western meadowlark
rusty blackbird
Brewer's blackbird
common grackle
brown-headed cowbird
orchard oriole
Baltimore oriole
purple finch
house finch
red crossbill
pine siskin
American goldfinch
evening grosbeak

Region 19

pied-billed grebe
American bittern
least bittern
great blue heron
great egret
little blue heron
cattle egret
green heron
black-crowned night-heron
yellow-crowned night-heron
black vulture
turkey vulture
Mississippi kite
bald eagle
northern harrier
sharp-shinned hawk
Cooper's hawk
red-shouldered hawk
broad-winged hawk
red-tailed hawk
American kestrel
peregrine falcon
sora
common moorhen

American coot
killdeer
spotted sandpiper
upland sandpiper
American woodcock
mourning dove
black-billed cuckoo
yellow-billed cuckoo
greater roadrunner
barn owl
eastern screech-owl
great horned owl
barred owl
long-eared owl
short-eared owl
common nighthawk
Chuck-Will's-widow
whip-poor-will
chimney swift
ruby-throated hummingbird
belted kingfisher
red-headed woodpecker
red-bellied woodpecker
downy woodpecker
hairy woodpecker
red-cockaded woodpecker
northern flicker
pileated woodpecker
eastern wood-pewee
acadian flycatcher
willow flycatcher
least flycatcher
eastern phoebe
great crested flycatcher
western kingbird
eastern kingbird
scissor-tailed flycatcher
horned lark
purple martin
tree swallow
northern rough-winged swallow
bank swallow
cliff swallow
barn swallow
blue jay
American crow

fish crow
black-capped chickadee
Carolina chickadee
tufted titmouse
white-breasted nuthatch
brown-headed nuthatch
brown creeper
Carolina wren
Bewick's wren
house wren
sedge wren
marsh wren
blue-gray gnatcatcher
eastern bluebird
American robin
gray catbird
northern mockingbird
brown thrasher
cedar waxwing
loggerhead shrike
white-eyed vireo
Bell's vireo
yellow-throated vireo
warbling vireo
red-eyed vireo
blue-winged warbler
northern parula
yellow warbler
chestnut-sided warbler
black-throated green warbler
yellow-throated warbler
pine warbler
prairie warbler
cerulean warbler
black-and-white warbler
American redstart
prothonotary warbler
worm-eating warbler
Swainson's warbler
ovenbird
Louisiana waterthrush
Kentucky warbler
common yellowthroat
hooded warbler
yellow-breasted chat
summer tanager

scarlet tanager
northern cardinal
rose-breasted grosbeak
blue grosbeak
indigo bunting
painted bunting
dickcissel
eastern towhee
Bachman's sparrow
rufous-crowned sparrow
chipping sparrow
field sparrow
vesper sparrow
lark sparrow
savannah sparrow
grasshopper sparrow
Henslow's sparrow
song sparrow
red-winged blackbird
eastern meadowlark
western meadowlark
great-tailed grackle
common grackle
brown-headed cowbird
orchard oriole
Baltimore oriole
house finch
pine siskin
American goldfinch

Region 20

common loon
pied-billed grebe
horned grebe
red-necked grebe
eared grebe
western grebe
American white pelican
double-crested cormorant
American bittern
least bittern
great blue heron
great egret
little blue heron

green heron
black-crowned night-heron
yellow-crowned night-heron
turkey vulture
osprey
bald eagle
northern harrier
sharp-shinned hawk
Cooper's hawk
northern goshawk
red-shouldered hawk
broad-winged hawk
red-tailed hawk
American kestrel
merlin
peregrine falcon
yellow rail
king rail
Virginia rail
sora
common moorhen
American coot
sandhill crane
piping plover
killdeer
spotted sandpiper
upland sandpiper
common snipe
American woodcock
Wilson's phalarope
mourning dove
black-billed cuckoo
yellow-billed cuckoo
barn owl
eastern screech-owl
great horned owl
northern hawk owl
barred owl
great gray owl
long-eared owl
short-eared owl
boreal owl
northern saw-whet owl
common nighthawk
whip-poor-will
chimney swift

ruby-throated hummingbird
belted kingfisher
red-headed woodpecker
red-bellied woodpecker
yellow-bellied sapsucker
downy woodpecker
hairy woodpecker
three-toed woodpecker
black-backed woodpecker
northern flicker
pileated woodpecker
olive-sided flycatcher
eastern wood-pewee
yellow-bellied flycatcher
alder flycatcher
willow flycatcher
least flycatcher
eastern phoebe
great crested flycatcher
western kingbird
eastern kingbird
horned lark
purple martin
tree swallow
northern rough-winged swallow
bank swallow
cliff swallow
barn swallow
gray jay
blue jay
black-billed magpie
American crow
common raven
black-capped chickadee
tufted titmouse
red-breasted nuthatch
white-breasted nuthatch
brown creeper
Bewick's wren
house wren
winter wren
sedge wren
marsh wren
golden-crowned kinglet
ruby-crowned kinglet
blue-gray gnatcatcher

eastern bluebird
veery
Swainson's thrush
hermit thrush
American robin
gray catbird
northern mockingbird
brown thrasher
cedar waxwing
loggerhead shrike
white-eyed vireo
blue-headed vireo
yellow-throated vireo
warbling vireo
Philadelphia vireo
red-eyed vireo
blue-winged warbler
golden-winged warbler
Tennessee warbler
Nashville warbler
northern parula
yellow warbler
chestnut-sided warbler
magnolia warbler
cape may warbler
black-throated blue warbler
yellow-rumped warbler
black-throated green warbler
blackburnian warbler
pine warbler
palm warbler
bay-breasted warbler
cerulean warbler
black-and-white warbler
American redstart
prothonotary warbler
worm-eating warbler
ovenbird
northern waterthrush
Louisiana waterthrush
Connecticut warbler
mourning warbler
common yellowthroat
hooded warbler
Wilson's warbler
Canada warbler

scarlet tanager
northern cardinal
rose-breasted grosbeak
indigo bunting
dickcissel
eastern towhee
chipping sparrow
clay-colored sparrow
field sparrow
vesper sparrow
lark sparrow
savannah sparrow
grasshopper sparrow
Henslow's sparrow
le Conte's sparrow
Nelson's sharp-tailed sparrow
song sparrow
Lincoln's sparrow
swamp sparrow
white-throated sparrow
dark-eyed junco
bobolink
red-winged blackbird
eastern meadowlark
western meadowlark
yellow-headed blackbird
rusty blackbird
Brewer's blackbird
common grackle
brown-headed cowbird
orchard oriole
Baltimore oriole
purple finch
house finch
red crossbill
pine siskin
American goldfinch
evening grosbeak

Region 21

pied-billed grebe
American bittern
least bittern
great blue heron

great egret
cattle egret
green heron
black-crowned night-heron
yellow-crowned night-heron
black vulture
turkey vulture
sharp-shinned hawk
Cooper's hawk
red-shouldered hawk
broad-winged hawk
red-tailed hawk
American kestrel
king rail
common moorhen
killdeer
American woodcock
mourning dove
black-billed cuckoo
yellow-billed cuckoo
barn owl
eastern screech-owl
great horned owl
barred owl
common nighthawk
Chuck-Will's-widow
whip-poor-will
chimney swift
ruby-throated hummingbird
belted kingfisher
red-headed woodpecker
red-bellied woodpecker
yellow-bellied sapsucker
downy woodpecker
hairy woodpecker
red-cockaded woodpecker
northern flicker
pileated woodpecker
eastern wood-pewee
acadian flycatcher
willow flycatcher
eastern phoebe
great crested flycatcher
eastern kingbird
horned lark
purple martin

tree swallow
northern rough-winged swallow
bank swallow
cliff swallow
barn swallow
blue jay
American crow
black-capped chickadee
Carolina chickadee
tufted titmouse
white-breasted nuthatch
Carolina wren
Bewick's wren
house wren
winter wren
ruby-crowned kinglet
blue-gray gnatcatcher
eastern bluebird
veery
hermit thrush
American robin
gray catbird
northern mockingbird
brown thrasher
cedar waxwing
loggerhead shrike
white-eyed vireo
blue-headed vireo
yellow-throated vireo
warbling vireo
red-eyed vireo
blue-winged warbler
golden-winged warbler
northern parula
yellow warbler
chestnut-sided warbler
magnolia warbler
black-throated blue warbler
black-throated green warbler
blackburnian warbler
yellow-throated warbler
pine warbler
prairie warbler
cerulean warbler
black-and-white warbler
American redstart

prothonotary warbler
worm-eating warbler
Swainson's warbler
ovenbird
Louisiana waterthrush
Kentucky warbler
mourning warbler
common yellowthroat
hooded warbler
Canada warbler
yellow-breasted chat
summer tanager
scarlet tanager
northern cardinal
rose-breasted grosbeak
blue grosbeak
indigo bunting
dickcissel
eastern towhee
Bachman's sparrow
chipping sparrow
field sparrow
vesper sparrow
lark sparrow
savannah sparrow
grasshopper sparrow
Henslow's sparrow
song sparrow
dark-eyed junco
red-winged blackbird
eastern meadowlark
common grackle
brown-headed cowbird
orchard oriole
Baltimore oriole
house finch
American goldfinch

Region 22

common loon
pied-billed grebe
American bittern
least bittern
great blue heron

green heron
yellow-crowned night-heron
black vulture
turkey vulture
osprey
northern harrier
sharp-shinned hawk
Cooper's hawk
red-shouldered hawk
broad-winged hawk
red-tailed hawk
American kestrel
king rail
Virginia rail
sora
common moorhen
American coot
killdeer
spotted sandpiper
upland sandpiper
common snipe
American woodcock
mourning dove
black-billed cuckoo
yellow-billed cuckoo
barn owl
eastern screech-owl
great horned owl
barred owl
long-eared owl
short-eared owl
northern saw-whet owl
common nighthawk
Chuck-Will's-widow
whip-poor-will
chimney swift
ruby-throated hummingbird
belted kingfisher
red-headed woodpecker
red-bellied woodpecker
yellow-bellied sapsucker
downy woodpecker
hairy woodpecker
northern flicker
pileated woodpecker
eastern wood-pewee

acadian flycatcher
alder flycatcher
willow flycatcher
least flycatcher
eastern phoebe
great crested flycatcher
eastern kingbird
horned lark
purple martin
tree swallow
northern rough-winged swallow
bank swallow
cliff swallow
barn swallow
blue jay
American crow
common raven
black-capped chickadee
Carolina chickadee
tufted titmouse
red-breasted nuthatch
white-breasted nuthatch
brown creeper
Carolina wren
Bewick's wren
house wren
winter wren
sedge wren
marsh wren
golden-crowned kinglet
blue-gray gnatcatcher
eastern bluebird
veery
hermit thrush
American robin
gray catbird
northern mockingbird
brown thrasher
cedar waxwing
loggerhead shrike
white-eyed vireo
blue-headed vireo
yellow-throated vireo
warbling vireo
red-eyed vireo
blue-winged warbler

golden-winged warbler
Nashville warbler
northern parula
yellow warbler
chestnut-sided warbler
magnolia warbler
black-throated blue warbler
yellow-rumped warbler
black-throated green warbler
blackburnian warbler
yellow-throated warbler
pine warbler
prairie warbler
cerulean warbler
black-and-white warbler
American redstart
prothonotary warbler
worm-eating warbler
Swainson's warbler
ovenbird
northern waterthrush
Louisiana waterthrush
Kentucky warbler
common yellowthroat
hooded warbler
Canada warbler
yellow-breasted chat
summer tanager
scarlet tanager
northern cardinal
rose-breasted grosbeak
blue grosbeak
indigo bunting
dickcissel
eastern towhee
chipping sparrow
field sparrow
vesper sparrow
lark sparrow
savannah sparrow
grasshopper sparrow
Henslow's sparrow
song sparrow
swamp sparrow
white-throated sparrow
dark-eyed junco

bobolink
red-winged blackbird
eastern meadowlark
common grackle
brown-headed cowbird
orchard oriole
Baltimore oriole
purple finch
house finch
red crossbill
pine siskin
American goldfinch

Region 23

pied-billed grebe
American bittern
least bittern
great blue heron
great egret
cattle egret
green heron
black-crowned night-heron
black vulture
turkey vulture
sharp-shinned hawk
Cooper's hawk
northern goshawk
red-shouldered hawk
broad-winged hawk
red-tailed hawk
American kestrel
peregrine falcon
common moorhen
killdeer
spotted sandpiper
American woodcock
mourning dove
black-billed cuckoo
yellow-billed cuckoo
barn owl
eastern screech-owl
great horned owl
barred owl
long-eared owl

northern saw-whet owl
common nighthawk
Chuck-Will's-widow
whip-poor-will
chimney swift
ruby-throated hummingbird
belted kingfisher
red-headed woodpecker
red-bellied woodpecker
yellow-bellied sapsucker
downy woodpecker
hairy woodpecker
red-cockaded woodpecker
northern flicker
pileated woodpecker
olive-sided flycatcher
eastern wood-pewee
yellow-bellied flycatcher
acadian flycatcher
alder flycatcher
willow flycatcher
least flycatcher
eastern phoebe
great crested flycatcher
eastern kingbird
horned lark
purple martin
tree swallow
northern rough-winged swallow
bank swallow
cliff swallow
barn swallow
blue jay
American crow
common raven
black-capped chickadee
Carolina chickadee
tufted titmouse
red-breasted nuthatch
white-breasted nuthatch
brown-headed nuthatch
brown creeper
Carolina wren
Bewick's wren
house wren
winter wren

golden-crowned kinglet
blue-gray gnatcatcher
eastern bluebird
veery
Swainson's thrush
hermit thrush
American robin
gray catbird
northern mockingbird
brown thrasher
cedar waxwing
loggerhead shrike
white-eyed vireo
blue-headed vireo
yellow-throated vireo
warbling vireo
red-eyed vireo
blue-winged warbler
golden-winged warbler
northern parula
yellow warbler
chestnut-sided warbler
magnolia warbler
black-throated blue warbler
black-throated green warbler
blackburnian warbler
yellow-throated warbler
pine warbler
prairie warbler
cerulean warbler
black-and-white warbler
American redstart
prothonotary warbler
worm-eating warbler
Swainson's warbler
ovenbird
northern waterthrush
Louisiana waterthrush
Kentucky warbler
mourning warbler
common yellowthroat
hooded warbler
Canada warbler
yellow-breasted chat
summer tanager
scarlet tanager

northern cardinal
rose-breasted grosbeak
blue grosbeak
indigo bunting
eastern towhee
Bachman's sparrow
chipping sparrow
field sparrow
vesper sparrow
savannah sparrow
grasshopper sparrow
song sparrow
dark-eyed junco
red-winged blackbird
eastern meadowlark
common grackle
brown-headed cowbird
orchard oriole
Baltimore oriole
purple finch
house finch
red crossbill
pine siskin
American goldfinch

Region 24

pied-billed grebe
American bittern
least bittern
great blue heron
green heron
black-crowned night-heron
yellow-crowned night-heron
turkey vulture
osprey
bald eagle
northern harrier
sharp-shinned hawk
Cooper's hawk
northern goshawk
red-shouldered hawk
broad-winged hawk
red-tailed hawk
American kestrel

king rail
Virginia rail
sora
common moorhen
American coot
killdeer
spotted sandpiper
upland sandpiper
common snipe
American woodcock
mourning dove
black-billed cuckoo
yellow-billed cuckoo
barn owl
eastern screech-owl
great horned owl
barred owl
long-eared owl
short-eared owl
northern saw-whet owl
common nighthawk
whip-poor-will
chimney swift
ruby-throated hummingbird
belted kingfisher
red-headed woodpecker
red-bellied woodpecker
yellow-bellied sapsucker
downy woodpecker
hairy woodpecker
northern flicker
pileated woodpecker
eastern wood-pewee
yellow-bellied flycatcher
acadian flycatcher
alder flycatcher
willow flycatcher
least flycatcher
eastern phoebe
great crested flycatcher
eastern kingbird
horned lark
purple martin
tree swallow
northern rough-winged swallow
bank swallow

cliff swallow
barn swallow
blue jay
American crow
fish crow
common raven
black-capped chickadee
Carolina chickadee
tufted titmouse
red-breasted nuthatch
white-breasted nuthatch
brown creeper
Carolina wren
house wren
winter wren
sedge wren
marsh wren
golden-crowned kinglet
blue-gray gnatcatcher
eastern bluebird
veery
Swainson's thrush
hermit thrush
American robin
gray catbird
northern mockingbird
brown thrasher
cedar waxwing
white-eyed vireo
blue-headed vireo
yellow-throated vireo
warbling vireo
red-eyed vireo
blue-winged warbler
golden-winged warbler
Nashville warbler
northern parula
yellow warbler
chestnut-sided warbler
magnolia warbler
black-throated blue warbler
yellow-rumped warbler
black-throated green warbler
blackburnian warbler
yellow-throated warbler
pine warbler

prairie warbler
cerulean warbler
black-and-white warbler
American redstart
prothonotary warbler
worm-eating warbler
ovenbird
northern waterthrush
Louisiana waterthrush
Kentucky warbler
mourning warbler
common yellowthroat
hooded warbler
Canada warbler
yellow-breasted chat
scarlet tanager
northern cardinal
rose-breasted grosbeak
indigo bunting
dickcissel
eastern towhee
chipping sparrow
clay-colored sparrow
field sparrow
vesper sparrow
savannah sparrow
grasshopper sparrow
Henslow's sparrow
song sparrow
swamp sparrow
white-throated sparrow
dark-eyed junco
bobolink
red-winged blackbird
eastern meadowlark
western meadowlark
common grackle
brown-headed cowbird
orchard oriole
Baltimore oriole
purple finch
house finch
red crossbill
pine siskin
American goldfinch
evening grosbeak

Region 26

common loon
pied-billed grebe
double-crested cormorant
American bittern
least bittern
great blue heron
green heron
turkey vulture
osprey
bald eagle
northern harrier
sharp-shinned hawk
Cooper's hawk
northern goshawk
red-shouldered hawk
broad-winged hawk
red-tailed hawk
golden eagle
American kestrel
merlin
peregrine falcon
Virginia rail
sora
common moorhen
killdeer
spotted sandpiper
upland sandpiper
common snipe
American woodcock
mourning dove
black-billed cuckoo
yellow-billed cuckoo
eastern screech-owl
great horned owl
barred owl
long-eared owl
short-eared owl
northern saw-whet owl
common nighthawk
whip-poor-will
chimney swift
ruby-throated hummingbird
belted kingfisher
red-headed woodpecker
yellow-bellied sapsucker
downy woodpecker
hairy woodpecker
three-toed woodpecker
black-backed woodpecker
northern flicker
pileated woodpecker
olive-sided flycatcher
eastern wood-pewee
yellow-bellied flycatcher
alder flycatcher
willow flycatcher
least flycatcher
eastern phoebe
great crested flycatcher
eastern kingbird
horned lark
purple martin
tree swallow
northern rough-winged swallow
bank swallow
cliff swallow
barn swallow
gray jay
blue jay
American crow
common raven
black-capped chickadee
tufted titmouse
red-breasted nuthatch
white-breasted nuthatch
brown creeper
house wren
winter wren
golden-crowned kinglet
ruby-crowned kinglet
eastern bluebird
veery
Bicknell's thrush
Swainson's thrush
hermit thrush
American robin
gray catbird
northern mockingbird
brown thrasher
cedar waxwing
blue-headed vireo

yellow-throated vireo
warbling vireo
Philadelphia vireo
red-eyed vireo
blue-winged warbler
golden-winged warbler
Tennessee warbler
Nashville warbler
northern parula
yellow warbler
chestnut-sided warbler
magnolia warbler
cape may warbler
black-throated blue warbler
yellow-rumped warbler
black-throated green warbler
blackburnian warbler
pine warbler
palm warbler
bay-breasted warbler
blackpoll warbler
cerulean warbler
black-and-white warbler
American redstart
ovenbird
northern waterthrush
Louisiana waterthrush
mourning warbler
common yellowthroat
hooded warbler
Wilson's warbler
Canada warbler
scarlet tanager
northern cardinal
rose-breasted grosbeak
indigo bunting
eastern towhee
chipping sparrow
field sparrow
vesper sparrow
savannah sparrow
grasshopper sparrow
song sparrow
Lincoln's sparrow
swamp sparrow
white-throated sparrow

dark-eyed junco
bobolink
red-winged blackbird
eastern meadowlark
rusty blackbird
common grackle
brown-headed cowbird
Baltimore oriole
purple finch
house finch
red crossbill
pine siskin
American goldfinch
evening grosbeak

Region 27

common loon
pied-billed grebe
double-crested cormorant
American bittern
least bittern
great blue heron
green heron
black-crowned night-heron
turkey vulture
osprey
sharp-shinned hawk
Cooper's hawk
northern goshawk
red-shouldered hawk
broad-winged hawk
red-tailed hawk
American kestrel
Virginia rail
sora
common moorhen
American coot
killdeer
spotted sandpiper
upland sandpiper
common snipe
American woodcock
mourning dove
black-billed cuckoo

yellow-billed cuckoo
eastern screech-owl
great horned owl
barred owl
long-eared owl
northern saw-whet owl
common nighthawk
whip-poor-will
chimney swift
ruby-throated hummingbird
belted kingfisher
red-headed woodpecker
yellow-bellied sapsucker
downy woodpecker
hairy woodpecker
black-backed woodpecker
northern flicker
pileated woodpecker
olive-sided flycatcher
eastern wood-pewee
yellow-bellied flycatcher
acadian flycatcher
alder flycatcher
willow flycatcher
least flycatcher
eastern phoebe
great crested flycatcher
eastern kingbird
horned lark
purple martin
tree swallow
northern rough-winged swallow
bank swallow
cliff swallow
barn swallow
blue jay
American crow
common raven
black-capped chickadee
tufted titmouse
red-breasted nuthatch
white-breasted nuthatch
brown creeper
house wren
winter wren
sedge wren

marsh wren
golden-crowned kinglet
ruby-crowned kinglet
blue-gray gnatcatcher
eastern bluebird
veery
Bicknell's thrush
Swainson's thrush
hermit thrush
American robin
gray catbird
northern mockingbird
brown thrasher
cedar waxwing
blue-headed vireo
yellow-throated vireo
warbling vireo
Philadelphia vireo
red-eyed vireo
blue-winged warbler
golden-winged warbler
Tennessee warbler
Nashville warbler
northern parula
yellow warbler
chestnut-sided warbler
magnolia warbler
cape may warbler
black-throated blue warbler
yellow-rumped warbler
black-throated green warbler
blackburnian warbler
pine warbler
prairie warbler
bay-breasted warbler
blackpoll warbler
black-and-white warbler
American redstart
ovenbird
northern waterthrush
Louisiana waterthrush
mourning warbler
common yellowthroat
Wilson's warbler
Canada warbler
scarlet tanager

northern cardinal
rose-breasted grosbeak
indigo bunting
eastern towhee
chipping sparrow
field sparrow
vesper sparrow
savannah sparrow
grasshopper sparrow
Nelson's sharp-tailed sparrow
song sparrow
Lincoln's sparrow
swamp sparrow
white-throated sparrow
dark-eyed junco
bobolink
red-winged blackbird
eastern meadowlark
rusty blackbird
common grackle
brown-headed cowbird
orchard oriole
Baltimore oriole
purple finch
house finch
red crossbill
pine siskin
American goldfinch
evening grosbeak

Region 28

common loon
pied-billed grebe
double-crested cormorant
American bittern
great blue heron
green heron
black-crowned night-heron
turkey vulture
osprey
bald eagle
northern harrier
sharp-shinned hawk
Cooper's hawk

northern goshawk
red-shouldered hawk
broad-winged hawk
red-tailed hawk
golden eagle
American kestrel
merlin
peregrine falcon
Virginia rail
sora
common moorhen
American coot
piping plover
killdeer
willet
spotted sandpiper
upland sandpiper
common snipe
American woodcock
Wilson's phalarope
mourning dove
black-billed cuckoo
yellow-billed cuckoo
eastern screech-owl
great horned owl
barred owl
long-eared owl
short-eared owl
boreal owl
northern saw-whet owl
common nighthawk
whip-poor-will
chimney swift
ruby-throated hummingbird
belted kingfisher
red-headed woodpecker
yellow-bellied sapsucker
downy woodpecker
hairy woodpecker
three-toed woodpecker
black-backed woodpecker
northern flicker
pileated woodpecker
olive-sided flycatcher
eastern wood-pewee
yellow-bellied flycatcher

alder flycatcher
willow flycatcher
least flycatcher
eastern phoebe
great crested flycatcher
eastern kingbird
horned lark
purple martin
tree swallow
northern rough-winged swallow
bank swallow
cliff swallow
barn swallow
gray jay
blue jay
American crow
common raven
black-capped chickadee
tufted titmouse
red-breasted nuthatch
white-breasted nuthatch
brown creeper
house wren
winter wren
marsh wren
golden-crowned kinglet
ruby-crowned kinglet
blue-gray gnatcatcher
eastern bluebird
veery
Bicknell's thrush
Swainson's thrush
hermit thrush
American robin
gray catbird
northern mockingbird
brown thrasher
cedar waxwing
blue-headed vireo
yellow-throated vireo
warbling vireo
Philadelphia vireo
red-eyed vireo
Tennessee warbler
Nashville warbler
northern parula

yellow warbler
chestnut-sided warbler
magnolia warbler
cape may warbler
black-throated blue warbler
yellow-rumped warbler
black-throated green warbler
blackburnian warbler
pine warbler
palm warbler
bay-breasted warbler
blackpoll warbler
black-and-white warbler
American redstart
ovenbird
northern waterthrush
Louisiana waterthrush
mourning warbler
common yellowthroat
Wilson's warbler
Canada warbler
scarlet tanager
northern cardinal
rose-breasted grosbeak
indigo bunting
eastern towhee
chipping sparrow
field sparrow
vesper sparrow
savannah sparrow
Nelson's sharp-tailed sparrow
fox sparrow
song sparrow
Lincoln's sparrow
swamp sparrow
white-throated sparrow
dark-eyed junco
bobolink
red-winged blackbird
eastern meadowlark
rusty blackbird
common grackle
brown-headed cowbird
Baltimore oriole
pine grosbeak
purple finch

house finch
red crossbill
pine siskin
American goldfinch
evening grosbeak

Region 30

common loon
pied-billed grebe
horned grebe
red-necked grebe
eared grebe
western grebe
double-crested cormorant
American bittern
least bittern
great blue heron
cattle egret
green heron
black-crowned night-heron
turkey vulture
osprey
bald eagle
northern harrier
sharp-shinned hawk
Cooper's hawk
broad-winged hawk
Swainson's hawk
red-tailed hawk
American kestrel
yellow rail
Virginia rail
sora
American coot
sandhill crane
killdeer
spotted sandpiper
upland sandpiper
marbled godwit
common snipe
American woodcock
Wilson's phalarope
mourning dove
black-billed cuckoo

yellow-billed cuckoo
great horned owl
barred owl
great gray owl
long-eared owl
short-eared owl
northern saw-whet owl
common nighthawk
whip-poor-will
chimney swift
ruby-throated hummingbird
belted kingfisher
red-headed woodpecker
red-bellied woodpecker
yellow-bellied sapsucker
downy woodpecker
hairy woodpecker
black-backed woodpecker
northern flicker
pileated woodpecker
olive-sided flycatcher
western wood-pewee
eastern wood-pewee
yellow-bellied flycatcher
alder flycatcher
willow flycatcher
least flycatcher
eastern phoebe
great crested flycatcher
western kingbird
eastern kingbird
horned lark
purple martin
tree swallow
northern rough-winged swallow
bank swallow
cliff swallow
barn swallow
gray jay
blue jay
black-billed magpie
American crow
common raven
black-capped chickadee
red-breasted nuthatch
white-breasted nuthatch

brown creeper
house wren
winter wren
sedge wren
marsh wren
golden-crowned kinglet
ruby-crowned kinglet
eastern bluebird
mountain bluebird
veery
Swainson's thrush
hermit thrush
American robin
gray catbird
brown thrasher
Sprague's pipit
cedar waxwing
blue-headed vireo
yellow-throated vireo
warbling vireo
red-eyed vireo
golden-winged warbler
Tennessee warbler
Nashville warbler
yellow warbler
chestnut-sided warbler
magnolia warbler
yellow-rumped warbler
black-throated green warbler
blackburnian warbler
pine warbler
palm warbler
black-and-white warbler
American redstart
ovenbird
northern waterthrush
Connecticut warbler
mourning warbler
common yellowthroat
scarlet tanager
northern cardinal
rose-breasted grosbeak
indigo bunting
eastern towhee
chipping sparrow
clay-colored sparrow

vesper sparrow
lark sparrow
savannah sparrow
grasshopper sparrow
le Conte's sparrow
Nelson's sharp-tailed sparrow
song sparrow
Lincoln's sparrow
swamp sparrow
white-throated sparrow
dark-eyed junco
bobolink
red-winged blackbird
western meadowlark
yellow-headed blackbird
Brewer's blackbird
common grackle
brown-headed cowbird
orchard oriole
Baltimore oriole
purple finch
house finch
red crossbill
pine siskin
American goldfinch
evening grosbeak

Region 31

pied-billed grebe
American bittern
least bittern
great blue heron
great egret
cattle egret
green heron
black-crowned night-heron
yellow-crowned night-heron
turkey vulture
osprey
Mississippi kite
bald eagle
northern harrier
sharp-shinned hawk
Cooper's hawk

red-shouldered hawk
broad-winged hawk
red-tailed hawk
American kestrel
peregrine falcon
black rail
king rail
Virginia rail
sora
common moorhen
American coot
killdeer
spotted sandpiper
upland sandpiper
common snipe
American woodcock
mourning dove
black-billed cuckoo
yellow-billed cuckoo
barn owl
eastern screech-owl
great horned owl
barred owl
short-eared owl
northern saw-whet owl
common nighthawk
Chuck-Will's-widow
whip-poor-will
chimney swift
ruby-throated hummingbird
belted kingfisher
red-headed woodpecker
red-bellied woodpecker
downy woodpecker
hairy woodpecker
northern flicker
pileated woodpecker
eastern wood-pewee
acadian flycatcher
willow flycatcher
least flycatcher
eastern phoebe
great crested flycatcher
western kingbird
eastern kingbird
scissor-tailed flycatcher

horned lark
purple martin
tree swallow
northern rough-winged swallow
bank swallow
cliff swallow
barn swallow
blue jay
American crow
black-capped chickadee
Carolina chickadee
tufted titmouse
red-breasted nuthatch
white-breasted nuthatch
brown creeper
Carolina wren
Bewick's wren
house wren
sedge wren
marsh wren
golden-crowned kinglet
blue-gray gnatcatcher
eastern bluebird
veery
American robin
gray catbird
northern mockingbird
brown thrasher
cedar waxwing
loggerhead shrike
white-eyed vireo
Bell's vireo
blue-headed vireo
yellow-throated vireo
warbling vireo
red-eyed vireo
blue-winged warbler
golden-winged warbler
northern parula
yellow warbler
chestnut-sided warbler
magnolia warbler
black-throated green warbler
yellow-throated warbler
pine warbler
prairie warbler

cerulean warbler
black-and-white warbler
American redstart
prothonotary warbler
worm-eating warbler
ovenbird
northern waterthrush
Louisiana waterthrush
Kentucky warbler
common yellowthroat
hooded warbler
Canada warbler
yellow-breasted chat
summer tanager
scarlet tanager
northern cardinal
rose-breasted grosbeak
blue grosbeak
indigo bunting
dickcissel
eastern towhee
chipping sparrow
field sparrow
vesper sparrow
lark sparrow
savannah sparrow
grasshopper sparrow
Henslow's sparrow
song sparrow
swamp sparrow
bobolink
red-winged blackbird
eastern meadowlark
western meadowlark
common grackle
brown-headed cowbird
orchard oriole
Baltimore oriole
house finch
pine siskin
American goldfinch

Region 32

pied-billed grebe
red-necked grebe

double-crested cormorant
American bittern
least bittern
great blue heron
great egret
little blue heron
cattle egret
green heron
black-crowned night-heron
yellow-crowned night-heron
white-faced ibis
turkey vulture
bald eagle
northern harrier
sharp-shinned hawk
Cooper's hawk
red-shouldered hawk
broad-winged hawk
Swainson's hawk
red-tailed hawk
American kestrel
peregrine falcon
black rail
king rail
Virginia rail
sora
common moorhen
American coot
sandhill crane
piping plover
killdeer
spotted sandpiper
upland sandpiper
common snipe
American woodcock
Wilson's phalarope
mourning dove
black-billed cuckoo
yellow-billed cuckoo
barn owl
eastern screech-owl
great horned owl
burrowing owl
barred owl
long-eared owl
short-eared owl

common nighthawk
common poorwill
Chuck-Will's-widow
whip-poor-will
chimney swift
ruby-throated hummingbird
belted kingfisher
red-headed woodpecker
red-bellied woodpecker
yellow-bellied sapsucker
downy woodpecker
hairy woodpecker
northern flicker
pileated woodpecker
eastern wood-pewee
acadian flycatcher
alder flycatcher
willow flycatcher
least flycatcher
eastern phoebe
Say's phoebe
great crested flycatcher
western kingbird
eastern kingbird
scissor-tailed flycatcher
horned lark
purple martin
tree swallow
northern rough-winged swallow
bank swallow
cliff swallow
barn swallow
blue jay
black-billed magpie
American crow
black-capped chickadee
tufted titmouse
white-breasted nuthatch
brown creeper
Carolina wren
Bewick's wren
house wren
sedge wren
marsh wren
blue-gray gnatcatcher
eastern bluebird

veery
American robin
gray catbird
northern mockingbird
brown thrasher
cedar waxwing
loggerhead shrike
white-eyed vireo
Bell's vireo
yellow-throated vireo
warbling vireo
red-eyed vireo
blue-winged warbler
northern parula
yellow warbler
chestnut-sided warbler
yellow-throated warbler
prairie warbler
cerulean warbler
black-and-white warbler
American redstart
prothonotary warbler
worm-eating warbler
ovenbird
Louisiana waterthrush
Kentucky warbler
common yellowthroat
hooded warbler
yellow-breasted chat
summer tanager
scarlet tanager
northern cardinal
rose-breasted grosbeak
blue grosbeak
indigo bunting
painted bunting
dickcissel
eastern towhee
chipping sparrow
clay-colored sparrow
field sparrow
vesper sparrow
lark sparrow
lark bunting
savannah sparrow
grasshopper sparrow

Henslow's sparrow
song sparrow
swamp sparrow
bobolink
red-winged blackbird
eastern meadowlark
western meadowlark
yellow-headed blackbird
Brewer's blackbird
great-tailed grackle
common grackle
brown-headed cowbird
orchard oriole
Baltimore oriole
house finch
pine siskin
American goldfinch

Region 33

pied-billed grebe
double-crested cormorant
American bittern
least bittern
great blue heron
great egret
snowy egret
little blue heron
cattle egret
green heron
black-crowned night-heron
yellow-crowned night-heron
black vulture
turkey vulture
Mississippi kite
bald eagle
northern harrier
sharp-shinned hawk
Cooper's hawk
red-shouldered hawk
broad-winged hawk
Swainson's hawk
red-tailed hawk
American kestrel
black rail

king rail
Virginia rail
sora
common moorhen
American coot
killdeer
spotted sandpiper
upland sandpiper
American woodcock
mourning dove
inca dove
black-billed cuckoo
yellow-billed cuckoo
greater roadrunner
barn owl
eastern screech-owl
great horned owl
burrowing owl
barred owl
long-eared owl
short-eared owl
lesser nighthawk
common nighthawk
common poorwill
Chuck-Will's-widow
whip-poor-will
chimney swift
ruby-throated hummingbird
black-chinned hummingbird
belted kingfisher
red-headed woodpecker
golden-fronted woodpecker
red-bellied woodpecker
ladder-backed woodpecker
downy woodpecker
hairy woodpecker
northern flicker
pileated woodpecker
western wood-pewee
eastern wood-pewee
acadian flycatcher
willow flycatcher
eastern phoebe
Say's phoebe
vermilion flycatcher
ash-throated flycatcher

great crested flycatcher
western kingbird
eastern kingbird
scissor-tailed flycatcher
horned lark
purple martin
tree swallow
northern rough-winged swallow
bank swallow
cliff swallow
barn swallow
blue jay
American crow
fish crow
chihuahuan raven
common raven
black-capped chickadee
Carolina chickadee
tufted titmouse
verdin
white-breasted nuthatch
cactus wren
rock wren
canyon wren
Carolina wren
Bewick's wren
house wren
sedge wren
marsh wren
blue-gray gnatcatcher
eastern bluebird
American robin
gray catbird
northern mockingbird
brown thrasher
curve-billed thrasher
cedar waxwing
loggerhead shrike
white-eyed vireo
Bell's vireo
black-capped vireo
yellow-throated vireo
warbling vireo
red-eyed vireo
blue-winged warbler
northern parula

yellow warbler
yellow-throated warbler
prairie warbler
cerulean warbler
black-and-white warbler
American redstart
prothonotary warbler
worm-eating warbler
ovenbird
Louisiana waterthrush
Kentucky warbler
common yellowthroat
hooded warbler
yellow-breasted chat
summer tanager
scarlet tanager
northern cardinal
rose-breasted grosbeak
blue grosbeak
lazuli bunting
indigo bunting
painted bunting
dickcissel
eastern towhee
Cassin's sparrow
rufous-crowned sparrow
chipping sparrow
field sparrow
vesper sparrow
lark sparrow
black-throated sparrow
lark bunting
savannah sparrow
grasshopper sparrow
Henslow's sparrow
song sparrow
bobolink
red-winged blackbird
eastern meadowlark
western meadowlark
yellow-headed blackbird
great-tailed grackle
common grackle
brown-headed cowbird
orchard oriole
Baltimore oriole

Bullock's oriole
house finch
pine siskin
lesser goldfinch
American goldfinch

Region 34

pied-billed grebe
horned grebe
eared grebe
western grebe
American white pelican
double-crested cormorant
American bittern
least bittern
great blue heron
great egret
snowy egret
little blue heron
cattle egret
green heron
black-crowned night-heron
yellow-crowned night-heron
white-faced ibis
turkey vulture
Mississippi kite
bald eagle
northern harrier
sharp-shinned hawk
Cooper's hawk
Swainson's hawk
red-tailed hawk
ferruginous hawk
golden eagle
American kestrel
black rail
king rail
Virginia rail
common moorhen
American coot
snowy plover
piping plover
killdeer
black-necked stilt

American avocet
willet
spotted sandpiper
upland sandpiper
common snipe
American woodcock
Wilson's phalarope
mourning dove
black-billed cuckoo
yellow-billed cuckoo
greater roadrunner
barn owl
eastern screech-owl
great horned owl
burrowing owl
barred owl
long-eared owl
short-eared owl
common nighthawk
common poorwill
Chuck-Will's-widow
chimney swift
ruby-throated hummingbird
belted kingfisher
red-headed woodpecker
red-bellied woodpecker
downy woodpecker
hairy woodpecker
northern flicker
western wood-pewee
eastern wood-pewee
willow flycatcher
least flycatcher
eastern phoebe
Say's phoebe
ash-throated flycatcher
great crested flycatcher
western kingbird
eastern kingbird
scissor-tailed flycatcher
horned lark
purple martin
tree swallow
northern rough-winged swallow
bank swallow
cliff swallow

barn swallow
blue jay
black-billed magpie
American crow
chihuahuan raven
black-capped chickadee
Carolina chickadee
tufted titmouse
red-breasted nuthatch
white-breasted nuthatch
brown creeper
rock wren
Carolina wren
Bewick's wren
house wren
sedge wren
marsh wren
blue-gray gnatcatcher
eastern bluebird
American robin
gray catbird
northern mockingbird
brown thrasher
cedar waxwing
loggerhead shrike
Bell's vireo
yellow-throated vireo
warbling vireo
red-eyed vireo
northern parula
yellow warbler
black-and-white warbler
American redstart
ovenbird
common yellowthroat
yellow-breasted chat
scarlet tanager
northern cardinal
rose-breasted grosbeak
black-headed grosbeak
blue grosbeak
indigo bunting
painted bunting
dickcissel
eastern towhee
spotted towhee

Cassin's sparrow
chipping sparrow
field sparrow
vesper sparrow
lark sparrow
lark bunting
savannah sparrow
grasshopper sparrow
song sparrow
swamp sparrow
chestnut-collared longspur
bobolink
red-winged blackbird
eastern meadowlark
western meadowlark
yellow-headed blackbird
Brewer's blackbird
great-tailed grackle
common grackle
brown-headed cowbird
orchard oriole
Baltimore oriole
Bullock's oriole
house finch
pine siskin
American goldfinch

Region 36

pied-billed grebe
eared grebe
western grebe
Clark's grebe
American white pelican
double-crested cormorant
American bittern
least bittern
great blue heron
great egret
snowy egret
cattle egret
green heron
black-crowned night-heron
yellow-crowned night-heron
turkey vulture

osprey
Mississippi kite
bald eagle
northern harrier
sharp-shinned hawk
Cooper's hawk
Swainson's hawk
red-tailed hawk
ferruginous hawk
golden eagle
American kestrel
prairie falcon
Virginia rail
sora
American coot
snowy plover
piping plover
killdeer
black-necked stilt
American avocet
willet
spotted sandpiper
upland sandpiper
common snipe
Wilson's phalarope
mourning dove
black-billed cuckoo
yellow-billed cuckoo
greater roadrunner
barn owl
eastern screech-owl
great horned owl
burrowing owl
long-eared owl
short-eared owl
common nighthawk
common poorwill
chimney swift
white-throated swift
belted kingfisher
Lewis's woodpecker
red-headed woodpecker
red-bellied woodpecker
ladder-backed woodpecker
downy woodpecker
hairy woodpecker

northern flicker
western wood-pewee
willow flycatcher
least flycatcher
eastern phoebe
Say's phoebe
vermilion flycatcher
ash-throated flycatcher
great crested flycatcher
Cassin's kingbird
western kingbird
eastern kingbird
scissor-tailed flycatcher
horned lark
purple martin
tree swallow
violet-green swallow
northern rough-winged swallow
bank swallow
cliff swallow
barn swallow
blue jay
pinyon jay
black-billed magpie
American crow
chihuahuan raven
common raven
black-capped chickadee
juniper titmouse
red-breasted nuthatch
white-breasted nuthatch
pygmy nuthatch
rock wren
canyon wren
Carolina wren
Bewick's wren
house wren
marsh wren
eastern bluebird
mountain bluebird
American robin
gray catbird
northern mockingbird
sage thrasher
brown thrasher
Bendire's thrasher

curve-billed thrasher
cedar waxwing
loggerhead shrike
Bell's vireo
warbling vireo
red-eyed vireo
yellow warbler
chestnut-sided warbler
American redstart
common yellowthroat
yellow-breasted chat
hepatic tanager
western tanager
northern cardinal
rose-breasted grosbeak
black-headed grosbeak
blue grosbeak
lazuli bunting
indigo bunting
dickcissel
green-tailed towhee
spotted towhee
canyon towhee
Cassin's sparrow
rufous-crowned sparrow
chipping sparrow
Brewer's sparrow
field sparrow
vesper sparrow
lark sparrow
black-throated sparrow
lark bunting
savannah sparrow
Baird's sparrow
grasshopper sparrow
song sparrow
white-crowned sparrow
McCown's longspur
chestnut-collared longspur
bobolink
red-winged blackbird
eastern meadowlark
western meadowlark
yellow-headed blackbird
Brewer's blackbird
great-tailed grackle

common grackle
brown-headed cowbird
orchard oriole
Baltimore oriole
Bullock's oriole
house finch
red crossbill
pine siskin
American goldfinch

Region 37

pied-billed grebe
horned grebe
eared grebe
western grebe
American white pelican
double-crested cormorant
American bittern
least bittern
great blue heron
great egret
snowy egret
cattle egret
green heron
black-crowned night-heron
white-faced ibis
turkey vulture
bald eagle
northern harrier
Cooper's hawk
Swainson's hawk
red-tailed hawk
ferruginous hawk
American kestrel
merlin
yellow rail
Virginia rail
sora
American coot
piping plover
killdeer
American avocet
willet
spotted sandpiper

upland sandpiper
marbled godwit
common snipe
American woodcock
Wilson's phalarope
mourning dove
black-billed cuckoo
yellow-billed cuckoo
eastern screech-owl
great horned owl
burrowing owl
long-eared owl
short-eared owl
common nighthawk
whip-poor-will
chimney swift
ruby-throated hummingbird
belted kingfisher
red-headed woodpecker
red-bellied woodpecker
yellow-bellied sapsucker
downy woodpecker
hairy woodpecker
northern flicker
western wood-pewee
eastern wood-pewee
alder flycatcher
willow flycatcher
least flycatcher
eastern phoebe
Say's phoebe
great crested flycatcher
western kingbird
eastern kingbird
horned lark
purple martin
tree swallow
northern rough-winged swallow
bank swallow
cliff swallow
barn swallow
blue jay
black-billed magpie
American crow
common raven
black-capped chickadee

red-breasted nuthatch
white-breasted nuthatch
house wren
sedge wren
marsh wren
eastern bluebird
mountain bluebird
veery
American robin
gray catbird
northern mockingbird
brown thrasher
Sprague's pipit
cedar waxwing
loggerhead shrike
Bell's vireo
yellow-throated vireo
warbling vireo
red-eyed vireo
yellow warbler
black-and-white warbler
American redstart
ovenbird
common yellowthroat
yellow-breasted chat
scarlet tanager
northern cardinal
rose-breasted grosbeak
black-headed grosbeak
blue grosbeak
lazuli bunting
indigo bunting
dickcissel
eastern towhee
spotted towhee
chipping sparrow
clay-colored sparrow
field sparrow
vesper sparrow
lark sparrow
lark bunting
savannah sparrow
Baird's sparrow
grasshopper sparrow
le Conte's sparrow
Nelson's sharp-tailed sparrow

song sparrow
swamp sparrow
McCown's longspur
chestnut-collared longspur
bobolink
red-winged blackbird
eastern meadowlark
western meadowlark
yellow-headed blackbird
Brewer's blackbird
common grackle
brown-headed cowbird
orchard oriole
Baltimore oriole
house finch
pine siskin
American goldfinch

Region 38

pied-billed grebe
eared grebe
American white pelican
double-crested cormorant
American bittern
great blue heron
black-crowned night-heron
turkey vulture
northern harrier
sharp-shinned hawk
Cooper's hawk
Swainson's hawk
red-tailed hawk
ferruginous hawk
golden eagle
American kestrel
merlin
prairie falcon
sora
American coot
killdeer
American avocet
willet
spotted sandpiper
upland sandpiper

marbled godwit
common snipe
Wilson's phalarope
mourning dove
black-billed cuckoo
yellow-billed cuckoo
barn owl
eastern screech-owl
great horned owl
burrowing owl
long-eared owl
short-eared owl
common nighthawk
common poorwill
chimney swift
white-throated swift
belted kingfisher
Lewis's woodpecker
red-headed woodpecker
downy woodpecker
hairy woodpecker
northern flicker
western wood-pewee
willow flycatcher
least flycatcher
cordilleran flycatcher
eastern phoebe
Say's phoebe
great crested flycatcher
Cassin's kingbird
western kingbird
eastern kingbird
horned lark
tree swallow
violet-green swallow
northern rough-winged swallow
bank swallow
cliff swallow
barn swallow
blue jay
pinyon jay
black-billed magpie
American crow
black-capped chickadee
red-breasted nuthatch
white-breasted nuthatch

pygmy nuthatch
rock wren
house wren
marsh wren
eastern bluebird
mountain bluebird
Townsend's solitaire
American robin
gray catbird
northern mockingbird
sage thrasher
brown thrasher
Sprague's pipit
cedar waxwing
loggerhead shrike
Bell's vireo
plumbeous vireo
warbling vireo
red-eyed vireo
yellow warbler
yellow-rumped warbler
American redstart
ovenbird
common yellowthroat
yellow-breasted chat
western tanager
black-headed grosbeak
blue grosbeak
lazuli bunting
indigo bunting
dickcissel
eastern towhee
spotted towhee
chipping sparrow
clay-colored sparrow
Brewer's sparrow
field sparrow
vesper sparrow
lark sparrow
lark bunting
savannah sparrow
Baird's sparrow
grasshopper sparrow
song sparrow
dark-eyed junco
McCown's longspur

chestnut-collared longspur
bobolink
red-winged blackbird
eastern meadowlark
western meadowlark
yellow-headed blackbird
Brewer's blackbird
common grackle
brown-headed cowbird
orchard oriole
Baltimore oriole
Bullock's oriole
house finch
red crossbill
pine siskin
American goldfinch

Region 39

pied-billed grebe
horned grebe
eared grebe
western grebe
Clark's grebe
American white pelican
double-crested cormorant
American bittern
great blue heron
black-crowned night-heron
white-faced ibis
turkey vulture
osprey
bald eagle
northern harrier
sharp-shinned hawk
Cooper's hawk
northern goshawk
Swainson's hawk
red-tailed hawk
ferruginous hawk
golden eagle
American kestrel
merlin
peregrine falcon
prairie falcon

yellow rail
Virginia rail
sora
American coot
sandhill crane
piping plover
killdeer
black-necked stilt
American avocet
willet
spotted sandpiper
upland sandpiper
marbled godwit
common snipe
Wilson's phalarope
mourning dove
black-billed cuckoo
yellow-billed cuckoo
barn owl
eastern screech-owl
great horned owl
burrowing owl
great gray owl
long-eared owl
short-eared owl
northern saw-whet owl
common nighthawk
common poorwill
chimney swift
white-throated swift
ruby-throated hummingbird
calliope hummingbird
rufous hummingbird
belted kingfisher
Lewis's woodpecker
red-headed woodpecker
red-naped sapsucker
downy woodpecker
hairy woodpecker
three-toed woodpecker
black-backed woodpecker
northern flicker
olive-sided flycatcher
western wood-pewee
willow flycatcher
least flycatcher

Hammond's flycatcher
dusky flycatcher
cordilleran flycatcher
eastern phoebe
Say's phoebe
Cassin's kingbird
western kingbird
eastern kingbird
horned lark
tree swallow
violet-green swallow
northern rough-winged swallow
bank swallow
cliff swallow
barn swallow
gray jay
Steller's jay
blue jay
pinyon jay
Clark's nutcracker
black-billed magpie
American crow
common raven
black-capped chickadee
mountain chickadee
red-breasted nuthatch
white-breasted nuthatch
brown creeper
rock wren
canyon wren
house wren
sedge wren
marsh wren
American dipper
golden-crowned kinglet
ruby-crowned kinglet
eastern bluebird
mountain bluebird
Townsend's solitaire
veery
Swainson's thrush
hermit thrush
American robin
gray catbird
northern mockingbird
sage thrasher

brown thrasher
American pipit
Sprague's pipit
cedar waxwing
loggerhead shrike
plumbeous vireo
warbling vireo
red-eyed vireo
orange-crowned warbler
yellow warbler
yellow-rumped warbler
black-and-white warbler
American redstart
ovenbird
northern waterthrush
MacGillivray's warbler
common yellowthroat
yellow-breasted chat
western tanager
black-headed grosbeak
lazuli bunting
indigo bunting
dickcissel
green-tailed towhee
spotted towhee
chipping sparrow
clay-colored sparrow
Brewer's sparrow
field sparrow
vesper sparrow
lark sparrow
sage sparrow
lark bunting
savannah sparrow
Baird's sparrow
grasshopper sparrow
le Conte's sparrow
Nelson's sharp-tailed sparrow
song sparrow
Lincoln's sparrow
white-crowned sparrow
dark-eyed junco
McCown's longspur
chestnut-collared longspur
bobolink
red-winged blackbird

western meadowlark
yellow-headed blackbird
Brewer's blackbird
common grackle
brown-headed cowbird
orchard oriole
Baltimore oriole
Bullock's oriole
pine grosbeak
Cassin's finch
house finch
red crossbill
pine siskin
American goldfinch
evening grosbeak

Region 40

common loon
pied-billed grebe
horned grebe
red-necked grebe
eared grebe
western grebe
Clark's grebe
American white pelican
double-crested cormorant
American bittern
least bittern
great blue heron
great egret
snowy egret
little blue heron
cattle egret
green heron
black-crowned night-heron
yellow-crowned night-heron
turkey vulture
osprey
bald eagle
northern harrier
Cooper's hawk
red-shouldered hawk
broad-winged hawk
Swainson's hawk

red-tailed hawk
American kestrel
peregrine falcon
yellow rail
king rail
Virginia rail
sora
common moorhen
American coot
sandhill crane
killdeer
American avocet
willet
spotted sandpiper
upland sandpiper
marbled godwit
common snipe
American woodcock
Wilson's phalarope
mourning dove
black-billed cuckoo
yellow-billed cuckoo
eastern screech-owl
great horned owl
burrowing owl
barred owl
long-eared owl
short-eared owl
northern saw-whet owl
common nighthawk
whip-poor-will
chimney swift
ruby-throated hummingbird
belted kingfisher
red-headed woodpecker
red-bellied woodpecker
yellow-bellied sapsucker
downy woodpecker
hairy woodpecker
northern flicker
pileated woodpecker
eastern wood-pewee
acadian flycatcher
alder flycatcher
willow flycatcher
least flycatcher

eastern phoebe
great crested flycatcher
western kingbird
eastern kingbird
horned lark
purple martin
tree swallow
northern rough-winged swallow
bank swallow
cliff swallow
barn swallow
blue jay
black-billed magpie
American crow
black-capped chickadee
tufted titmouse
red-breasted nuthatch
white-breasted nuthatch
brown creeper
house wren
sedge wren
marsh wren
blue-gray gnatcatcher
eastern bluebird
veery
American robin
gray catbird
brown thrasher
cedar waxwing
loggerhead shrike
Bell's vireo
yellow-throated vireo
warbling vireo
red-eyed vireo
blue-winged warbler
northern parula
yellow warbler
yellow-throated warbler
cerulean warbler
black-and-white warbler
American redstart
prothonotary warbler
ovenbird
Louisiana waterthrush
Kentucky warbler
common yellowthroat

scarlet tanager
northern cardinal
rose-breasted grosbeak
blue grosbeak
indigo bunting
dickcissel
eastern towhee
chipping sparrow
clay-colored sparrow
field sparrow
vesper sparrow
lark sparrow
savannah sparrow
Baird's sparrow
grasshopper sparrow
Henslow's sparrow
le Conte's sparrow
Nelson's sharp-tailed sparrow
song sparrow
swamp sparrow
chestnut-collared longspur
bobolink
red-winged blackbird
eastern meadowlark
western meadowlark
yellow-headed blackbird
Brewer's blackbird
great-tailed grackle
common grackle
brown-headed cowbird
orchard oriole
Baltimore oriole
house finch
pine siskin
American goldfinch

Region 42

double-crested cormorant
anhinga
great blue heron
great egret
little blue heron
cattle egret
green heron

black-crowned night-heron
yellow-crowned night-heron
black vulture
turkey vulture
swallow-tailed kite
white-tailed kite
Mississippi kite
bald eagle
sharp-shinned hawk
Cooper's hawk
red-shouldered hawk
broad-winged hawk
red-tailed hawk
American kestrel
killdeer
American woodcock
mourning dove
inca dove
common ground-dove
yellow-billed cuckoo
greater roadrunner
barn owl
eastern screech-owl
great horned owl
barred owl
common nighthawk
Chuck-Will's-widow
whip-poor-will
chimney swift
ruby-throated hummingbird
belted kingfisher
red-headed woodpecker
red-bellied woodpecker
downy woodpecker
hairy woodpecker
red-cockaded woodpecker
northern flicker
pileated woodpecker
eastern wood-pewee
acadian flycatcher
willow flycatcher
eastern phoebe
great crested flycatcher
western kingbird
eastern kingbird
scissor-tailed flycatcher

horned lark
purple martin
northern rough-winged swallow
cliff swallow
barn swallow
blue jay
American crow
fish crow
Carolina chickadee
tufted titmouse
white-breasted nuthatch
brown-headed nuthatch
Carolina wren
Bewick's wren
house wren
blue-gray gnatcatcher
eastern bluebird
American robin
gray catbird
northern mockingbird
brown thrasher
cedar waxwing
loggerhead shrike
white-eyed vireo
Bell's vireo
yellow-throated vireo
warbling vireo
red-eyed vireo
northern parula
yellow warbler
yellow-throated warbler
pine warbler
prairie warbler
cerulean warbler
black-and-white warbler
American redstart
prothonotary warbler
worm-eating warbler
Swainson's warbler
ovenbird
Louisiana waterthrush
Kentucky warbler
common yellowthroat
hooded warbler
yellow-breasted chat
summer tanager

scarlet tanager
northern cardinal
blue grosbeak
indigo bunting
painted bunting
dickcissel
eastern towhee
Bachman's sparrow
rufous-crowned sparrow
chipping sparrow
field sparrow
lark sparrow
grasshopper sparrow
red-winged blackbird
eastern meadowlark
western meadowlark
great-tailed grackle
common grackle
brown-headed cowbird
orchard oriole
Baltimore oriole
American goldfinch

Region 44

pied-billed grebe
double-crested cormorant
American bittern
least bittern
great blue heron
great egret
snowy egret
little blue heron
tricolored heron
cattle egret
green heron
black-crowned night-heron
yellow-crowned night-heron
glossy ibis
black vulture
turkey vulture
osprey
Mississippi kite
bald eagle
northern harrier

sharp-shinned hawk
Cooper's hawk
red-shouldered hawk
broad-winged hawk
red-tailed hawk
American kestrel
peregrine falcon
black rail
clapper rail
king rail
Virginia rail
sora
common moorhen
American coot
Wilson's plover
piping plover
killdeer
American oystercatcher
black-necked stilt
willet
spotted sandpiper
upland sandpiper
common snipe
American woodcock
mourning dove
black-billed cuckoo
yellow-billed cuckoo
barn owl
eastern screech-owl
great horned owl
barred owl
long-eared owl
short-eared owl
northern saw-whet owl
common nighthawk
Chuck-Will's-widow
whip-poor-will
chimney swift
ruby-throated hummingbird
belted kingfisher
red-headed woodpecker
red-bellied woodpecker
downy woodpecker
hairy woodpecker
red-cockaded woodpecker
northern flicker

pileated woodpecker
eastern wood-pewee
acadian flycatcher
willow flycatcher
eastern phoebe
great crested flycatcher
eastern kingbird
horned lark
purple martin
tree swallow
northern rough-winged swallow
bank swallow
cliff swallow
barn swallow
blue jay
American crow
fish crow
black-capped chickadee
Carolina chickadee
tufted titmouse
red-breasted nuthatch
white-breasted nuthatch
brown-headed nuthatch
brown creeper
Carolina wren
house wren
sedge wren
marsh wren
blue-gray gnatcatcher
eastern bluebird
veery
hermit thrush
American robin
gray catbird
northern mockingbird
brown thrasher
cedar waxwing
loggerhead shrike
white-eyed vireo
blue-headed vireo
yellow-throated vireo
warbling vireo
red-eyed vireo
blue-winged warbler
northern parula
yellow warbler

black-throated green warbler
yellow-throated warbler
pine warbler
prairie warbler
cerulean warbler
black-and-white warbler
American redstart
prothonotary warbler
worm-eating warbler
Swainson's warbler
ovenbird
Louisiana waterthrush
Kentucky warbler
common yellowthroat
hooded warbler
yellow-breasted chat
summer tanager
scarlet tanager
northern cardinal
rose-breasted grosbeak
blue grosbeak
indigo bunting
dickcissel
eastern towhee
Bachman's sparrow
chipping sparrow
field sparrow
vesper sparrow
savannah sparrow
grasshopper sparrow
Henslow's sparrow
saltmarsh sharp-tailed sparrow
seaside sparrow
song sparrow
swamp sparrow
bobolink
red-winged blackbird
eastern meadowlark
boat-tailed grackle
common grackle
brown-headed cowbird
orchard oriole
Baltimore oriole
house finch
red crossbill
American goldfinch

Region 53

great blue heron
green heron
black vulture
turkey vulture
osprey
northern harrier
Cooper's hawk
Harris's hawk
red-shouldered hawk
Swainson's hawk
zone-tailed hawk
red-tailed hawk
golden eagle
American kestrel
killdeer
white-winged dove
mourning dove
inca dove
common ground-dove
yellow-billed cuckoo
greater roadrunner
barn owl
eastern screech-owl
great horned owl
elf owl
burrowing owl
barred owl
long-eared owl
lesser nighthawk
common nighthawk
common poorwill
Chuck-Will's-widow
chimney swift
ruby-throated hummingbird
black-chinned hummingbird
belted kingfisher
green kingfisher
red-headed woodpecker
golden-fronted woodpecker
red-bellied woodpecker
ladder-backed woodpecker
downy woodpecker
northern flicker
pileated woodpecker
western wood-pewee

eastern wood-pewee
acadian flycatcher
black phoebe
eastern phoebe
vermilion flycatcher
ash-throated flycatcher
great crested flycatcher
western kingbird
eastern kingbird
scissor-tailed flycatcher
horned lark
purple martin
northern rough-winged swallow
cliff swallow
cave swallow
barn swallow
blue jay
American crow
chihuahuan raven
common raven
Carolina chickadee
tufted titmouse
verdin
bushtit
white-breasted nuthatch
cactus wren
rock wren
canyon wren
Carolina wren
Bewick's wren
blue-gray gnatcatcher
eastern bluebird
American robin
northern mockingbird
curve-billed thrasher
loggerhead shrike
white-eyed vireo
Bell's vireo
black-capped vireo
gray vireo
yellow-throated vireo
red-eyed vireo
northern parula
yellow warbler
golden-cheeked warbler
yellow-throated warbler

black-and-white warbler
prothonotary warbler
Louisiana waterthrush
Kentucky warbler
common yellowthroat
yellow-breasted chat
summer tanager
northern cardinal
pyrrhuloxia
blue grosbeak
indigo bunting
varied bunting
painted bunting
dickcissel
canyon towhee
Cassin's sparrow
rufous-crowned sparrow
chipping sparrow
field sparrow
lark sparrow
black-throated sparrow
lark bunting
grasshopper sparrow
red-winged blackbird
eastern meadowlark
western meadowlark
yellow-headed blackbird
great-tailed grackle
common grackle
bronzed cowbird
brown-headed cowbird
orchard oriole
hooded oriole
Bullock's oriole
Scott's oriole
house finch
lesser goldfinch
American goldfinch

Region 54

great blue heron
little blue heron
cattle egret
green heron

black-crowned night-heron
yellow-crowned night-heron
black vulture
turkey vulture
Mississippi kite
northern harrier
Harris's hawk
Swainson's hawk
red-tailed hawk
ferruginous hawk
golden eagle
American kestrel
American coot
killdeer
American avocet
upland sandpiper
mourning dove
yellow-billed cuckoo
greater roadrunner
barn owl
eastern screech-owl
great horned owl
burrowing owl
long-eared owl
common nighthawk
common poorwill
Chuck-Will's-widow
chimney swift
black-chinned hummingbird
belted kingfisher
red-headed woodpecker
golden-fronted woodpecker
red-bellied woodpecker
ladder-backed woodpecker
downy woodpecker
hairy woodpecker
northern flicker
eastern wood-pewee
eastern phoebe
Say's phoebe
ash-throated flycatcher
great crested flycatcher
western kingbird
eastern kingbird
scissor-tailed flycatcher
horned lark

purple martin
northern rough-winged swallow
bank swallow
cliff swallow
barn swallow
blue jay
American crow
chihuahuan raven
common raven
Carolina chickadee
tufted titmouse
verdin
bushtit
cactus wren
rock wren
canyon wren
Carolina wren
Bewick's wren
house wren
marsh wren
blue-gray gnatcatcher
eastern bluebird
American robin
gray catbird
northern mockingbird
brown thrasher
curve-billed thrasher
cedar waxwing
loggerhead shrike
Bell's vireo
black-capped vireo
warbling vireo
yellow warbler
common yellowthroat
yellow-breasted chat
summer tanager
northern cardinal
pyrrhuloxia
blue grosbeak
lazuli bunting
indigo bunting
painted bunting
dickcissel
canyon towhee
Cassin's sparrow
rufous-crowned sparrow

chipping sparrow
field sparrow
lark sparrow
black-throated sparrow
lark bunting
grasshopper sparrow
red-winged blackbird
eastern meadowlark
western meadowlark
yellow-headed blackbird
Brewer's blackbird
great-tailed grackle
common grackle
brown-headed cowbird
orchard oriole
Baltimore oriole
Bullock's oriole
house finch
lesser goldfinch
American goldfinch

Region 55

pied-billed grebe
eared grebe
double-crested cormorant
American bittern
least bittern
great blue heron
great egret
cattle egret
green heron
black-crowned night-heron
white-faced ibis
black vulture
turkey vulture
Mississippi kite
northern harrier
Cooper's hawk
Swainson's hawk
red-tailed hawk
ferruginous hawk
golden eagle
American kestrel
prairie falcon

Virginia rail
sora
American coot
snowy plover
killdeer
American avocet
mourning dove
yellow-billed cuckoo
greater roadrunner
barn owl
western screech-owl
great horned owl
burrowing owl
long-eared owl
lesser nighthawk
common nighthawk
common poorwill
chimney swift
black-chinned hummingbird
broad-tailed hummingbird
belted kingfisher
red-headed woodpecker
golden-fronted woodpecker
red-bellied woodpecker
ladder-backed woodpecker
downy woodpecker
hairy woodpecker
northern flicker
western wood-pewee
black phoebe
eastern phoebe
Say's phoebe
vermilion flycatcher
ash-throated flycatcher
Cassin's kingbird
western kingbird
eastern kingbird
scissor-tailed flycatcher
horned lark
northern rough-winged swallow
cliff swallow
barn swallow
blue jay
chihuahuan raven
common raven
tufted titmouse

verdin
cactus wren
rock wren
canyon wren
Bewick's wren
house wren
blue-gray gnatcatcher
eastern bluebird
American robin
northern mockingbird
brown thrasher
curve-billed thrasher
loggerhead shrike
warbling vireo
yellow warbler
common yellowthroat
yellow-breasted chat
northern cardinal
pyrrhuloxia
blue grosbeak
lazuli bunting
indigo bunting
painted bunting
dickcissel
Cassin's sparrow
lark sparrow
black-throated sparrow
lark bunting
grasshopper sparrow
red-winged blackbird
eastern meadowlark
western meadowlark
great-tailed grackle
common grackle
brown-headed cowbird
orchard oriole
Bullock's oriole
house finch
lesser goldfinch

Region 56

pied-billed grebe
western grebe
Clark's grebe

double-crested cormorant
American bittern
least bittern
great blue heron
great egret
snowy egret
little blue heron
cattle egret
green heron
black-crowned night-heron
white-faced ibis
black vulture
turkey vulture
Mississippi kite
bald eagle
northern harrier
Cooper's hawk
common black-hawk
Harris's hawk
Swainson's hawk
zone-tailed hawk
red-tailed hawk
golden eagle
American kestrel
peregrine falcon
prairie falcon
Virginia rail
sora
common moorhen
American coot
snowy plover
killdeer
black-necked stilt
American avocet
spotted sandpiper
band-tailed pigeon
white-winged dove
mourning dove
inca dove
common ground-dove
yellow-billed cuckoo
greater roadrunner
barn owl
flammulated owl
eastern screech-owl
western screech-owl

great horned owl
northern pygmy-owl
elf owl
burrowing owl
spotted owl
northern saw-whet owl
lesser nighthawk
common nighthawk
common poorwill
whip-poor-will
chimney swift
white-throated swift
black-chinned hummingbird
Costa's hummingbird
broad-tailed hummingbird
green kingfisher
acorn woodpecker
gila woodpecker
golden-fronted woodpecker
red-naped sapsucker
ladder-backed woodpecker
hairy woodpecker
northern flicker
olive-sided flycatcher
western wood-pewee
willow flycatcher
gray flycatcher
cordilleran flycatcher
black phoebe
Say's phoebe
vermilion flycatcher
ash-throated flycatcher
Cassin's kingbird
western kingbird
scissor-tailed flycatcher
horned lark
violet-green swallow
northern rough-winged swallow
cliff swallow
cave swallow
barn swallow
Steller's jay
blue jay
western scrub-jay
Mexican jay
chihuahuan raven

common raven
mountain chickadee
juniper titmouse
tufted titmouse
verdin
bushtit
white-breasted nuthatch
pygmy nuthatch
brown creeper
cactus wren
rock wren
canyon wren
Carolina wren
Bewick's wren
house wren
marsh wren
blue-gray gnatcatcher
black-tailed gnatcatcher
eastern bluebird
western bluebird
hermit thrush
American robin
northern mockingbird
long-billed thrasher
Bendire's thrasher
curve-billed thrasher
crissal thrasher
phainopepla
loggerhead shrike
white-eyed vireo
Bell's vireo
black-capped vireo
gray vireo
plumbeous vireo
yellow-throated vireo
Hutton's vireo
warbling vireo
orange-crowned warbler
Virginia's warbler
Lucy's warbler
yellow warbler
black-throated gray warbler
Grace's warbler
common yellowthroat
red-faced warbler
painted redstart

yellow-breasted chat
hepatic tanager
summer tanager
western tanager
northern cardinal
pyrrhuloxia
black-headed grosbeak
blue grosbeak
indigo bunting
varied bunting
painted bunting
dickcissel
spotted towhee
canyon towhee
Abert's towhee
Cassin's sparrow
rufous-crowned sparrow
chipping sparrow
black-chinned sparrow
lark sparrow
black-throated sparrow
lark bunting
red-winged blackbird
eastern meadowlark
western meadowlark
great-tailed grackle
bronzed cowbird
brown-headed cowbird
orchard oriole
hooded oriole
Bullock's oriole
Scott's oriole
house finch
red crossbill
lesser goldfinch

Region 62

pied-billed grebe
eared grebe
western grebe
American white pelican
double-crested cormorant
great blue heron
black-crowned night-heron

white-faced ibis
turkey vulture
osprey
northern harrier
sharp-shinned hawk
Cooper's hawk
northern goshawk
Swainson's hawk
zone-tailed hawk
red-tailed hawk
ferruginous hawk
golden eagle
American kestrel
peregrine falcon
prairie falcon
Virginia rail
sora
American coot
sandhill crane
killdeer
spotted sandpiper
common snipe
Wilson's phalarope
band-tailed pigeon
mourning dove
flammulated owl
western screech-owl
great horned owl
northern pygmy-owl
spotted owl
long-eared owl
short-eared owl
boreal owl
northern saw-whet owl
common nighthawk
common poorwill
black swift
white-throated swift
broad-tailed hummingbird
belted kingfisher
Lewis's woodpecker
red-naped sapsucker
Williamson's sapsucker
downy woodpecker
hairy woodpecker
three-toed woodpecker

northern flicker
olive-sided flycatcher
western wood-pewee
willow flycatcher
Hammond's flycatcher
dusky flycatcher
cordilleran flycatcher
Say's phoebe
ash-throated flycatcher
Cassin's kingbird
horned lark
purple martin
tree swallow
violet-green swallow
northern rough-winged swallow
bank swallow
cliff swallow
barn swallow
gray jay
Steller's jay
western scrub-jay
pinyon jay
Clark's nutcracker
black-billed magpie
American crow
common raven
black-capped chickadee
mountain chickadee
red-breasted nuthatch
white-breasted nuthatch
pygmy nuthatch
brown creeper
rock wren
canyon wren
Bewick's wren
house wren
marsh wren
American dipper
golden-crowned kinglet
ruby-crowned kinglet
blue-gray gnatcatcher
western bluebird
mountain bluebird
Townsend's solitaire
veery
Swainson's thrush

hermit thrush
American robin
gray catbird
northern mockingbird
sage thrasher
American pipit
cedar waxwing
loggerhead shrike
plumbeous vireo
warbling vireo
red-eyed vireo
orange-crowned warbler
Virginia's warbler
yellow warbler
yellow-rumped warbler
black-throated gray warbler
Grace's warbler
American redstart
MacGillivray's warbler
common yellowthroat
Wilson's warbler
yellow-breasted chat
hepatic tanager
western tanager
black-headed grosbeak
lazuli bunting
green-tailed towhee
spotted towhee
canyon towhee
chipping sparrow
Brewer's sparrow
vesper sparrow
lark sparrow
sage sparrow
savannah sparrow
fox sparrow
song sparrow
Lincoln's sparrow
white-crowned sparrow
dark-eyed junco
bobolink
red-winged blackbird
western meadowlark
yellow-headed blackbird
Brewer's blackbird
great-tailed grackle

common grackle
brown-headed cowbird
Bullock's oriole
pine grosbeak
Cassin's finch
house finch
red crossbill
pine siskin
lesser goldfinch
American goldfinch
evening grosbeak

Region 64

common loon
pied-billed grebe
horned grebe
red-necked grebe
eared grebe
western grebe
Clark's grebe
American white pelican
double-crested cormorant
American bittern
great blue heron
black-crowned night-heron
white-faced ibis
turkey vulture
osprey
bald eagle
northern harrier
sharp-shinned hawk
Cooper's hawk
northern goshawk
Swainson's hawk
red-tailed hawk
ferruginous hawk
golden eagle
American kestrel
merlin
peregrine falcon
prairie falcon
Virginia rail
sora
American coot

sandhill crane
killdeer
American avocet
willet
spotted sandpiper
upland sandpiper
marbled godwit
common snipe
Wilson's phalarope
mourning dove
black-billed cuckoo
yellow-billed cuckoo
barn owl
flammulated owl
eastern screech-owl
western screech-owl
great horned owl
northern hawk owl
northern pygmy-owl
burrowing owl
barred owl
great gray owl
long-eared owl
short-eared owl
boreal owl
northern saw-whet owl
common nighthawk
common poorwill
black swift
Vaux's swift
white-throated swift
black-chinned hummingbird
calliope hummingbird
rufous hummingbird
belted kingfisher
Lewis's woodpecker
red-headed woodpecker
red-naped sapsucker
Williamson's sapsucker
downy woodpecker
hairy woodpecker
three-toed woodpecker
black-backed woodpecker
northern flicker
pileated woodpecker
olive-sided flycatcher

western wood-pewee
alder flycatcher
willow flycatcher
least flycatcher
Hammond's flycatcher
dusky flycatcher
cordilleran flycatcher
Say's phoebe
western kingbird
eastern kingbird
horned lark
tree swallow
violet-green swallow
northern rough-winged swallow
bank swallow
cliff swallow
barn swallow
gray jay
Steller's jay
blue jay
pinyon jay
Clark's nutcracker
black-billed magpie
American crow
common raven
black-capped chickadee
mountain chickadee
chestnut-backed chickadee
red-breasted nuthatch
white-breasted nuthatch
pygmy nuthatch
brown creeper
rock wren
canyon wren
house wren
winter wren
marsh wren
American dipper
golden-crowned kinglet
ruby-crowned kinglet
western bluebird
mountain bluebird
Townsend's solitaire
veery
Swainson's thrush
hermit thrush

American robin
varied thrush
gray catbird
northern mockingbird
sage thrasher
brown thrasher
American pipit
Sprague's pipit
cedar waxwing
loggerhead shrike
Cassin's vireo
plumbeous vireo
warbling vireo
red-eyed vireo
Tennessee warbler
orange-crowned warbler
Nashville warbler
yellow warbler
magnolia warbler
yellow-rumped warbler
Townsend's warbler
American redstart
ovenbird
northern waterthrush
MacGillivray's warbler
common yellowthroat
Wilson's warbler
yellow-breasted chat
western tanager
black-headed grosbeak
lazuli bunting
indigo bunting
green-tailed towhee
spotted towhee
chipping sparrow
clay-colored sparrow
Brewer's sparrow
vesper sparrow
lark sparrow
black-throated sparrow
sage sparrow
lark bunting
savannah sparrow
Baird's sparrow
grasshopper sparrow
le Conte's sparrow

fox sparrow
song sparrow
Lincoln's sparrow
white-crowned sparrow
dark-eyed junco
McCown's longspur
chestnut-collared longspur
bobolink
red-winged blackbird
western meadowlark
yellow-headed blackbird
Brewer's blackbird
common grackle
brown-headed cowbird
Bullock's oriole
pine grosbeak
purple finch
Cassin's finch
house finch
red crossbill
pine siskin
American goldfinch
evening grosbeak

Region 66

pied-billed grebe
eared grebe
western grebe
Clark's grebe
double-crested cormorant
American bittern
least bittern
great blue heron
great egret
snowy egret
black-crowned night-heron
turkey vulture
white-tailed kite
northern harrier
sharp-shinned hawk
Cooper's hawk
northern goshawk
red-shouldered hawk
Swainson's hawk

red-tailed hawk
golden eagle
American kestrel
peregrine falcon
prairie falcon
Virginia rail
sora
American coot
sandhill crane
killdeer
black-necked stilt
American avocet
spotted sandpiper
common snipe
Wilson's phalarope
band-tailed pigeon
mourning dove
groove-billed ani
barn owl
flammulated owl
western screech-owl
great horned owl
northern pygmy-owl
burrowing owl
spotted owl
great gray owl
long-eared owl
short-eared owl
northern saw-whet owl
common nighthawk
common poorwill
black swift
Vaux's swift
white-throated swift
black-chinned hummingbird
Anna's hummingbird
calliope hummingbird
belted kingfisher
Lewis's woodpecker
acorn woodpecker
red-breasted sapsucker
Williamson's sapsucker
Nuttall's woodpecker
downy woodpecker
hairy woodpecker
white-headed woodpecker

black-backed woodpecker
northern flicker
pileated woodpecker
olive-sided flycatcher
western wood-pewee
willow flycatcher
Hammond's flycatcher
dusky flycatcher
pacific-slope flycatcher
black phoebe
Say's phoebe
ash-throated flycatcher
western kingbird
horned lark
purple martin
tree swallow
violet-green swallow
northern rough-winged swallow
bank swallow
cliff swallow
barn swallow
Steller's jay
western scrub-jay
Clark's nutcracker
black-billed magpie
yellow-billed magpie
American crow
common raven
mountain chickadee
oak titmouse
bushtit
red-breasted nuthatch
white-breasted nuthatch
pygmy nuthatch
brown creeper
rock wren
canyon wren
Bewick's wren
house wren
winter wren
marsh wren
American dipper
golden-crowned kinglet
ruby-crowned kinglet
blue-gray gnatcatcher
western bluebird

mountain bluebird
Townsend's solitaire
Swainson's thrush
hermit thrush
American robin
wrentit
northern mockingbird
sage thrasher
California thrasher
cedar waxwing
loggerhead shrike
Cassin's vireo
Hutton's vireo
warbling vireo
orange-crowned warbler
Nashville warbler
yellow warbler
yellow-rumped warbler
black-throated gray warbler
hermit warbler
MacGillivray's warbler
common yellowthroat
Wilson's warbler
yellow-breasted chat
western tanager
black-headed grosbeak
blue grosbeak
lazuli bunting
green-tailed towhee
spotted towhee
California towhee
rufous-crowned sparrow
chipping sparrow
black-chinned sparrow
lark sparrow
sage sparrow
savannah sparrow
song sparrow
dark-eyed junco
red-winged blackbird
tricolored blackbird
western meadowlark
yellow-headed blackbird
Brewer's blackbird
brown-headed cowbird
Bullock's oriole

pine grosbeak
purple finch
house finch
red crossbill
pine siskin

Region 67

common loon
red-necked grebe
eared grebe
western grebe
American white pelican
American bittern
least bittern
great blue heron
great egret
snowy egret
green heron
black-crowned night-heron
white-faced ibis
turkey vulture
osprey
bald eagle
northern harrier
sharp-shinned hawk
Cooper's hawk
northern goshawk
Swainson's hawk
red-tailed hawk
golden eagle
American kestrel
merlin
peregrine falcon
prairie falcon
yellow rail
Virginia rail
sora
American coot
sandhill crane
snowy plover
killdeer
black-necked stilt
American avocet
willet

spotted sandpiper
common snipe
Wilson's phalarope
band-tailed pigeon
mourning dove
barn owl
flammulated owl
western screech-owl
great horned owl
northern pygmy-owl
burrowing owl
spotted owl
barred owl
great gray owl
long-eared owl
short-eared owl
northern saw-whet owl
common nighthawk
common poorwill
black swift
Vaux's swift
calliope hummingbird
rufous hummingbird
belted kingfisher
Lewis's woodpecker
acorn woodpecker
red-naped sapsucker
red-breasted sapsucker
Williamson's sapsucker
downy woodpecker
hairy woodpecker
white-headed woodpecker
three-toed woodpecker
black-backed woodpecker
northern flicker
pileated woodpecker
olive-sided flycatcher
western wood-pewee
willow flycatcher
Hammond's flycatcher
dusky flycatcher
gray flycatcher
cordilleran flycatcher
Say's phoebe
ash-throated flycatcher
eastern kingbird

horned lark
purple martin
tree swallow
violet-green swallow
northern rough-winged swallow
bank swallow
cliff swallow
barn swallow
gray jay
Steller's jay
western scrub-jay
pinyon jay
Clark's nutcracker
black-billed magpie
American crow
common raven
black-capped chickadee
mountain chickadee
chestnut-backed chickadee
oak titmouse
red-breasted nuthatch
white-breasted nuthatch
pygmy nuthatch
brown creeper
Bewick's wren
house wren
winter wren
marsh wren
American dipper
golden-crowned kinglet
ruby-crowned kinglet
blue-gray gnatcatcher
western bluebird
mountain bluebird
Townsend's solitaire
veery
Swainson's thrush
hermit thrush
American robin
varied thrush
gray catbird
sage thrasher
American pipit
cedar waxwing
loggerhead shrike
Cassin's vireo

Hutton's vireo
warbling vireo
red-eyed vireo
orange-crowned warbler
Nashville warbler
yellow warbler
yellow-rumped warbler
black-throated gray warbler
Townsend's warbler
hermit warbler
American redstart
northern waterthrush
MacGillivray's warbler
common yellowthroat
Wilson's warbler
yellow-breasted chat
western tanager
black-headed grosbeak
lazuli bunting
spotted towhee
California towhee
chipping sparrow
Brewer's sparrow
black-chinned sparrow
vesper sparrow
lark sparrow
sage sparrow
savannah sparrow
fox sparrow
song sparrow
Lincoln's sparrow
white-crowned sparrow
dark-eyed junco
tricolored blackbird
western meadowlark
yellow-headed blackbird
Brewer's blackbird
brown-headed cowbird
Bullock's oriole
pine grosbeak
purple finch
Cassin's finch
house finch
red crossbill
pine siskin
lesser goldfinch

American goldfinch
evening grosbeak

Region 69

turkey vulture
Swainson's hawk
red-tailed hawk
golden eagle
American kestrel
prairie falcon
mourning dove
great horned owl
common nighthawk
common poorwill
calliope hummingbird
belted kingfisher
Lewis's woodpecker
northern flicker
western wood-pewee
dusky flycatcher
gray flycatcher
ash-throated flycatcher
violet-green swallow
northern rough-winged swallow
bank swallow
cliff swallow
barn swallow
western scrub-jay
pinyon jay
Clark's nutcracker
black-billed magpie
American crow
common raven
black-capped chickadee
mountain chickadee
juniper titmouse
bushtit
rock wren
canyon wren
Bewick's wren
ruby-crowned kinglet
blue-gray gnatcatcher
western bluebird
mountain bluebird

Townsend's solitaire
Swainson's thrush
hermit thrush
American robin
cedar waxwing
loggerhead shrike
Virginia's warbler
black-throated gray warbler
lazuli bunting
green-tailed towhee
spotted towhee
lark sparrow
brown-headed cowbird
Scott's oriole

Region 80

pied-billed grebe
eared grebe
western grebe
Clark's grebe
American white pelican
double-crested cormorant
American bittern
great blue heron
great egret
snowy egret
cattle egret
black-crowned night-heron
white-faced ibis
turkey vulture
osprey
bald eagle
northern harrier
sharp-shinned hawk
Cooper's hawk
northern goshawk
Swainson's hawk
red-tailed hawk
ferruginous hawk
golden eagle
American kestrel
merlin
peregrine falcon
prairie falcon

Virginia rail
sora
common moorhen
American coot
sandhill crane
snowy plover
killdeer
black-necked stilt
American avocet
willet
spotted sandpiper
common snipe
Wilson's phalarope
mourning dove
black-billed cuckoo
yellow-billed cuckoo
barn owl
flammulated owl
western screech-owl
great horned owl
northern pygmy-owl
burrowing owl
great gray owl
long-eared owl
short-eared owl
boreal owl
northern saw-whet owl
common nighthawk
common poorwill
white-throated swift
black-chinned hummingbird
calliope hummingbird
broad-tailed hummingbird
rufous hummingbird
belted kingfisher
Lewis's woodpecker
red-naped sapsucker
red-breasted sapsucker
Williamson's sapsucker
downy woodpecker
hairy woodpecker
three-toed woodpecker
northern flicker
olive-sided flycatcher
western wood-pewee
willow flycatcher

Hammond's flycatcher
dusky flycatcher
gray flycatcher
cordilleran flycatcher
Say's phoebe
ash-throated flycatcher
western kingbird
eastern kingbird
horned lark
tree swallow
violet-green swallow
northern rough-winged swallow
bank swallow
cliff swallow
barn swallow
Steller's jay
western scrub-jay
pinyon jay
Clark's nutcracker
black-billed magpie
American crow
common raven
black-capped chickadee
mountain chickadee
juniper titmouse
bushtit
red-breasted nuthatch
white-breasted nuthatch
brown creeper
rock wren
canyon wren
Bewick's wren
house wren
marsh wren
American dipper
golden-crowned kinglet
ruby-crowned kinglet
blue-gray gnatcatcher
mountain bluebird
Townsend's solitaire
veery
Swainson's thrush
hermit thrush
American robin
gray catbird
northern mockingbird

sage thrasher
cedar waxwing
loggerhead shrike
plumbeous vireo
warbling vireo
orange-crowned warbler
Virginia's warbler
yellow warbler
yellow-rumped warbler
black-throated gray warbler
Townsend's warbler
American redstart
MacGillivray's warbler
common yellowthroat
Wilson's warbler
yellow-breasted chat
western tanager
black-headed grosbeak
blue grosbeak
lazuli bunting
green-tailed towhee
spotted towhee
chipping sparrow
Brewer's sparrow
vesper sparrow
lark sparrow
black-throated sparrow
sage sparrow
lark bunting
savannah sparrow
grasshopper sparrow
fox sparrow
song sparrow
Lincoln's sparrow
white-crowned sparrow
dark-eyed junco
bobolink
red-winged blackbird
western meadowlark
yellow-headed blackbird
Brewer's blackbird
great-tailed grackle
common grackle
brown-headed cowbird
Bullock's oriole
Scott's oriole

Cassin's finch
house finch
red crossbill
pine siskin
lesser goldfinch
American goldfinch
evening grosbeak

Region 81

pied-billed grebe
American white pelican
great blue heron
cattle egret
green heron
black-crowned night-heron
black vulture
turkey vulture
Mississippi kite
sharp-shinned hawk
Cooper's hawk
northern goshawk
common black-hawk
Swainson's hawk
zone-tailed hawk
red-tailed hawk
golden eagle
crested caracara
American kestrel
peregrine falcon
prairie falcon
common moorhen
American coot
snowy plover
killdeer
black-necked stilt
American avocet
band-tailed pigeon
white-winged dove
mourning dove
inca dove
common ground-dove
yellow-billed cuckoo
greater roadrunner
barn owl

flammulated owl
western screech-owl
great horned owl
northern pygmy-owl
elf owl
burrowing owl
spotted owl
northern saw-whet owl
lesser nighthawk
common nighthawk
common poorwill
whip-poor-will
white-throated swift
black-chinned hummingbird
Anna's hummingbird
Costa's hummingbird
broad-tailed hummingbird
green kingfisher
acorn woodpecker
gila woodpecker
ladder-backed woodpecker
hairy woodpecker
Strickland's woodpecker
northern flicker
greater pewee
western wood-pewee
willow flycatcher
cordilleran flycatcher
black phoebe
Say's phoebe
vermilion flycatcher
ash-throated flycatcher
Cassin's kingbird
western kingbird
horned lark
purple martin
violet-green swallow
northern rough-winged swallow
cliff swallow
barn swallow
Steller's jay
western scrub-jay
Mexican jay
chihuahuan raven
common raven
mountain chickadee

bridled titmouse
juniper titmouse
verdin
bushtit
white-breasted nuthatch
pygmy nuthatch
brown creeper
cactus wren
rock wren
canyon wren
Bewick's wren
house wren
blue-gray gnatcatcher
black-tailed gnatcatcher
eastern bluebird
western bluebird
hermit thrush
American robin
northern mockingbird
Bendire's thrasher
curve-billed thrasher
crissal thrasher
phainopepla
loggerhead shrike
Bell's vireo
plumbeous vireo
Hutton's vireo
warbling vireo
orange-crowned warbler
Virginia's warbler
Lucy's warbler
yellow warbler
yellow-rumped warbler
black-throated gray warbler
Grace's warbler
common yellowthroat
red-faced warbler
painted redstart
yellow-breasted chat
olive warbler
hepatic tanager
summer tanager
western tanager
northern cardinal
pyrrhuloxia
black-headed grosbeak

blue grosbeak
indigo bunting
varied bunting
spotted towhee
canyon towhee
Abert's towhee
Cassin's sparrow
rufous-crowned sparrow
chipping sparrow
lark sparrow
black-throated sparrow
grasshopper sparrow
song sparrow
yellow-eyed junco
red-winged blackbird
eastern meadowlark
western meadowlark
great-tailed grackle
bronzed cowbird
brown-headed cowbird
hooded oriole
Bullock's oriole
Scott's oriole
house finch
red crossbill
pine siskin
lesser goldfinch
evening grosbeak

Region 82

pied-billed grebe
eared grebe
western grebe
Clark's grebe
double-crested cormorant
least bittern
great blue heron
great egret
snowy egret
cattle egret
green heron
black-crowned night-heron
black vulture
turkey vulture

osprey
white-tailed kite
bald eagle
Cooper's hawk
common black-hawk
Harris's hawk
red-shouldered hawk
Swainson's hawk
zone-tailed hawk
red-tailed hawk
golden eagle
crested caracara
American kestrel
peregrine falcon
prairie falcon
black rail
clapper rail
Virginia rail
common moorhen
American coot
snowy plover
killdeer
black-necked stilt
American avocet
white-winged dove
mourning dove
inca dove
common ground-dove
yellow-billed cuckoo
greater roadrunner
barn owl
flammulated owl
western screech-owl
great horned owl
northern pygmy-owl
elf owl
burrowing owl
long-eared owl
lesser nighthawk
common poorwill
whip-poor-will
white-throated swift
black-chinned hummingbird
Anna's hummingbird
Costa's hummingbird
acorn woodpecker

gila woodpecker
ladder-backed woodpecker
Strickland's woodpecker
gilded flicker
northern flicker
western wood-pewee
willow flycatcher
cordilleran flycatcher
black phoebe
Say's phoebe
vermilion flycatcher
ash-throated flycatcher
Cassin's kingbird
western kingbird
horned lark
purple martin
violet-green swallow
northern rough-winged swallow
cliff swallow
barn swallow
Steller's jay
western scrub-jay
chihuahuan raven
common raven
mountain chickadee
verdin
bushtit
cactus wren
rock wren
canyon wren
Bewick's wren
house wren
marsh wren
American dipper
blue-gray gnatcatcher
black-tailed gnatcatcher
American robin
northern mockingbird
Bendire's thrasher
curve-billed thrasher
crissal thrasher
le Conte's thrasher
phainopepla
loggerhead shrike
Bell's vireo
plumbeous vireo

Virginia's warbler
Lucy's warbler
yellow warbler
yellow-rumped warbler
black-throated gray warbler
common yellowthroat
red-faced warbler
yellow-breasted chat
hepatic tanager
summer tanager
northern cardinal
pyrrhuloxia
black-headed grosbeak
blue grosbeak
indigo bunting
varied bunting
spotted towhee
canyon towhee
Abert's towhee
rufous-winged sparrow
rufous-crowned sparrow
lark sparrow
black-throated sparrow
grasshopper sparrow
song sparrow
red-winged blackbird
western meadowlark
yellow-headed blackbird
great-tailed grackle
bronzed cowbird
brown-headed cowbird
hooded oriole
Bullock's oriole
Scott's oriole
house finch
red crossbill
lesser goldfinch
Lawrence's goldfinch

Region 83

pied-billed grebe
eared grebe
western grebe
Clark's grebe

double-crested cormorant
least bittern
great blue heron
great egret
snowy egret
green heron
black-crowned night-heron
turkey vulture
northern harrier
common black-hawk
red-tailed hawk
golden eagle
American kestrel
peregrine falcon
prairie falcon
black rail
clapper rail
Virginia rail
common moorhen
American coot
snowy plover
killdeer
black-necked stilt
white-winged dove
mourning dove
inca dove
yellow-billed cuckoo
greater roadrunner
barn owl
western screech-owl
great horned owl
elf owl
burrowing owl
long-eared owl
lesser nighthawk
common poorwill
white-throated swift
black-chinned hummingbird
Costa's hummingbird
broad-tailed hummingbird
gila woodpecker
ladder-backed woodpecker
northern flicker
willow flycatcher
black phoebe
Say's phoebe

vermilion flycatcher
ash-throated flycatcher
western kingbird
horned lark
violet-green swallow
northern rough-winged swallow
cliff swallow
Steller's jay
common raven
verdin
bushtit
cactus wren
rock wren
canyon wren
Bewick's wren
house wren
marsh wren
blue-gray gnatcatcher
black-tailed gnatcatcher
northern mockingbird
Bendire's thrasher
crissal thrasher
le Conte's thrasher
phainopepla
loggerhead shrike
Bell's vireo
gray vireo
Lucy's warbler
yellow warbler
common yellowthroat
yellow-breasted chat
summer tanager
blue grosbeak
indigo bunting
canyon towhee
Abert's towhee
black-throated sparrow
song sparrow
red-winged blackbird
western meadowlark
yellow-headed blackbird
great-tailed grackle
bronzed cowbird
brown-headed cowbird
hooded oriole
Bullock's oriole

Scott's oriole
house finch
lesser goldfinch

Region 84

pied-billed grebe
eared grebe
western grebe
double-crested cormorant
great blue heron
cattle egret
green heron
black-crowned night-heron
turkey vulture
osprey
Mississippi kite
bald eagle
sharp-shinned hawk
Cooper's hawk
northern goshawk
common black-hawk
Swainson's hawk
zone-tailed hawk
red-tailed hawk
ferruginous hawk
golden eagle
American kestrel
peregrine falcon
prairie falcon
Virginia rail
sora
common moorhen
American coot
snowy plover
killdeer
American avocet
common snipe
band-tailed pigeon
white-winged dove
mourning dove
common ground-dove
yellow-billed cuckoo
greater roadrunner
barn owl

flammulated owl
western screech-owl
great horned owl
northern pygmy-owl
elf owl
burrowing owl
spotted owl
long-eared owl
northern saw-whet owl
lesser nighthawk
common nighthawk
common poorwill
whip-poor-will
white-throated swift
black-chinned hummingbird
Costa's hummingbird
broad-tailed hummingbird
belted kingfisher
Lewis's woodpecker
red-headed woodpecker
acorn woodpecker
gila woodpecker
red-naped sapsucker
Williamson's sapsucker
ladder-backed woodpecker
downy woodpecker
hairy woodpecker
Strickland's woodpecker
three-toed woodpecker
gilded flicker
northern flicker
olive-sided flycatcher
greater pewee
western wood-pewee
willow flycatcher
dusky flycatcher
gray flycatcher
cordilleran flycatcher
black phoebe
Say's phoebe
vermilion flycatcher
ash-throated flycatcher
Cassin's kingbird
western kingbird
horned lark
purple martin

tree swallow
violet-green swallow
northern rough-winged swallow
cliff swallow
barn swallow
gray jay
Steller's jay
western scrub-jay
Mexican jay
pinyon jay
Clark's nutcracker
American crow
common raven
mountain chickadee
bridled titmouse
juniper titmouse
bushtit
red-breasted nuthatch
white-breasted nuthatch
pygmy nuthatch
brown creeper
rock wren
canyon wren
Bewick's wren
house wren
American dipper
golden-crowned kinglet
ruby-crowned kinglet
blue-gray gnatcatcher
western bluebird
mountain bluebird
Townsend's solitaire
veery
Swainson's thrush
hermit thrush
American robin
wrentit
gray catbird
northern mockingbird
Bendire's thrasher
curve-billed thrasher
crissal thrasher
American pipit
phainopepla
loggerhead shrike
Bell's vireo

gray vireo
plumbeous vireo
Hutton's vireo
warbling vireo
orange-crowned warbler
Virginia's warbler
yellow warbler
yellow-rumped warbler
black-throated gray warbler
Grace's warbler
American redstart
MacGillivray's warbler
common yellowthroat
red-faced warbler
painted redstart
yellow-breasted chat
olive warbler
hepatic tanager
summer tanager
western tanager
black-headed grosbeak
blue grosbeak
lazuli bunting
indigo bunting
green-tailed towhee
spotted towhee
canyon towhee
rufous-crowned sparrow
chipping sparrow
black-chinned sparrow
vesper sparrow
lark sparrow
black-throated sparrow
savannah sparrow
song sparrow
Lincoln's sparrow
white-crowned sparrow
dark-eyed junco
red-winged blackbird
eastern meadowlark
western meadowlark
yellow-headed blackbird
Brewer's blackbird
great-tailed grackle
brown-headed cowbird
hooded oriole

Bullock's oriole
Scott's oriole
pine grosbeak
Cassin's finch
house finch
red crossbill
pine siskin
lesser goldfinch
American goldfinch
evening grosbeak

Region 86

pied-billed grebe
eared grebe
western grebe
Clark's grebe
American white pelican
double-crested cormorant
American bittern
great blue heron
snowy egret
cattle egret
black-crowned night-heron
white-faced ibis
turkey vulture
osprey
bald eagle
northern harrier
sharp-shinned hawk
Cooper's hawk
northern goshawk
Swainson's hawk
red-tailed hawk
ferruginous hawk
golden eagle
American kestrel
merlin
prairie falcon
Virginia rail
sora
American coot
sandhill crane
snowy plover
killdeer

black-necked stilt
American avocet
willet
spotted sandpiper
upland sandpiper
common snipe
Wilson's phalarope
mourning dove
black-billed cuckoo
yellow-billed cuckoo
barn owl
western screech-owl
great horned owl
burrowing owl
long-eared owl
short-eared owl
common nighthawk
common poorwill
chimney swift
white-throated swift
black-chinned hummingbird
broad-tailed hummingbird
rufous hummingbird
belted kingfisher
Lewis's woodpecker
red-naped sapsucker
downy woodpecker
hairy woodpecker
northern flicker
olive-sided flycatcher
western wood-pewee
willow flycatcher
least flycatcher
Hammond's flycatcher
dusky flycatcher
gray flycatcher
cordilleran flycatcher
Say's phoebe
ash-throated flycatcher
Cassin's kingbird
western kingbird
eastern kingbird
horned lark
purple martin
tree swallow
violet-green swallow

northern rough-winged swallow
bank swallow
cliff swallow
barn swallow
Steller's jay
blue jay
pinyon jay
Clark's nutcracker
black-billed magpie
American crow
common raven
black-capped chickadee
mountain chickadee
juniper titmouse
red-breasted nuthatch
white-breasted nuthatch
rock wren
canyon wren
Bewick's wren
house wren
marsh wren
ruby-crowned kinglet
blue-gray gnatcatcher
mountain bluebird
Townsend's solitaire
veery
Swainson's thrush
hermit thrush
American robin
gray catbird
northern mockingbird
sage thrasher
brown thrasher
cedar waxwing
loggerhead shrike
warbling vireo
orange-crowned warbler
Virginia's warbler
yellow warbler
yellow-rumped warbler
black-throated gray warbler
American redstart
MacGillivray's warbler
common yellowthroat
Wilson's warbler
yellow-breasted chat

western tanager
rose-breasted grosbeak
black-headed grosbeak
blue grosbeak
lazuli bunting
green-tailed towhee
spotted towhee
chipping sparrow
clay-colored sparrow
Brewer's sparrow
vesper sparrow
lark sparrow
black-throated sparrow
sage sparrow
lark bunting
savannah sparrow
grasshopper sparrow
fox sparrow
song sparrow
Lincoln's sparrow
white-crowned sparrow
dark-eyed junco
McCown's longspur
chestnut-collared longspur
bobolink
red-winged blackbird
western meadowlark
yellow-headed blackbird
Brewer's blackbird
common grackle
brown-headed cowbird
orchard oriole
Bullock's oriole
Scott's oriole
Cassin's finch
house finch
pine siskin
American goldfinch
evening grosbeak

Region 87

pied-billed grebe
eared grebe
western grebe

Clark's grebe
double-crested cormorant
American bittern
least bittern
great blue heron
snowy egret
little blue heron
cattle egret
green heron
black-crowned night-heron
white-faced ibis
turkey vulture
osprey
Mississippi kite
bald eagle
northern harrier
sharp-shinned hawk
Cooper's hawk
northern goshawk
Swainson's hawk
zone-tailed hawk
red-tailed hawk
ferruginous hawk
golden eagle
American kestrel
peregrine falcon
prairie falcon
Virginia rail
sora
common moorhen
American coot
sandhill crane
killdeer
black-necked stilt
American avocet
willet
spotted sandpiper
common snipe
Wilson's phalarope
band-tailed pigeon
white-winged dove
mourning dove
yellow-billed cuckoo
greater roadrunner
barn owl
flammulated owl

western screech-owl
great horned owl
northern pygmy-owl
burrowing owl
spotted owl
long-eared owl
short-eared owl
northern saw-whet owl
lesser nighthawk
common nighthawk
common poorwill
whip-poor-will
white-throated swift
black-chinned hummingbird
broad-tailed hummingbird
belted kingfisher
Lewis's woodpecker
red-headed woodpecker
acorn woodpecker
red-naped sapsucker
Williamson's sapsucker
ladder-backed woodpecker
downy woodpecker
hairy woodpecker
three-toed woodpecker
northern flicker
olive-sided flycatcher
western wood-pewee
willow flycatcher
Hammond's flycatcher
dusky flycatcher
gray flycatcher
cordilleran flycatcher
black phoebe
eastern phoebe
Say's phoebe
ash-throated flycatcher
Cassin's kingbird
western kingbird
eastern kingbird
horned lark
tree swallow
violet-green swallow
northern rough-winged swallow
bank swallow
cliff swallow

barn swallow
Steller's jay
blue jay
western scrub-jay
pinyon jay
Clark's nutcracker
black-billed magpie
American crow
chihuahuan raven
common raven
black-capped chickadee
mountain chickadee
juniper titmouse
verdin
bushtit
red-breasted nuthatch
white-breasted nuthatch
pygmy nuthatch
brown creeper
cactus wren
rock wren
canyon wren
Bewick's wren
house wren
marsh wren
American dipper
golden-crowned kinglet
ruby-crowned kinglet
blue-gray gnatcatcher
eastern bluebird
western bluebird
mountain bluebird
Townsend's solitaire
veery
Swainson's thrush
hermit thrush
American robin
gray catbird
northern mockingbird
sage thrasher
Bendire's thrasher
curve-billed thrasher
crissal thrasher
phainopepla
loggerhead shrike
Bell's vireo

gray vireo
plumbeous vireo
warbling vireo
orange-crowned warbler
Virginia's warbler
Lucy's warbler
yellow warbler
yellow-rumped warbler
black-throated gray warbler
Grace's warbler
American redstart
MacGillivray's warbler
common yellowthroat
red-faced warbler
yellow-breasted chat
hepatic tanager
summer tanager
western tanager
pyrrhuloxia
black-headed grosbeak
blue grosbeak
lazuli bunting
indigo bunting
dickcissel
green-tailed towhee
spotted towhee
canyon towhee
Cassin's sparrow
rufous-crowned sparrow
chipping sparrow
Brewer's sparrow
black-chinned sparrow
vesper sparrow
lark sparrow
black-throated sparrow
sage sparrow
lark bunting
savannah sparrow
grasshopper sparrow
fox sparrow
song sparrow
Lincoln's sparrow
white-crowned sparrow
dark-eyed junco
bobolink
red-winged blackbird

eastern meadowlark
western meadowlark
yellow-headed blackbird
Brewer's blackbird
great-tailed grackle
common grackle
brown-headed cowbird
Bullock's oriole
Scott's oriole
pine grosbeak
Cassin's finch
house finch
red crossbill
pine siskin
lesser goldfinch
American goldfinch
evening grosbeak

Region 89

common loon
pied-billed grebe
horned grebe
red-necked grebe
eared grebe
western grebe
Clark's grebe
American white pelican
double-crested cormorant
American bittern
great blue heron
great egret
snowy egret
cattle egret
black-crowned night-heron
white-faced ibis
turkey vulture
osprey
bald eagle
northern harrier
sharp-shinned hawk
Cooper's hawk
northern goshawk
Swainson's hawk
red-tailed hawk

ferruginous hawk
golden eagle
American kestrel
merlin
peregrine falcon
prairie falcon
Virginia rail
sora
American coot
sandhill crane
snowy plover
killdeer
black-necked stilt
American avocet
willet
spotted sandpiper
common snipe
Wilson's phalarope
mourning dove
black-billed cuckoo
yellow-billed cuckoo
barn owl
flammulated owl
western screech-owl
great horned owl
northern pygmy-owl
burrowing owl
barred owl
great gray owl
long-eared owl
short-eared owl
northern saw-whet owl
common nighthawk
common poorwill
Vaux's swift
white-throated swift
black-chinned hummingbird
calliope hummingbird
broad-tailed hummingbird
rufous hummingbird
belted kingfisher
Lewis's woodpecker
red-naped sapsucker
Williamson's sapsucker
downy woodpecker
hairy woodpecker

white-headed woodpecker
three-toed woodpecker
black-backed woodpecker
northern flicker
pileated woodpecker
olive-sided flycatcher
western wood-pewee
willow flycatcher
Hammond's flycatcher
dusky flycatcher
gray flycatcher
cordilleran flycatcher
Say's phoebe
ash-throated flycatcher
western kingbird
eastern kingbird
horned lark
tree swallow
violet-green swallow
northern rough-winged swallow
bank swallow
cliff swallow
barn swallow
gray jay
Steller's jay
western scrub-jay
pinyon jay
Clark's nutcracker
black-billed magpie
American crow
common raven
black-capped chickadee
mountain chickadee
juniper titmouse
bushtit
red-breasted nuthatch
white-breasted nuthatch
pygmy nuthatch
brown creeper
rock wren
canyon wren
Bewick's wren
house wren
winter wren
marsh wren
American dipper

golden-crowned kinglet
ruby-crowned kinglet
blue-gray gnatcatcher
western bluebird
mountain bluebird
Townsend's solitaire
veery
Swainson's thrush
hermit thrush
American robin
varied thrush
gray catbird
northern mockingbird
sage thrasher
American pipit
cedar waxwing
loggerhead shrike
Cassin's vireo
warbling vireo
red-eyed vireo
orange-crowned warbler
Nashville warbler
Virginia's warbler
yellow warbler
yellow-rumped warbler
black-throated gray warbler
Townsend's warbler
American redstart
northern waterthrush
MacGillivray's warbler
common yellowthroat
Wilson's warbler
yellow-breasted chat
western tanager
black-headed grosbeak
blue grosbeak
lazuli bunting
green-tailed towhee
spotted towhee
chipping sparrow
Brewer's sparrow
vesper sparrow
lark sparrow
black-throated sparrow
sage sparrow
lark bunting

savannah sparrow
grasshopper sparrow
fox sparrow
song sparrow
Lincoln's sparrow
white-crowned sparrow
dark-eyed junco
bobolink
red-winged blackbird
tricolored blackbird
western meadowlark
yellow-headed blackbird
Brewer's blackbird
great-tailed grackle
common grackle
brown-headed cowbird
Bullock's oriole
Scott's oriole
pine grosbeak
Cassin's finch
house finch
red crossbill
pine siskin
lesser goldfinch
American goldfinch
evening grosbeak

Region 90

pied-billed grebe
eared grebe
brown pelican
least bittern
great blue heron
cattle egret
green heron
black-crowned night-heron
white-faced ibis
turkey vulture
white-tailed kite
northern harrier
Cooper's hawk
red-shouldered hawk
red-tailed hawk
golden eagle

American kestrel
prairie falcon
Virginia rail
sora
common moorhen
American coot
snowy plover
killdeer
American avocet
spotted sandpiper
band-tailed pigeon
mourning dove
yellow-billed cuckoo
greater roadrunner
barn owl
flammulated owl
western screech-owl
great horned owl
northern pygmy-owl
burrowing owl
spotted owl
northern saw-whet owl
lesser nighthawk
common poorwill
white-throated swift
black-chinned hummingbird
Anna's hummingbird
Costa's hummingbird
belted kingfisher
Lewis's woodpecker
acorn woodpecker
Nuttall's woodpecker
downy woodpecker
hairy woodpecker
gilded flicker
northern flicker
olive-sided flycatcher
western wood-pewee
dusky flycatcher
pacific-slope flycatcher
black phoebe
ash-throated flycatcher
Cassin's kingbird
western kingbird
horned lark
purple martin

tree swallow
violet-green swallow
northern rough-winged swallow
cliff swallow
barn swallow
Steller's jay
western scrub-jay
Clark's nutcracker
yellow-billed magpie
American crow
common raven
oak titmouse
bushtit
white-breasted nuthatch
pygmy nuthatch
brown creeper
cactus wren
rock wren
canyon wren
Bewick's wren
house wren
winter wren
marsh wren
American dipper
golden-crowned kinglet
blue-gray gnatcatcher
western bluebird
American robin
wrentit
northern mockingbird
California thrasher
phainopepla
loggerhead shrike
Cassin's vireo
Hutton's vireo
warbling vireo
orange-crowned warbler
yellow warbler
yellow-rumped warbler
black-throated gray warbler
common yellowthroat
Wilson's warbler
yellow-breasted chat
western tanager
black-headed grosbeak
blue grosbeak

lazuli bunting
spotted towhee
California towhee
rufous-crowned sparrow
chipping sparrow
Brewer's sparrow
black-chinned sparrow
lark sparrow
black-throated sparrow
grasshopper sparrow
song sparrow
dark-eyed junco
red-winged blackbird
tricolored blackbird
western meadowlark
yellow-headed blackbird
Brewer's blackbird
brown-headed cowbird
hooded oriole
Bullock's oriole
Scott's oriole
purple finch
house finch
red crossbill
lesser goldfinch
Lawrence's goldfinch
American goldfinch

Region 91

pied-billed grebe
eared grebe
western grebe
Clark's grebe
double-crested cormorant
American bittern
least bittern
great blue heron
great egret
snowy egret
green heron
black-crowned night-heron
turkey vulture
white-tailed kite
northern harrier

Cooper's hawk
red-shouldered hawk
red-tailed hawk
golden eagle
American kestrel
prairie falcon
Virginia rail
sora
common moorhen
American coot
killdeer
American avocet
spotted sandpiper
mourning dove
greater roadrunner
barn owl
western screech-owl
great horned owl
northern pygmy-owl
burrowing owl
long-eared owl
short-eared owl
northern saw-whet owl
lesser nighthawk
common nighthawk
black swift
white-throated swift
black-chinned hummingbird
Anna's hummingbird
Lewis's woodpecker
acorn woodpecker
Williamson's sapsucker
Nuttall's woodpecker
downy woodpecker
hairy woodpecker
black-backed woodpecker
northern flicker
pileated woodpecker
western wood-pewee
black phoebe
Say's phoebe
ash-throated flycatcher
western kingbird
horned lark
purple martin
tree swallow

violet-green swallow
northern rough-winged swallow
cliff swallow
barn swallow
western scrub-jay
yellow-billed magpie
American crow
common raven
oak titmouse
bushtit
white-breasted nuthatch
brown creeper
rock wren
canyon wren
Bewick's wren
house wren
winter wren
marsh wren
western bluebird
Townsend's solitaire
American robin
wrentit
northern mockingbird
California thrasher
le Conte's thrasher
cedar waxwing
phainopepla
loggerhead shrike
Cassin's vireo
Hutton's vireo
warbling vireo
orange-crowned warbler
yellow warbler
MacGillivray's warbler
common yellowthroat
Wilson's warbler
yellow-breasted chat
western tanager
black-headed grosbeak
blue grosbeak
lazuli bunting
spotted towhee
California towhee
rufous-crowned sparrow
chipping sparrow
black-chinned sparrow

lark sparrow
grasshopper sparrow
song sparrow
red-winged blackbird
tricolored blackbird
western meadowlark
yellow-headed blackbird
Brewer's blackbird
brown-headed cowbird
hooded oriole
Bullock's oriole
pine grosbeak
house finch
lesser goldfinch
Lawrence's goldfinch
American goldfinch

Region 92

pied-billed grebe
eared grebe
western grebe
Clark's grebe
brown pelican
double-crested cormorant
American bittern
least bittern
great blue heron
great egret
snowy egret
green heron
black-crowned night-heron
turkey vulture
white-tailed kite
northern harrier
Cooper's hawk
red-shouldered hawk
red-tailed hawk
golden eagle
American kestrel
peregrine falcon
black rail
Virginia rail
sora
common moorhen

American coot
snowy plover
killdeer
spotted sandpiper
band-tailed pigeon
mourning dove
barn owl
western screech-owl
great horned owl
northern pygmy-owl
burrowing owl
spotted owl
short-eared owl
northern saw-whet owl
common poorwill
white-throated swift
black-chinned hummingbird
Anna's hummingbird
Costa's hummingbird
Allen's hummingbird
belted kingfisher
Lewis's woodpecker
acorn woodpecker
Nuttall's woodpecker
downy woodpecker
hairy woodpecker
northern flicker
olive-sided flycatcher
western wood-pewee
pacific-slope flycatcher
black phoebe
ash-throated flycatcher
Cassin's kingbird
western kingbird
horned lark
purple martin
tree swallow
violet-green swallow
northern rough-winged swallow
cliff swallow
barn swallow
Steller's jay
western scrub-jay
American crow
common raven
oak titmouse

bushtit
white-breasted nuthatch
pygmy nuthatch
brown creeper
rock wren
canyon wren
Bewick's wren
house wren
winter wren
marsh wren
American dipper
western bluebird
Swainson's thrush
American robin
northern mockingbird
California thrasher
loggerhead shrike
Cassin's vireo
Hutton's vireo
warbling vireo
orange-crowned warbler
yellow warbler
yellow-rumped warbler
black-throated gray warbler
common yellowthroat
Wilson's warbler
yellow-breasted chat
western tanager
black-headed grosbeak
lazuli bunting
spotted towhee
California towhee
rufous-crowned sparrow
chipping sparrow
black-chinned sparrow
lark sparrow
grasshopper sparrow
song sparrow
dark-eyed junco
red-winged blackbird
tricolored blackbird
western meadowlark
yellow-headed blackbird
Brewer's blackbird
brown-headed cowbird
hooded oriole

Bullock's oriole
purple finch
house finch
lesser goldfinch
Lawrence's goldfinch
American goldfinch

Region 93

common loon
pied-billed grebe
horned grebe
red-necked grebe
eared grebe
western grebe
American white pelican
brown pelican
double-crested cormorant
American bittern
great blue heron
great egret
green heron
black-crowned night-heron
turkey vulture
osprey
bald eagle
northern harrier
sharp-shinned hawk
Cooper's hawk
northern goshawk
red-shouldered hawk
red-tailed hawk
golden eagle
American kestrel
merlin
peregrine falcon
prairie falcon
Virginia rail
sora
American coot
sandhill crane
snowy plover
killdeer
black oystercatcher
spotted sandpiper

common snipe
Wilson's phalarope
band-tailed pigeon
mourning dove
barn owl
western screech-owl
great horned owl
northern pygmy-owl
burrowing owl
spotted owl
barred owl
great gray owl
long-eared owl
short-eared owl
northern saw-whet owl
common nighthawk
common poorwill
black swift
Vaux's swift
white-throated swift
Anna's hummingbird
rufous hummingbird
Allen's hummingbird
belted kingfisher
Lewis's woodpecker
red-breasted sapsucker
Nuttall's woodpecker
downy woodpecker
hairy woodpecker
white-headed woodpecker
black-backed woodpecker
northern flicker
pileated woodpecker
olive-sided flycatcher
western wood-pewee
willow flycatcher
Hammond's flycatcher
dusky flycatcher
pacific-slope flycatcher
black phoebe
Say's phoebe
western kingbird
horned lark
purple martin
tree swallow
violet-green swallow

northern rough-winged swallow
bank swallow
cliff swallow
barn swallow
gray jay
Steller's jay
western scrub-jay
black-billed magpie
American crow
northwestern crow
common raven
black-capped chickadee
mountain chickadee
chestnut-backed chickadee
bushtit
red-breasted nuthatch
white-breasted nuthatch
pygmy nuthatch
brown creeper
Bewick's wren
house wren
winter wren
marsh wren
American dipper
golden-crowned kinglet
ruby-crowned kinglet
western bluebird
mountain bluebird
Townsend's solitaire
Swainson's thrush
hermit thrush
American robin
varied thrush
northern mockingbird
California thrasher
American pipit
cedar waxwing
Cassin's vireo
Hutton's vireo
warbling vireo
red-eyed vireo
orange-crowned warbler
Nashville warbler
yellow warbler
yellow-rumped warbler
black-throated gray warbler

Townsend's warbler
hermit warbler
MacGillivray's warbler
common yellowthroat
Wilson's warbler
western tanager
black-headed grosbeak
spotted towhee
rufous-crowned sparrow
chipping sparrow
Brewer's sparrow
black-chinned sparrow
vesper sparrow
savannah sparrow
fox sparrow
song sparrow
Lincoln's sparrow

white-crowned sparrow
dark-eyed junco
red-winged blackbird
tricolored blackbird
western meadowlark
yellow-headed blackbird
Brewer's blackbird
brown-headed cowbird
Bullock's oriole
pine grosbeak
purple finch
house finch
red crossbill
pine siskin
lesser goldfinch
American goldfinch
evening grosbeak

HABITAT REQUIREMENTS OF BREEDING BIRDS

What follows is a list of the specific habitat needs of about 400 bird species (organized in taxonomic order) that breed in North America. This information comes from field research done by biologists, and represents the best information currently available.

Explanation of information contained in each column:

Species: Common name and scientific name of each species. Naming of North American bird species is governed by the American Ornithologists' Union (AOU). The names used here follow the AOU's *41st Supplement to the Checklist of North American Birds,* published in 1997.

Breeding habitat: Some species have specialized habitat requirements, and those requirements are presented here as very specific measurements of habitat features. Other species are more flexible in their habitat requirements, and those requirements are presented in general terms. "Mixed" forest refers to a wooded area containing both deciduous and coniferous trees.

Area requirements: Most bird species regularly search for food in an area around the nest called the **home range**. Within the home range, most species defend an area around their nest from other members of their species—and sometimes from other species—in their territory. For many species, the home range and the territory are identical, but generally the home range is larger. Estimates of home range size and territory size are included; keep in mind, however, that the territory size given is probably the *minimum* area required, and the species may need much more. Try to set aside more habitat than the minimum required. The area requirements of some species have been studied very little; for those species, either no figure is given or an exact figure is given (because it is from a single study). For better-studied species, a range of values is given, because they come from many different studies. The estimates included in the range sometimes vary greatly because of different methods used by biologists to gather the information, or differences in the amount of food available in different areas (birds often need less area when food is abundant). Some species will not nest in a small habitat patch, even if the patch is many times larger than the species' territory size. For those species, the minimum required patch sizes are given.

Feeding: Food items most commonly eaten during the breeding season.

Nesting: Type of nest and its typical location.

Conservation status: Species that are in imminent danger of going extinct are given protected status by the federal government as *endangered*; species that could become endangered in the near future are given federal protection as *threatened*. Those designations are listed for all threatened or endangered birds. All species are assigned a Partners in Flight conservation priority score. This score is based on six factors: relative abundance, population trend, breeding and nonbreeding distribution, and threats to the species during the breeding and nonbreeding seasons. The maximum possible score is 30. These scores change regularly based on updated information and alterations to habitat. The scores given here are current as of early 1998, but updated scores can be found on the Colorado Bird Observatory's World Wide Web site. (See Appendix 1.) Each year, Partners in Flight also creates the WatchList, which includes species that are not yet endangered or threatened, but whose conservation status is perilous nevertheless. Species that appeared on the 1998 WatchList are indicated. *Species with* *endangered or threatened status, WatchList designation, or conserva-tion scores of 17 or higher are the species that should be the focus of your efforts.* Whenever possible, try to address their habitat needs when pre-serving, creating, or maintaining habitat on the golf course.

Species	Breeding Habitat	Area Requirements
common loon *Gavia immer*	large lakes and ponds	territory = 180 ac
least grebe *Tachybaptus dominicus*	lakes, ponds, and quiet, slow-moving streams; will accept wide range of vegetation densities	no information available
pied-billed grebe *Podilymbus podiceps*	lakes, ponds, marshes (<3 ft water); will accept wide range of vegetation densities	territory = 0.2–1 ac, but each pair may need ≥7 ac to meet all habitat needs
horned grebe *Podiceps auritus*	lakes, ponds, marshes	no information available
red-necked grebe *Podiceps grisegena*	shallow lakes or ponds (<3 ft), with emergent shoreline vegetation	territory = 75–100 yd of shoreline; will nest on ponds as small as 2.5 ac
eared grebe *Podiceps nigricollis*	lakes, ponds, marshes	no information available
western grebe *Aechmophorus occidentalis*	large lakes ringed with emergent vegetation, or marshes with extensive open water areas	breeding areas generally have several square miles of open water
Clark's grebe *Aechmophorus clarkii*	large lakes ringed with emergent vegetation, or marshes with extensive open water areas	breeding areas generally have several square miles of open water
American white pelican *Pelecanus erythrorhynchus*	islands on lakes, rivers, bays	will travel up to 50 mi from nest to find food

Feeding	Nesting	Conservation Status	Comments
fish, crustaceans	platform of aquatic vegetation in shallow water	14	
aquatic insects, crustaceans, tadpoles, fish	floating platform of vegetation in shallow water	11	
aquatic insects, mollusks, fish, amphibians	shallow platform in emergent vegetation, in water 18–30 in. deep	9	
aquatic insects, crustaceans, mollusks, fish	floating platform in shallow water	15	
aquatic insects, fish, amphibians	floating platform in shallow water	12	
aquatic insects, fish, crustaceans, mollusks	floating platform in shallow water	12	
fish, aquatic insects	floating platform of vegetation in water >15 in. deep, in area of dense emergent vegetation	17	
fish, aquatic insects	floating platform of vegetation in water >15 in. deep, in area of dense emergent vegetation	17	
primarily fish, occasionally amphibians	shallow depression on ground; forms colonies of up to 900 nests	16	

Species	Breeding Habitat	Area Requirements
brown pelican *Pelecanus occidentalis*	coastal islands	nesting colony needs ≥2.5 ac of nesting habitat, plus an equal area of sandy beach for resting
double-crested cormorant *Phalacrocorax auritus*	lakes, rivers, swamps, coastal areas	no information available
anhinga *Anhinga anhinga*	swamps, lakes, slow-moving streams	no information available
American bittern *Botaurus lentiginosus*	marshes with abundant tall emergent vegetation, shallow water (about 4 in.); favors areas with abundant amphibians	In IA, found only in wetlands >25 ac; in NY, found only in wetlands >10 ac; usually <1 nesting pair per ac of marsh
least bittern *Ixobrychus exilis*	marshes with abundant tall emergent vegetation, deep water (about 20 in.), and woody vegetation over water	In ME, found in wetlands as small as 1 ac; in IA, most common in wetlands >12 ac; densities of up to 6 nesting pairs per ac
great blue heron *Ardea herodias*	wetlands, slow-moving waters, shallow saltwater areas	Will search for food up to 20 mi from nest
great egret *Ardea alba*	wetlands with large trees	Will travel up to 6 mi from nest to find food
snowy egret *Egretta thula*	wetlands, coastal areas	no information available

Feeding	Nesting	Conservation Status	Comments
fish	stick nest in tops of mangrove trees; nests in colonies	endangered 14	sensitive to disturbance; nest colony should be protected by a buffer zone of ≥100 yd
fish, aquatic insects	platform of sticks in tree or on ground, especially in rocky area; nests in colonies	9	
fish, aquatic insects	platform of sticks 5–25 ft above water in tree or shrub	11	
fish, amphibians, aquatic insects, small mammals	platform of sticks and vegetation in dense emergent vegetation with 2–8 in. water, or on ground in shoreline vegetation	17	
fish, aquatic invertebrates, amphibians, small mammals	platform of sticks or other vegetation, usually in emergent vegetation or shrub 6–30 in. tall, over water 3–40 in. deep	15	
fish, aquatic insects, amphibians, small birds and mammals	platform of sticks in tree, up to 100 ft above ground; nests in colonies of up to several hundred pairs	9	
fish, small birds and mammals, aquatic insects	platform of sticks 3–30 ft above water in tree or shrub	9	
aquatic insects, fish	platform of sticks 5–10 ft above ground in tree or shrub	9	

Species	Breeding Habitat	Area Requirements
little blue heron *Egretta caerulea*	wetlands, hardwood swamps, riparian areas	will travel up to 7 mi from nest to find food
tricolored heron *Egretta tricolor*	wetlands, hardwood swamps, often near saltwater	no information available
reddish egret *Egretta rufescens*	marshes and coastal areas	no information available
cattle egret *Bubulcus ibis*	broad preferences, including shallow wetlands and dry, open areas	colonies often in isolated, closed-canopy forest of 2.5–7.5 ac; will travel up to 20 mi to find food during nesting season
green heron *Butorides virescens*	wetlands with wooded areas	no information available

Feeding	Nesting	Conservation Status	Comments
fish, crustaceans, amphibians, aquatic insects	platform of sticks up to 12 ft above ground in tree or shrub, often over water; breeds in colonies	12	nesting colonies are sensitive to human disturbance
fish, amphibians, aquatic insects	platform of sticks 6–15 ft above ground in tree or shrub	14	
fish, aquatic insects	platform of sticks in tree or shrub	WatchList 22	
grasshoppers, crickets, spiders, flies, frogs, small birds and mammals, mollusks, crustaceans	platform of sticks in tree or shrub; breeds in colonies, usually about 5000 pairs	7	colonies often considered nuisances because of noise and odor, or considered hazardous when near airports; such colonies can be discouraged by harassing with noise, water sprays, balloons, etc., or by removing or trimming nest trees, *but not during nesting season*
primarily fish; also crustaceans, insects, earthworms, dragonflies, snails, amphibians, lizards	platform of sticks 0–35 ft above ground in tree or shrub near or over water; sometimes nests in colonies of up to 70 pairs	10	

Species	Breeding Habitat	Area Requirements
black-crowned night-heron *Nycticorax nycticorax*	coastal and inland wetlands, especially with 50:50 mix of open water and vegetation	will travel up to 15 mi from nest to find food
yellow-crowned night-heron *Nyctanassa violacea*	wooded wetlands; also open wooded uplands with little understory vegetation, near water	will travel 150 yd from nest to find food
white ibis *Eudocimus albus*	coastal or inland islands with shallow wetlands, especially where mangroves or cypress are present	will travel up to 25 mi from nest to find food
glossy ibis *Plegadis falcinellus*	marshes, swamps	no information available
white-faced ibis *Plegadis chihi*	shallow wetlands, especially with cattails and bulrushes; flooded meadows or wetlands with short vegetation	will travel up to 11 mi from nest to find food
roseate spoonbill *Ajaia ajaja*	marshes, swamps, ponds, rivers	no information available
wood stork *Mycteria americana*	wetlands, streams, bald cypress forest	will travel up to 80 mi from nest to find food (but usually less than 40 mi)

Feeding	Nesting	Conservation Status	Comments
fish, aquatic insects, mollusks, crustaceans, bird eggs and young	platform of sticks and other vegetation in tree, shrub, or cattails; nest in colonies, with up to 12 nests per tree	9	
primarily crustaceans (crayfish, crabs); also fish, insects, young birds	platform of sticks 6–60 ft above ground in tree or shrub; often nest alone, but will nest in colonies of up to 1000 pairs	14	will nest near buildings in wooded areas
crabs, crayfish, snails, fish, frogs, snakes, insects	platform of sticks 0–12 ft high in tree or shrub near water; nests in colonies of 25–50 pairs	18	
aquatic insects, crayfish, water snakes	platform of sticks 1–25 ft above water in tree or shrub	11	
aquatic insects, crayfish, earthworms, small fish, leeches, spiders, snails	platform of vegetation and sticks on ground in emergent vegetation, or in tree or shrub; nests in colonies	12	nesting colonies sensitive to human activities
fish, crustaceans, aquatic insects	platform of sticks 10–15 ft above ground in tree or shrub over water	13	
fish, amphibians, aquatic insects	platform of sticks 0–100 ft above shallow, standing water in tree, usually large cypress; nests in colonies	16	

Species	Breeding Habitat	Area Requirements
black vulture *Coragyps atratus*	open country, open forest	no information available
turkey vulture *Cathartes aura*	open country, open forest	no information available
osprey *Pandion haliaetus*	lakes, rivers, coastal areas	will use ponds as small as 10 ac; will travel up to 6 mi from nest to find food
swallow-tailed kite *Elanoides forficatus*	open areas with tall trees, either scattered or clustered	territory size highly variable, depending on food supply; home range = 12 sq mi
white-tailed kite *Elanus leucurus*	grasslands with scattered trees or wooded patches; wetlands, open shrublands	territory = 4–110 ac; size highly variable, depending on amount of food available
snail kite *Rostrhamus sociabilis*	wetlands (water depth <4 ft) with areas of open water and submerged and emergent vegetation	no information available

Feeding	Nesting	Conservation Status	Comments
dead animals: mammals, birds, fish, amphibians, reptiles	no nest *per se;* lays eggs on ground on cliff, sometimes up to 8 ft above the ground in snag	7	
dead animals: mammals, birds, fish, amphibians, reptiles	no nest *per se;* lays eggs on ground on cliff or in cave, sometimes up to 20 ft above the ground in snag	10	
fish	platform of sticks 10–60 ft above ground in tall tree or snag, ≥18 in. diameter, close to water	11	
primarily insects, especially wasps; also frogs, young birds, reptiles	open cup of sticks near top of one of the tallest trees available, usually at the edge of an open area	WatchList 21	relatively insensitive to human activity, and will nest in suburban areas
small mammals (voles and mice)	large open cup of sticks, near top of tree, 10–150 ft above ground; tree may be isolated or part of wooded patch	10	
diet is almost exclusively apple snails, captured at or just below water surface in areas of open water	platform of sticks and vegetation 3–40 ft above ground (avg = 7 ft) in small tree, shrub, or emergent vegetation <16 ft tall, with 5–45 in. of water (avg = 20 in.) below nest	WatchList 26	wetlands must be continuously flooded for at least 1 yr for growth of apple snail population

Species	Breeding Habitat	Area Requirements
Mississippi kite *Ictinia mississippiensis*	mature, open deciduous forest, streamside woods	no information available
bald eagle *Haliaeetus leucocephalus*	rivers, large lakes, coastal areas	territory = 2–3 sq mi
northern harrier *Circus cyaneus*	open wetlands with dense, low vegetation	home range = 300–35,000 ac (avg = 640 ac); will travel ≥6 mi from nest to find food
sharp-shinned hawk *Accipiter striatus*	coniferous and mixed forest	territory = 160–1200 ac; in Vancouver, found in forest patches as small as 10 ac
Cooper's hawk *Accipiter cooperii*	deciduous, coniferous, and mixed forests and forest edges, with 100–450 trees per ac, 65–95% canopy closure, and trees >40 ft tall	home range = 250–1900 ac; has nested in woodlots as small as 2.5 ac in WI, although 25 ac is more common
northern goshawk *Accipiter gentilis*	coniferous and mixed forest with dense canopy and scattered small openings	territory = 2–8 ac; home range = 500–6000 ac; requires patches of forest >200 ac

Feeding	Nesting	Conservation Status	Comments
large insects, including cicadas	platform of sticks 30–135 ft above ground in tree; nests in colonies	18	very protective of nest, will dive at humans
mostly fish, also small to medium-sized mammals, birds	platform of sticks 30–60 ft above ground in tree	threatened 15	
small mammals (primarily voles, also ground squirrels), small birds, frogs	open cup on ground or elevated on mound of vegetation, in area of dense, tall vegetation (e.g., cattails, sedges)	16	sensitive to human activity
small birds	platform of sticks 10–60 ft above ground in tree	11	
birds (including robins, jays, flickers, and starlings), also small mammals (including chipmunks and squirrels)	Platform of sticks 25–50 ft above ground in large trees (for example, in WI, 65–80 ft tall, 8–16 in. diameter)	11	breeds in urban areas, sometimes close to houses, although in NJ, researchers recommended that no development occur within 650 yd of nest
birds, mammals	platform of sticks 20–60 ft above the ground in tree	15	fairly intolerant of human activity

Species	Breeding Habitat	Area Requirements
common black hawk *Buteogallus anthracinus*	riparian forest with clusters of mature trees, and perennial streams <12 in. deep with riffles and perches (boulders, branches)	requires 0.5–1.5 mi of forested stream
Harris's hawk *Parabuteo unicinctus*	open areas (desert scrub, grasslands, wetlands) with sparse ground vegetation and scattered large trees for perching and nesting	home range = 725 ac
red-shouldered hawk *Buteo lineatus*	mature deciduous and mixed forest, especially flooded or riparian forest, with 100–400 trees per ac of 8–25 in. diameter, 75% canopy cover, sparse shrubs and ground vegetation; prefers areas with small (2.5 ac) wetlands and pools, small (7 ac) openings	home range = 100–835 ac; in NJ, found in forests as small as 25 ac, but only as part of a larger network of forest patches
broad-winged hawk *Buteo platypterus*	deciduous or mixed forests that contain open areas and water	no information available
short-tailed hawk *Buteo brachyurus*	grasslands, mature open forest, swampy forest	no information available

Feeding	Nesting	Conservation Status	Comments
fish, frogs, crustaceans, snakes, lizards	platform of sticks 30–100 ft above ground (avg = 60 ft) in large tree (avg diameter = 40 in.), usually cottonwood	18	in some areas, native tree species used for nesting (cottonwood, mesquite, etc.) are being crowded out by exotic salt cedar (*Tamarix chinensis*), which is too small to support nest
hares, rabbits, ground squirrels, birds, lizards	Platform of sticks 8–50 ft above ground in large tree or cactus	13	sensitive to human activity, and will abandon nest until humans have left the area
small mammals (voles and chipmunks), snakes, toads, frogs, small birds, crayfish	platform of sticks 40–65 ft above ground in tree (usually deciduous) near water but far from forest edge (>75 yd); prefer trees >15 in. diameter; select largest (or nearly so) tree in an area	12	fairly tolerant of human activity in the West, not so in the East; adapted to open forests, but not open nonforested areas
small mammals, amphibians, young birds, insects	platform of sticks 18–60 ft above ground (avg = 37 ft) in tree (avg diameter = 15 in.)	12	generally avoids areas of human activity
birds	platform of sticks 15–60 ft above ground in tree	WatchList 22	

Species	Breeding Habitat	Area Requirements
Swainson's hawk *Buteo swainsoni*	grasslands with scattered large trees, open forest	home range = 1–35 sq mi
white-tailed hawk *Buteo albicaudatus*	open grasslands with up to 40% shrub cover (>5 ft tall)	home range ≥80 ac
zone-tailed hawk *Buteo albonotatus*	arid open pine-oak forest, canyons	no information available
red-tailed hawk *Buteo jamaicensis*	open areas with scattered or clustered tall trees	territory = 45–400 ac
ferruginous hawk *Buteo regalis*	grasslands, deserts, open areas with scattered shrubs or trees	home range = 2.5–75 sq mi
golden eagle *Aquila chrysaetos*	open, often mountainous country	territory = 6–70 sq mi
crested caracara *Caracara plancus*	open areas with low (<3 ft tall) ground vegetation and scattered tall trees or cacti	home range = 4000 ac

Feeding	Nesting	Conservation Status	Comments
small mammals, reptiles, amphibians, young birds, grasshoppers	platform of sticks 20–30 ft above ground in tree, usually an isolated tree	16	typically a bird of the open prairie, but has nested in urban parks
small mammals, birds, reptiles	platform of twigs and grasses in shrub, 2–6 ft above ground	15	sensitive to human disturbance; will fly away from humans approaching within 500 yd
reptiles, small birds, amphibians	platform of sticks 25–50 ft above ground in tree along stream	15	
small to medium-sized mammals, including voles, mice, rabbits; also birds, reptiles	platform of sticks near top of large tree	8	
jackrabbits, rabbits, ground squirrels, prairie dogs; occasionally songbirds, reptiles	platform of sticks 0–65 ft above ground in tree, tall shrub, rock outcrop	17	highly sensitive to disturbance from humans; will not nest near areas of human activity
mammals (including jackrabbits, rabbits, ground squirrels), birds, reptiles	platform of sticks on cliff, occasionally in tree 10–100 ft above ground	16	
grasshoppers, beetles, ants, millipedes; live or dead fish, reptiles, amphibians, birds, mammals	platform of sticks 5–60 ft above ground (avg = 22 ft) in tall tree or cactus	11	

Species	Breeding Habitat	Area Requirements
American kestrel *Falco sparverius*	open country with elevated perches, forest edges	territory = 30–1000 ac
merlin *Falco columbarius*	open areas with trees or tall shrubs	home range = 5–15 sq mi
prairie falcon *Falco mexicanus*	open, mountainous country, grasslands	territory = 2–10 sq mi; home range = 10–50 sq mi
peregrine falcon *Falco peregrinus*	open areas with cliffs	home range = 20–180 sq mi; will travel up to 10 mi from nest to find food
Montezuma quail *Cyrtonyx montezumae*	oak and pine-oak forest with dense grass	no information available
northern bobwhite *Colinus virginianus*	tall grasslands or open forest, with vegetation <20 in. tall	territory = 40 ac
scaled quail *Callipepla squamata*	open, arid areas with scattered shrubs	no information available
Gambel's quail *Callipepla gambelii*	arid areas with thorny shrubs, also open riparian forest	home range = 3 ac
California quail *Callipepla californica*	open areas with scattered shrubs and patches of grass and bare ground, or open forest	home range = 10–54 ac
mountain quail *Oreortyx pictus*	open coniferous forest or open areas with shrubs; also open areas in denser coniferous forest	no information available

Feeding	Nesting	Conservation Status	Comments
large insects (grasshoppers, beetles, dragon-flies), small birds and mammals	cavity 10–30 above ground in tree, snag, or cactus	10	will use nest boxes (see Appendix 3)
small to medium sized birds	platform of sticks abandoned by crow or hawk, high in tree	12	populations growing in urban areas, at least in Canada
birds, small mammals, large insects, reptiles	shallow depression on cliff ledge, facing open area	16	
birds, including doves, pigeons, shorebirds, songbirds	shallow depression on a cliff ledge 200 ft high	14	will nest on tall buildings in urban areas
plant roots, insects, seeds	shallow depression on ground with overhanging grass	22	
leaves, buds, tubers, seeds, insects	shallow depression on ground with overhanging vegetation	17	
forb and grass seeds, leaves, insects	shallow depression on ground under shrub or in dense grass	20	
seeds, leaves	shallow depression on ground under shrub	16	
seeds, leaves	shallow depression on ground in grass or under shrub, or next to log, rock, or other structure	20	
seeds, roots, leaves, insects	shallow depression on ground under shrub or next to tree or log	21	

Species	Breeding Habitat	Area Requirements
yellow rail *Coturnicops noveboracensis*	shallow wetlands (<18 in. water) with sedges and grasses	territory = 14–26 ac (avg = 19 ac)
black rail *Laterallus jamaicensis*	salt marshes and freshwater wetlands with dense, tall, grassy vegetation in <1 in. of water, also exposed mud and scattered small pools	territory = 7–10 ac
clapper rail *Rallus longirostris*	salt marshes and freshwater wetlands	territory = 1–25 ac
king rail *Rallus elegans*	wetlands and marshes with dense grasses, sedges, rushes, and cattails; water depth 4–18 in.	home range = 2 ac
Virginia rail *Rallus limicola*	freshwater wetlands with shallow water (<6 in.), areas of exposed mud and open water, and 40–70% emergent vegetation cover	home range = 0.4–4 ac

Feeding	Nesting	Conservation Status	Comments
primarily snails; also beetles, grasshoppers, spiders, ants, crustaceans, seeds	open cup with overhanging vegetation, on or near ground, where water <6 in. deep	WatchList 22	prefer the drier, outer parts of wetlands, where invading woody vegetation could reduce habitat if not cut or burned (burn <10% of the habitat, on a 10-yr rotation)
small crustaceans, aquatic and terrestrial invertebrates	open cup with overhanging vegetation, on ground	WatchList 24	prefer the drier, outer parts of wetlands, where invading woody vegetation could reduce habitat if not cut or burned (burn <10% of the habitat, on a 10-yr rotation)
aquatic and terrestrial invertebrates (including crabs), fish	open cup with overhanging vegetation, on ground	17	
crustaceans, aquatic and terrestrial insects	platform of vegetation with shallow cup in top, in shallow water (2–3 in.)	15	part of the wetlands should be allowed to dry out during the summer
beetles, snails, spiders, worms, diptera larvae	open cup with overhanging vegetation 6 in. above water surface in dense emergent vegetation; water depth usually <12 in.	11	

Species	Breeding Habitat	Area Requirements
sora *Porzana carolina*	wetlands (where avg water depth = 15 in.) with patches of dense emergent vegetation, such as cattails and sedges, interspersed with areas of open water	home range = 0.5 ac; found on wetlands as small as 1 ac, but more common on wetlands ≥5 ac
purple gallinule *Porphyrula martinica*	wetlands with dense emergent vegetation	territory = 0.1 ac
common moorhen *Gallinula chloropus*	marshes, lakes, ponds with emergent vegetation	no information available
American coot *Fulica americana*	marshes, lakes, ponds with emergent vegetation	territory = 1 ac
limpkin *Aramus guarauna*	swampy forests	no information available
sandhill crane *Grus canadensis*	small ponds (<10 ac), shallow, sparsely vegetated marshes and flooded open meadows surrounded by shrubs or open forest	territory = 40–210 ac
snowy plover *Charadrius alexandrinus*	sparsely vegetated salt flats, beaches, river sandbars, shallow alkaline lakes	territory = 1.2–2.5 ac, although will travel up to 5 mi from nest to find food

Feeding	Nesting	Conservation Status	Comments
seeds of wetland plants, aquatic insects	open cup on or near ground or water surface, often with overhanging vegetation, in area with 6–8 in. water	11	
seeds, plants, snails, aquatic insects, amphibians	platform of vegetation floating in 1–10 ft of water	12	
aquatic plants, snails, worms, seeds	platform of vegetation floating or on ground	9	
aquatic plants, fish, crustaceans, snails, worms	platform of vegetation floating in 1–4 ft of water	10	
snails, mussels, aquatic invertebrates, frogs, worms	platform of vegetation on ground, under shrub, or in streambank	13	
aquatic and terrestrial invertebrates, seeds, berries	a mound of vegetation in 1 ft of water; if water levels rise and flood the nest or fall too low, they will desert the nest	18	
terrestrial and aquatic invertebrates captured on ground or in water <1 in. deep	shallow depression in sand, with some vegetation present	WatchList 19	sensitive to disturbance from human activities; 35-yd buffer zone recommended for breeding birds, with fences and signs to ensure compliance

Species	Breeding Habitat	Area Requirements
Wilson's plover *Charadrius wilsonia*	beaches, mud flats, shallow water areas with sparse vegetation	no information available
piping plover *Charadrius melodus*	sandy or gravelly beaches with little vegetation on freshwater or alkali lakes, seacoasts, or rivers	territory = 1–7 ac
killdeer *Charadrius vociferus*	open areas with sparse, low vegetation, mud flats, or along streams, ponds, lakes	density ≤1 pair per 8 ac
mountain plover *Charadrius montanus*	dry, open areas with very short grass and about 30% bare ground	territory = 40 ac
American oystercatcher *Haematopus palliatus*	coastal areas with little or no vegetation, including sandy beaches, dunes, marsh islands	may travel >1 mi from nest to find food
black oystercatcher *Haematopus bachmani*	primarily rocky shorelines, also sandy or gravelly beaches with sparse vegetation	territory = 0.1–4.5 ac, but highly variable and may be as large as 90 ac
black-necked stilt *Himantopus mexicanus*	marshes, mud flats, shallow ponds	no information available
American avocet *Recurvirostra americana*	marshes, mud flats, ponds, lakes	territory = 0.3–13 ac
willet *Catoptrophorus semipalmatus*	marshes and lakes, nearby upland areas	home range = 110 ac

Feeding	Nesting	Conservation Status	Comments
crabs, sand worms, insects	shallow depression on ground	19	
freshwater, marine, and terrestrial invertebrates, especially worms and crustaceans	shallow depression in sand	threatened 24	
beetles, grasshoppers, caterpillars, ants, spiders	shallow depression on ground, often in gravelly area with little or no vegetation	15	
grasshoppers, beetles, crickets, ants	shallow depression in ground	WatchList 26	
marine bivalves, molluscs, worms of intertidal zones	shallow depression in sand, usually on elevated site with at least 180° visibility, 25–100 ft from water	17	sensitive to human disturbance; 75-yd buffer zone recommended for breeding birds
marine bivalves and molluscs; also crabs, sea urchins, barnacles	shallow depression in sand or on rock in area of little or no vegetation, 1–40 yd from high tide	WatchList 23	
flies, crayfish, shrimp, snails	shallow depression on ground, often in the open on mud flats	11	
crustaceans, insects, aquatic plants	shallow depression on ground in area of sparse ground vegetation	19	
aquatic insects, worms, crustaceans	shallow depression on ground in area of dense low vegetation	WatchList 18	

Species	Breeding Habitat	Area Requirements
spotted sandpiper *Actitis macularia*	open areas near water, with low vegetation	territory = 0.3–1.6 ac
upland sandpiper *Bartramia longicauda*	grasslands	in ME, rare in patches <125 ac; in IL, not found in patches <50 ac
long-billed curlew *Numenius americanus*	areas of short vegetation (2–8 in.), with clumps of taller vegetation for nest cover; usually near water	territory = 8–200 ac
marbled godwit *Limosa fedoa*	thick, short grass (<1 ft)	home range = 220 ac
common snipe *Gallinago gallinago*	shallow wetlands, wet meadows, with vegetation <16 in. tall	territory ≤25 ac
American woodcock *Scolopax minor*	shallow wetlands; wet meadows; wet, open deciduous or mixed forest; riparian shrubs	no information available
Wilson's phalarope *Phalaropus tricolor*	shallow wetlands, especially saline lakes, with grassy uplands for nesting	will travel up to 1100 yd from nest to find food
black skimmer *Rynchops niger*	sand or gravel coastline or island with sparse vegetation	no information available

Feeding	Nesting	Conservation Status	Comments
insects, worms, crustaceans	shallow depression on ground in area of grass, forbs, or rocks	8	
insects, seeds	shallow depression on ground in grass	15	sensitive to habitat fragmentation
insects, crustaceans	shallow depression on ground in grass	WatchList 21	
grasshoppers and other insects, molluscs, snails, worms	shallow depression on ground	20	
beetles, larvae of flies, craneflies, midges	open cup on ground among grasses	12	
earthworms, insect larvae, spiders, snails, seeds	shallow depression on ground, where dead leaves are abundant	18	
aquatic and terrestrial invertebrates	open cup in area of dense grass or rushes, <100 yd from wetland	17	
primarily small fish, occasionally small crustaceans	shallow depression in sand; nests in colonies of up to many thousands of pairs	17	very sensitive to human disturbance; embryos and chicks die quickly if parent not present to provide shade and protection from predators

Species	Breeding Habitat	Area Requirements
marbled murrelet *Brachyramphus marmoratus*	mature coniferous forest in coastal areas; nests within 15 mi of coast	no information available
rock dove *Columba livia*	areas of human habitation, rocky areas, riparian deciduous woods	no information available
band-tailed pigeon *Columba fasciata*	open forest or shrublands, especially oak shrubs	territory = 20–500 ac; in Vancouver, found only in patches >180 ac
white-winged dove *Zenaida asiatica*	semiarid woodlands, riparian woodlands, desert scrub	will travel up to 25 mi from nest to find food
mourning dove *Zenaida macroura*	broad preferences, including open forest and field/forest edges	territory = 0.7–3.2 ac, but will travel over 3 mi from nest to find food; in NJ, found in forests as small as 0.5 ac; in SD, found in the smallest shelterbelts examined (0.25 ac)
Inca dove *Columbina inca*	open, dry habitats; common in suburban areas	territory = 0.5 ac
common ground-dove *Columbina passerina*	arid riparian woods, desert scrub	no information available
black-billed cuckoo *Coccyzus erythropthalmus*	open deciduous or mixed forest, forest edges	in NJ, found only in forests ≥18.5 ac, but in SD, found in shelterbelts as small as 1.1 ac

Feeding	Nesting	Conservation Status	Comments
fish, crustaceans	open cup up to 150 ft above ground in tree	threatened 20	
seeds	shallow platform on rooftops, cliff ledges	8	introduced from the Mediterranean; considered a pest in many areas
seeds, acorns, berries	platform of sticks 15–40 ft above ground in tree	WatchList 18	
seeds, berries	open cup 4–30 ft above ground in shrub, tree, or cactus	14	
seeds of herbaceous plants, agricultural grains	open cup up to 100 ft above ground (avg = 16 ft) in coniferous or deciduous tree, or on ground with vegetation around nest for cover	8	common in suburban areas
grass and weed seeds	platform of twigs and vegetation in tree or shrub, 2–50 ft high (avg = 12 ft); often near buildings	14	in AZ, respond positively to increasing urbanization— attracted to lawns
seeds	open cup 0–21 ft above ground (usually <6 ft) in tree or shrub	16	
mostly caterpillars, also beetles, grasshoppers, crickets	platform of sticks 0–20 ft above ground in tree or shrub	16	

Species	Breeding Habitat	Area Requirements
yellow-billed cuckoo *Coccyzus americanus*	deciduous forest, riparian forest, or forest edges, with some areas (>7.5 ac) of closed canopy, also dense shrubs	territory = 5.5 ac; home range = 42 ac; in KS, found only in windbreaks >2.5 ac; in NJ, found only in forests ≥10 ac; in CA, found only in riparian areas >300 yd long and 100 yd wide
mangrove cuckoo *Coccyzus minor*	mangrove swamps	in FL, found only in patches >32 ac
greater roadrunner *Geococcyx californianus*	open, arid areas with scattered shrubs and trees 6–10 ft tall	territory = 110–125 ac
smooth-billed ani *Crotophaga ani*	edges of areas with dense shrubs and openings	no information available
groove-billed ani *Crotophaga sulcirostris*	edges of areas with dense shrubs and openings, forest edges	no information available
barn owl *Tyto alba*	open areas with high densities of small mammals; suitable nest sites must be available	home range = 1750 ac
flammulated owl *Otus flammeolus*	mature, open conifer (especially ponderosa pine) or aspen forest	territory = 4–10 ac; home range = 7.5–50 ac

Feeding	Nesting	Conservation Status	Comments
mostly caterpillars, also beetles, grasshoppers, crickets, berries	platform of sticks 4–35 ft above ground (usually < 10 ft)	17	
caterpillars, grasshoppers, moths, and flies	platform of sticks up to 10 ft above ground or water, in tree	18	
grasshoppers, beetles, spiders, scorpions, lizards, snakes, birds, eggs, small mammals	platform of sticks 3–10 ft above ground (avg = 4.5 ft) in thorny bush, tree, or cactus, located in small thicket adjacent to open area (short grass)	14	will inhabit low-density suburban areas, so should be able to live on golf courses provided appropriate habitat and adequate prey exist there
grasshoppers, beetles, moths, caterpillars	open cup 5–30 ft above ground in shrub or tree	12	
grasshoppers, beetles, spiders, ants, cockroaches	open cup 5–15 ft above ground in tree	14	
small mammals	large cavity in tree, cliff, riverbank; also in buildings that are seldom used by humans	14	will use nest boxes (see Appendix 3)
moths, beetles, crickets, grasshoppers	natural cavity or abandoned woodpecker cavity 10–55 ft above ground in tree with > 18 in. diameter	19	

Species	Breeding Habitat	Area Requirements
eastern screech owl *Otus asio*	mature deciduous or mixed forest with open understory	home range in suburban areas = 15–20 ac
western screech owl *Otus kennicottii*	deciduous, coniferous, or mixed forest, desert scrub, grasslands	no information available
great horned owl *Bubo virginianus*	widespread; found in virtually any habitat that contains some trees or dense shrubs	territory = 125–1600 ac; in KS, found only in wind-breaks >2.5 ac
northern hawk owl *Surnia ulula*	open coniferous or mixed forest	home range = 345–2100 ac (avg = 920 ac)
northern pygmy owl *Glaucidium gnoma*	open coniferous or mixed forest, riparian deciduous forest	territory = 250–400 ac
elf owl *Micrathene whitneyi*	arid regions with saguaro cactus, riparian deciduous forest	no information available

Feeding	Nesting	Conservation Status	Comments
beetles, moths, caterpillars, crickets, crayfish, earthworms, small birds and mammals	cavity 5–65 ft above ground (avg = 16 ft) in tree	13	relatively common in suburban areas with large trees available for nesting; readily accepts nest box (see Appendix 3)
beetles, moths, caterpillars, crickets, crayfish, earthworms, small birds and mammals	cavity 5–35 ft above ground in tree, ≥12 in. diameter, or large cactus	13	relatively common in suburban areas with large trees available for nesting; readily accepts nest box (see Appendix 3)
small to medium sized mammals, large insects	platform of sticks abandoned by another bird species, 20–60 ft above ground in tree	8	
small mammals	cavity 10–40 ft above ground in tree, or broken treetop	17	
small birds and mammals, insects	cavity 8–25 ft above ground in tree	14	
moths, beetles, crickets, katydids, scorpions, spiders	cavity 10–50 ft above ground in cactus or tree	WatchList 20	

Species	Breeding Habitat	Area Requirements
burrowing owl *Athene cunicularia*	open, treeless areas with bare ground and short grasses; in the West, shares habitat with prairie dogs	territory = 0.1–4 ac (avg = 2 ac); home range = 600 ac
spotted owl *Strix occidentalis*	mature coniferous or deciduous (oak) forest (closed canopy, large trees, multiple canopy layers)	home range >3000 ac (OR)
barred owl *Strix varia*	dense, mature deciduous or mixed forest with ≥60% canopy cover, sparse shrubs and ground vegetation	home range = 200–900 ac; each pair needs ≥250 ac of forest
great gray owl *Strix nebulosa*	deciduous or coniferous forests with large-diameter trees and closed canopy, adjacent to meadows with ample small mammal prey	home range = 40 sq mi
long-eared owl *Asio otus*	open coniferous, deciduous, or mixed forest, and dense forest adjacent to grasslands or shrublands; often nests in riparian forests	home range = 80–500 ac; will nest in dense clusters of trees as small as 35 ft across

Feeding	Nesting	Conservation Status	Comments
beetles, scorpions, locusts, grasshoppers, crickets, small birds and mammals, amphibians, reptiles	underground burrows; nests in loose colonies	16	eastern sub-species digs its own burrows; can be found in urban areas (including golf courses), so long as pesticide use is restricted within 250 yd of the burrows
small and medium sized mammals (flying squirrels, wood rats, mice, voles, rabbits)	cavity in tree, or abandoned stick nest or similar structure (broken-top trees, mistletoe brooms)	threatened 23	
small mammals	in cavity in tree or snag with ≥20 in. diameter, 5–100 ft above ground (avg = 30 ft)	12	
small mammals, especially voles and pocket gophers	platform of sticks abandoned by other large birds, such as ravens or goshawks, 10–50 ft above ground in tree	15	readily accepts artificial nesting platforms
primarily small mammals (mostly voles and mice); also small birds	platform of sticks abandoned by other large birds, such as magpies and crows, 4–30 ft above ground in tree	15	nests in forest, hunts in open areas; prefers to nest in a cluster of trees rather than an isolated tree or a row of single trees

Species	Breeding Habitat	Area Requirements
short-eared owl *Asio flammeus*	open grassy areas, sometimes with scattered shrubs, with ample small mammal prey	home range = 35–500 ac
boreal owl *Aegolius funereus*	mature, closed-canopy coniferous or conifer-aspen forests with open understory	home range = 230–870 ac
northern saw-whet owl *Aegolius acadicus*	wide range of forest types, but especially coniferous	home range = 280–390 ac
lesser nighthawk *Chordeiles acutipennis*	desert scrub, grasslands	no information available
common nighthawk *Chordeiles minor*	nests in open areas, including beaches, forest clearings, and prairies; forages over any habitat that provides flying insects	territory = 10–70 ac
pauraque *Nyctidromus albicollis*	deciduous forest, areas of tall, dense shrubs	no information available
common poorwill *Phalaenoptilus nuttallii*	dry, open, grassy or shrubby areas, sometimes with rocky outcrops	will travel up to 550 yd from nest to find food

Feeding	Nesting	Conservation Status	Comments
small mammals (primarily voles) and birds	scrape on the ground, often on a slight rise, in area of dense grasses up to 20 in. tall	WatchList 19	woody vegetation in the habitat can be controlled by burning
small mammals, including voles, shrews, mice; small birds	adopts old woodpecker nest cavities or natural cavities, in large (15 in. diameter) trees	15	will use nest boxes if in suitable habitat (mature forest); see Appendix 3
small mammals, especially woodland mice	cavity 15–60 ft above ground in large snag	12	readily accepts nest boxes (see Appendix 3); sensitive to human disturbance during breeding, less so during winter, when it is more likely to be found near human settlements
flying insects, including grasshoppers, beetles, moths	no nest *per se;* lays eggs on the ground in open areas	9	
flying insects, including flying ants, moths, beetles, and flies	no nest *per se;* lays eggs on the ground in open areas	12	will nest on flat, gravel rooftops in cities; will also use gravel pads placed on flat, smooth rooftops
flying insects, including moths, beetles	no nest *per se;* lays eggs on the ground in open areas	15	
night-flying moths and beetles	slight depression in bare ground, often shaded by vegetation or rocks	16	

Species	Breeding Habitat	Area Requirements
whippoorwill *Caprimulgus vociferus*	open, young deciduous and coniferous forest with thick leaf litter	territory = 7–25 ac
black swift *Cypseloides niger*	areas of mountains, cliffs, with waterfalls	no information available
chimney swift *Chaetura pelagica*	urban areas, open areas with scattered trees	no information available
Vaux's swift *Chaetura vauxi*	mature coniferous and deciduous forests with large hollow trees for nesting and roosting	will travel up to 3 mi from nest to find food
white-throated swift *Aeronautes saxatilis*	steep canyons with cliffs ≥50 ft high	no information available
broad-billed hummingbird *Cynanthus latirostris*	riparian deciduous forest, open oak forest	no information available
ruby-throated hummingbird *Archilochus colubris*	deciduous and mixed forests with open areas	territory = 0.3 ac
black-chinned hummingbird *Archilochus alexandri*	riparian deciduous forest, open forest, canyons	territory = 0.25 ac

Feeding	Nesting	Conservation Status	Comments
flying insects, including moths, mosquitoes, caddisflies, grasshoppers	no nest *per se;* lays eggs on the ground in shrubby area near forest edge	17	
flying insects, including wasps, flies, caddisflies, mayflies	cup on cliff ledge or cavity in rocks near stream or waterfall; nests in colonies of up to 100 pairs	WatchList 20	
flying insects, including beetles, flies, moths	open cup attached to vertical surface, such as chimney wall	17	formerly nested in hollow trees or snags
flies, ants, bees, aphids, beetles, moths, spiders	cavity in large hollow tree (avg height = 82 ft, avg diameter = 26 in.); nests in loose colonies	18	
flying insects, including flies, beetles, wasps, bees	open cup on cliff ledge or rock crevice	14	
flower nectar, small invertebrates	open cup 3–12 ft above ground in shrub or tree	19	
flower nectar, insects (including mosquitoes, spiders, and gnats), tree sap	open cup 1.5–50 above ground (avg = 20 ft) in tree, near sources of nectar	14	
flower nectar, small invertebrates	open cup 3–8 ft above ground in tree	18	

Species	Breeding Habitat	Area Requirements
Anna's hummingbird *Calypte anna*	chaparral with open evergreen forest, streamside woods, urban areas	territory = 2.2–3.2 ac
Costa's hummingbird *Calypte costae*	arid areas with scattered scrub vegetation (sage, yucca, paloverde, creosote bush, etc.), and riparian woodlands	territory = 2–4 ac
calliope hummingbird *Stellula calliope*	young coniferous forest or aspen stands, with shrubs and small trees, or shrubby streamsides with forest nearby	territory = 0.5–0.75 ac
broad-tailed hummingbird *Selasphorus platycercus*	open or shrubby meadows near woods	territory = 0.5–1.1 ac
rufous hummingbird *Selasphorus rufus*	open areas in forested or brushy areas	territory = 0.1–0.8 ac
Allen's hummingbird *Selasphorus sasin*	riparian deciduous forest, meadows	no information available
belted kingfisher *Ceryle alcyon*	streams, rivers, ponds, or estuaries with clear water and little emergent vegetation; needs bare branch or other perch over water	territory = 1200 ac; will travel up to 5 mi from nest to find food
green kingfisher *Chloroceryle americana*	streams, rivers with tree or shrub branches low over water	no information available

Feeding	Nesting	Conservation Status	Comments
flower nectar, small invertebrates (midges, spiders, flies), tree sap	open cup 1–50 ft above ground (avg = 28 ft) in deciduous tree or shrub	13	
flower nectar, small flying insects, other small insects, spiders	open cup 3–7 ft above the ground in shrub, tree, or cactus	19	
flower nectar, small insects, spiders, tree sap	open cup 6–40 ft above ground in tree, usually with overhead protection from a tree limb	18	smallest breeding bird in North America: adults weigh only about 0.10 oz
flower nectar; gnats, aphids, spiders, other small invertebrates; tree sap	open cup in tree or shrub, 1–5 ft above ground, with overhanging branch or vegetation	17	
flower nectar, small invertebrates, tree sap	open cup in tree or shrub, usually less than 15 ft above ground	WatchList 20	
flower nectar, small invertebrates, tree sap	open cup in tree or shrub	WatchList 20	
primarily fish; also molluscs, crustaceans, insects, amphibians, small mammals	burrow in steambank or other earthen bank without vegetation	10	sensitive to human disturbance
small fish	burrow in earthen bank near water	13	

Species	Breeding Habitat	Area Requirements
Lewis's woodpecker *Melanerpes lewis*	open pine forest or riparian forest, with tall trees, shrubs	territory = 15 ac
red-headed woodpecker *Melanerpes erythrocephalus*	open deciduous forest, riparian woods, open areas with scattered trees, lush ground vegetation	in VA, found in forests as small as 1.2 ac; in WI, found mostly in forests ≥3 ac
acorn woodpecker *Melanerpes formicivorus*	primarily pine-oak forests; also other open forests where oaks are present	territory = 10–15 ac
gila woodpecker *Melanerpes uropygialis*	open forest, open areas with scattered cacti, riparian woods	no information available
golden-fronted woodpecker *Melanerpes aurifrons*	open deciduous forest, riparian deciduous forest	no information available
red-bellied woodpecker *Melanerpes carolinus*	mature riparian deciduous forest, also coniferous and mixed forest	territory = 2–6 ac; each pair may need 20–30 ac; in KS, found only in wind-breaks >2.5 ac, but much more common in wind-breaks ≥10 ac; in NJ, found only in forests ≥7.5 ac
yellow-bellied sapsucker *Sphyrapicus varius*	deciduous or mixed forest, especially near water and forest openings	territory = 5–12 ac

Feeding	Nesting	Conservation Status	Comments
insects, acorns	cavity, usually in snag >12 in. diameter; in CO, cottonwood nest trees averaged 67 ft tall, 44 in. diameter	WatchList 21	regarded as sensitive to human activity
insects, acorns	cavity, usually in dead tree of 14–20 in. diameter	WatchList 18	
insects, including flying ants, and beetles; also acorns, tree sap, oak catkins	cavity 7–60 ft above the ground (avg = 27 ft) in live tree or snag >10 in. diameter; forms breeding group of up to 12 birds	14	stores acorns in holes that it drills in tree trunks—one acorn per hole, up to 50,000 holes per tree
insects, berries	cavity 8–30 ft above ground in tree or saguaro cactus	17	
insects, seeds, berries	cavity 6–25 ft above ground in tree or snag	17	
ants, beetles, grasshoppers, cockroaches, berries	cavity 3–90 ft high (usually <40 ft) in tree or snag ≥14 in. diameter	14	
insects, tree sap	cavity 3–30 ft above ground (avg = 13 ft), usually in tree 10–18 in. diameter	14	

Species	Breeding Habitat	Area Requirements
red-naped sapsucker *Sphyrapicus nuchalis*	coniferous or mixed forest near willows	territory = 1.5–15 ac
red-breasted sapsucker *Sphyrapicus ruber*	coniferous or mixed forest	territory = 15 ac
Williamson's sapsucker *Sphyrapicus thryoideus*	riparian forest, shrublands, coniferous or mixed forest	territory = 10–22 ac
ladder-backed woodpecker *Picoides scalaris*	open arid areas with scattered trees, shrubs, or cacti; riparian deciduous forest	no information available
Nuttall's woodpecker *Picoides nuttallii*	riparian deciduous forest, especially oaks	no information available
downy woodpecker *Picoides pubescens*	widespread; almost anywhere with deciduous trees	territory = 3–10 ac; in KS, found only in windbreaks >2.5 ac; in NJ, found only in forests ≥3 ac
hairy woodpecker *Picoides villosus*	mature deciduous and mixed forest with dense canopy	territory = 1.5–25 ac; in KS, found only in windbreaks >2.5 ac; in NJ, found only in forests ≥5 ac
Strickland's woodpecker *Picoides stricklandi*	riparian deciduous forest (especially oak), desert scrub with cacti	no information available
red-cockaded woodpecker *Picoides borealis*	mature open pine forest with little or no shrub cover	home range of breeding group = 200–2000 ac (varies with habitat quality)

Feeding	Nesting	Conservation Status	Comments
insects, tree sap	cavity 3–35 ft above ground in tree or snag	18	
insects, tree sap	cavity 50–60 ft above ground in tree	19	
insects, tree sap	cavity 3–60 ft above ground (avg = 8 ft) in live tree or snag >12 in. diameter	18	
beetles, beetle larvae, caterpillars, ants, berries	cavity 4–25 ft above ground (avg = 12 ft) in live tree or snag	16	
beetles, caterpillars, ants	cavity 3–35 ft above ground in tree or snag	WatchList 20	
beetles, wood-boring larvae, ants, caterpillars	nest cavity 3–50 ft above ground, usually in snag or rotten tree 6–9 in. diameter	11	
beetles, wood-boring larvae, ants, caterpillars	cavity 5–40 ft above ground in snag or live tree with heart rot, ≥10 in. diameter	1	
insects, especially wood-boring larvae	cavity 9–50 ft above ground in snag	WatchList 22	
mostly adult and larval pine beetles and bark beetles; also termites	cavity 30–50 ft above the ground in live pine with decaying heartwood	endangered 28	breeding colonies found on several golf courses in NC

Species	Breeding Habitat	Area Requirements
white-headed woodpecker *Picoides albolarvatus*	mature open pine forest with ≥2 pine species present, 50–70% canopy closure, and large-diameter (≥24 in.) tall (100 ft) trees	territory = 140–1700 ac (larger in fragmented forest)
three-toed woodpecker *Picoides tridactylus*	mature coniferous forest, especially in areas of bark beetles (such as burned forest)	territory = 75 ac
black-backed woodpecker *Picoides arcticus*	coniferous forest, especially in areas of bark beetles (such as burned forest)	territory = 75 ac
northern flicker *Colaptes auratus*	open deciduous, coniferous, or mixed forest with little understory, forest edge, and cactus forest	territory = 40 ac; in WI, found only in forests ≥1.3 ac; in NJ, found in forests as small as 0.5 ac
gilded flicker *Colaptes chrysoides*	open areas with scattered cacti	no information available
pileated woodpecker *Dryocopus pileatus*	mature coniferous or deciduous forest with >60% canopy cover and large-diameter trees (≥12 in.) and snags (≥21 in.)	territory = 130–400 ac; in Vancouver, found in patches as small as 10 ac; in MD, not found in patches <50 ac
olive-sided flycatcher *Contopus cooperi*	edge of mature coniferous forest, wooded streams	territory = 20–45 ac; in Vancouver, found in patches as small as 10 ac (smallest patch examined)

Feeding	Nesting	Conservation Status	Comments
adult and larval ants, termites, beetles, and scale insects; also conifer seeds	cavity 8–14 ft above ground (avg = 11 ft) in snag >10 in. diameter (but avg = 28 in.)	WatchList 21	
wood-boring larvae, caterpillars	cavity 2–80 ft above ground (usually 2–15 ft) in snag or live tree with heart rot, >12 in. diameter	16	
wood-boring larvae, caterpillars	cavity 2–15 ft above ground in snag >12 in. diameter	18	
primarily ants; also beetles and other insects	cavity 4–90 ft above ground (avg = 25 ft) in dead or diseased tree, or cactus, with 12–24 in. diameter	11	
insects	cavity in saguaro cactus	WatchList 20	
carpenter ants and woodboring beetle larvae excavated from under the bark of trees, snags, and logs; also berries	cavity 15–80 ft above ground (avg = 45 ft) in dead tree 40–70 ft tall and ≥20 in. diameter	10	
flying insects, including wasps, ants, bees, beetles	open cup 7–70 ft above ground (avg = 45 ft) in tree	17	

Species	Breeding Habitat	Area Requirements
greater pewee *Contopus pertinax*	riparian deciduous or mixed forest, open mixed forest	no information available
western wood-pewee *Contopus sordidulus*	open deciduous, coniferous, and mixed forest, often near water	territory = 0.7–4 ac
eastern wood-pewee *Contopus virens*	deciduous, coniferous, and mixed forest with clearings, <650 trees/ac of 3–9 in. diameter, open understory with few tall shrubs (15–24 ft)	territory = 2–20 ac; in NJ, found only in forests ≥5 ac; found in riparian corridors as narrow as 20 yd
yellow-bellied flycatcher *Empidonax flaviventris*	coniferous forest, especially wet, swampy forest	no information available
Acadian flycatcher *Empidonax virescens*	dense, mature, swampy deciduous forest with high, dense canopy, 70–100% canopy closure, and open understory	territory = 1.5–6.5 ac; in MD, found in patches as small as 13 ac; in FL, not found in corridors <60 yd wide
alder flycatcher *Empidonax alnorum*	open, swampy areas with low shrubs	territory = 3–7 ac
willow flycatcher *Empidonax traillii*	wet meadows with dense willows interspersed with openings; also open deciduous, coniferous, or mixed forest with <30% canopy cover and dense tall shrubs	territory = 0.2–4 ac; rarely found in meadows <10 ac, much more common in meadows ≥20 ac

Feeding	Nesting	Conservation Status	Comments
insects	open cup 10–40 ft above ground in tree	WatchList 20	
flying insects	open cup 10–75 ft above ground in tree	15	
flying insects, including flies, gnats, mosquitoes, moths, beetles; also caterpillars, spiders	open cup 6–70 ft above ground (avg = 27 ft) in tree	17	sensitive to forest fragmentation
flying insects	open cup on ground, at base of tree or in clump of other vegetation; occasionally up to 2 ft above ground	16	
wasps, bees, ants, caterpillars, flies, moths	open cup 4–20 ft above ground or water; avg distance to forest edge = 50 yd	18	sensitive to forest fragmentation: significantly less abundant near forest edges
beetles, ants, bees, wasps, flies, moths, caterpillars	open cup 15–33 ft above ground in shrub	13	
wasps, bees, ants, beetles, flies, caterpillars, moths	open cup 1–16 ft above ground (avg = 4.5 ft)	16	

Species	Breeding Habitat	Area Requirements
least flycatcher *Empidonax minimus*	Semiopen to mature deciduous or mixed forest with high canopy	territory = 0.1–0.5 ac
Hammond's flycatcher *Empidonax hammondii*	mature coniferous or coniferous-aspen forests, with few small trees (<4 in. diameter)	territory = 1.5–3.8 ac (avg = 2.6 ac); in Vancouver, found in patches as small as 10 ac (smallest patch examined)
dusky flycatcher *Empidonax oberholseri*	shrubby areas with scattered trees, open forest with shrubby understory, or streamsides with dense shrubs	territory = 1.8–6 ac
gray flycatcher *Empidonax wrightii*	open shrublands and forests	territory = 1–5 ac
Pacific-slope flycatcher *Empidonax difficilis*	moist coniferous or mixed forest, riparian deciduous forest	in Vancouver, found in patches as small as 10 ac (smallest patch examined)
Cordilleran flycatcher *Empidonax occidentalis*	moist coniferous or mixed forest, riparian deciduous forest	territory = 1.4 ac
black phoebe *Sayornis nigricans*	areas with a source of water and mud: near rivers, streams, ponds, ocean	territory = 1.2–2 ac

Feeding	Nesting	Conservation Status	Comments
flying insects, including ants, wasps, and beetles	open cup 5–65 ft above ground (avg = 24 ft) in tree	16	
caterpillars, butterflies, moths, and other insects	open cup 10–50 ft above ground (avg = 25 ft) in conifer tree	18	
caterpillars, wasps, bees, grasshoppers, damselflies, moths, butterflies	open cup 1–11 ft above ground (avg = 5 ft) in shrub or tree	17	
beetles, wasps, moths, grasshoppers	open cup 3–21 ft above ground (avg = 13 ft) in conifer tree, or shrub	16	
wasps, bees, flies, caterpillars, moths, beetles	cavity 0–30 ft above ground in streambank or roots of upturned tree	18	
wasps, bees, flies, caterpillars, moths, beetles	cavity 0–30 ft above ground in streambank or roots of upturned tree	17	
flying insects, including bees, wasps, flies, beetles, and damselflies	open cup of mud and vegetation 3–10 ft above ground, attached to vertical surface such as rock face, bridge, or building	13	in AZ, responded positively to urbanization, apparently due to increase of water

Species	Breeding Habitat	Area Requirements
eastern phoebe *Sayornis phoebe*	open woodlands, especially near rock outcrops for nesting	territory = 0.7 ac
Say's phoebe *Sayornis saya*	open, often arid, areas with shrubs	no information available
vermilion flycatcher *Pyrocephalus rubinus*	riparian deciduous forest with shrubs	no information available
ash-throated flycatcher *Myiarchus cinerascens*	open, arid areas with shrubs, cacti	territory = 3.5–25 ac
great crested flycatcher *Myiarchus crinitus*	deciduous or mixed forest	territory = 0.6–5 ac; in KS, found only in windbreaks >2.5 ac; in WI, found mostly in forests ≥3 ac
brown-crested flycatcher *Myiarchus tyrannulus*	desert scrub with cacti; riparian deciduous woods	no information available
Cassin's kingbird *Tyrannus vociferans*	open coniferous or mixed forest, riparian deciduous forest	no information available
western kingbird *Tyrannus verticalis*	open areas with trees or tall cacti, riparian forests	density = 1 pair per 9–35 ac; in SD, found in shelterbelts as small as 0.36 ac; will travel up to 0.25 mi from nest to find food

Feeding	Nesting	Conservation Status	Comments
flying insects, including bees, beetles, moths, captured in flight	open cup 5–15 ft above ground (avg = 8 ft) on a natural or artificial shelf with overhead cover (e.g., rock outcrop, bridge, or building)	11	
bees, wasps, ants	crevice in dirt bank, cave, building, or cliff	14	
flying insects, grasshoppers, beetles, flies, bees	open cup 8–60 ft above ground in tree	13	
caterpillars, beetles, grasshoppers, wasps, flies	cavity 2–25 ft above ground in tree, snag, or cactus	12	
caterpillars, moths, butterflies, katydids, crickets, beetles	cavity 3–50 ft above ground in tree	14	
cicadas, grasshoppers, beetles, dragonflies	cavity 10–30 ft above ground in tree or cactus	14	
wasps, beetles, caterpillars, moths, grasshoppers	open cup 20–50 ft above ground	19	
bees, wasps, grasshoppers, caterpillars, moths	open cup 10–60 ft above ground in tree or shrub	12	

Species	Breeding Habitat	Area Requirements
eastern kingbird *Tyrannus tyrannus*	open areas with scattered shrubs or trees; forest edge	territory = 14–35 ac
scissor-tailed flycatcher *Tyrannus forficatus*	open areas with scattered shrubs or trees; forest edge	home range = 15 ac
horned lark *Eremophila alpestris*	open areas with bare ground and short grasses	territory = 0.7–12 ac
purple martin *Progne subis*	open areas with scattered trees or cacti, forest edges	no information available
tree swallow *Tachycineta bicolor*	open areas near water, with snags available for nesting; prefer taller grasses than bluebirds	will fly up to 3 mi from nest to find food
violet-green swallow *Tachycineta thalassina*	open woods, forest edges	no information available
northern rough-winged swallow *Stelgidopteryx stelgidopteryx*	open areas near exposed banks of rocks, sand, or soil	will travel several hundred yards from nest to find food
bank swallow *Riparia riparia*	open areas with riverbanks or other steep soil areas for nesting	no information available

Feeding	Nesting	Conservation Status	Comments
bees, wasps, beetles, flies, grasshoppers; also berries	open cup 6–30 ft above ground in tree located in open area	12	
grasshoppers, beetles, wasps, bees, flies, caterpillars	open cup 5–35 ft above ground in shrub or tree	19	
mostly grass seeds, also grasshoppers and beetles	open cup on the ground in area with sparse vegetation; often next to grass clump or rock	11	
wasps, flying ants, bees, flies, beetles, moths, butterflies	cavity in tree or cactus, or artificial nest box	13 long-term decline in the northern part of its range	will use nest boxes (see Appendix 3)
flying insects, beetles, ants	cavity in snag ≥10 in. diameter, 3–24 ft above ground	10	
flying insects, especially leafhoppers, ants, bees, wasps	cavity in live tree or snag; also cavity in cliff or earthen bank; nest in small colonies, up to 25 pairs	14	
flying insects, including ants, flies, midges, beetles	burrow 3–15 ft above ground or water in exposed bank; may nest in colonies of up to 25 pairs	13	
flying insects	burrow in soil bank; nest in colonies	11	

Species	Breeding Habitat	Area Requirements
cliff swallow *Petrochelidon pyrrhonota*	open areas (grass-lands, forest edges, open forest) with vertical surfaces for nesting, and a source of mud for nest construction	will travel up to 1 mi from nest to find food
cave swallow *Petrochelidon fulva*	open areas, often near water	no information available
barn swallow *Hirundo rustica*	open or semiopen areas, especially near water	will travel up to 0.5 mi from nest to find food
gray jay *Perisoreus canadensis*	coniferous and mixed forest, especially where spruce is present	territory = 160 ac; in Vancouver, found in patches as small as 10 ac (smallest patch examined)
Steller's jay *Cyanocitta stelleri*	coniferous forest	in Vancouver, found in patches as small as 10 ac (smallest patch examined)
blue jay *Cyanocitta cristata*	deciduous or mixed forest, forest edges, open areas	territory = 3–16 ac; in NJ, found in forests as small as 2 ac; in SD, found in shelterbelts as small as 0.75 ac

Feeding	Nesting	Conservation Status	Comments
flying insects	enclosed cup of mud ≥5 ft above ground on cliff face, under eave of building or under bridge; nest in colonies of up to 3500 pairs	7	old nests can be knocked down after the nesting season to prevent occupation by house sparrows
flying insects, including grasshoppers, lacewings, beetles, aphids, flies, and moths	open to partially closed cup of mud, up to 115 ft above ground on side of vertical surface such as cave, bridge, culvert	18	often shares caves with bats
flying insects	mud cup on vertical surface, usually on building	9	
insects, berries, dead animals, small birds and mammals, fungi	platform of twigs 5–40 ft above ground (avg = 7 ft) in tree	10	
acorns, pine seeds, fruit, insects, bird eggs, young birds, small mammals	open cup 8–40 ft above ground (avg = 20 ft)	13	
acorns, nuts, grains, fruits, small mammals, insects, beetles, caterpillars, grasshoppers, bird eggs, young birds	open cup 5–50 ft above ground (avg = 15 ft) in tree	12	

Species	Breeding Habitat	Area Requirements
Florida scrub jay *Aphelocoma coerulescens*	shrubby areas, especially oak scrub, <6.5 ft tall, with bare ground or very sparse ground vegetation, <15% pine cover	breeding group territory = 22 ac
western scrub jay *Aphelocoma californica*	areas of shrubs (especially oaks), pinyon-juniper forest	territory = 2–3 ac
Mexican jay *Aphelocoma ultramarina*	oak-juniper and oak-pine forests	home range of social group = 90 ac
pinyon jay *Gymnorhinus cyanocephalus*	open coniferous forest (pinyon pine, ponderosa pine)	home range of social group = 8 sq mi
Clark's nutcracker *Nucifraga columbiana*	coniferous forest	no information available
black-billed magpie *Pica pica*	open areas with scattered trees, riparian deciduous forest	no information available
yellow-billed magpie *Pica nuttalli*	open areas with scattered large trees (oaks), near water	territory = 3 ac, with much overlap between individuals; home range = 25 ac

Feeding	Nesting	Conservation Status	Comments
insects (including grasshoppers, crickets, caterpillars), acorns, tree-frogs, small mammals, reptiles	open cup 3–6 ft above ground in dense shrub; breeding pair assisted by up to six non-breeding "helpers"	threatened 30	very tolerant of human activity; oak scrub habitat should be maintained by burning every 8–15 years, in patchy pattern (rather than burning entire area)
insects	open cup 5–30 ft above ground in shrub or tree	18	
grasshoppers, crickets, caterpillars, other insects, lizards	open cup 6–60 ft (avg = 20 ft) above ground in upper half of tree; nests in groups of 5–25 birds	18	will tolerate human distur-bance, even in area of nest
mostly pine seeds; also berries, insects, eggs and young birds	open cup 3–20 ft above ground in tree	14	
mostly pine seeds; also berries, insects, eggs and young birds	open cup 8–40 ft above ground in tree	12	
insects, dead animals, small mammals, eggs and young birds	domed cup 15–30 ft above ground in tree	15	
primarily ground-dwelling insects; also acorns, small mammals	large, domed stick structure, high above ground (avg height = 47 ft) in tree; sometimes nests in colonies of 3–30 pairs	19	

Species	Breeding Habitat	Area Requirements
American crow *Corvus brachyrhynchos*	open areas with scattered trees, forest edges, coastal areas	territory = 105 ac
northwestern crow *Corvus caurinus*	coastal areas	no information available
fish crow *Corvus ossifragus*	coastal areas (wetlands, woods, beaches)	no information available
Chihuahuan raven *Corvus cryptoleucus*	dry, open areas	no information available
common raven *Corvus corax*	coniferous forest, coastal areas with cliffs, desert	territory = 2–10 sq mi
black-capped chickadee *Poecile atricapillus*	deciduous or mixed forest, willow thickets, often more common near the forest edge	territory = 3–11 ac; in KS, found only in windbreaks >2.5 ac; in NJ, found only in forests ≥5 ac
Carolina chickadee *Poecile carolinensis*	mixed forest with ≥70% canopy closure, short ground vegetation (<1 ft)	territory = 3.5–5 ac; home range = 35 ac
mountain chickadee *Poecile gambeli*	coniferous or deciduous forest	territory = 3.1–3.7 ac

Feeding	Nesting	Conservation Status	Comments
beetle larvae, grasshoppers, seeds, fruits, eggs and young birds, dead animals	platform of sticks 6–70 ft (avg = 32 ft) above the ground in tree or shrub	6	
fish, crabs, dead animals, insects, berries, seeds, bird eggs	platform of sticks in tree or shrub	15	
insects, grains, fruits, bird eggs, aquatic animals, dead animals	platform of sticks 20–80 ft high in tree	12	
insects, small mammals, lizards, eggs and young birds, dead animals	platform of sticks 5–40 ft above ground in isolated tree or building	13	
small mammals, reptiles, eggs or young birds, insects, dead animals, nuts, berries	platform of sticks 45–80 ft above ground in tree or on cliff ledge	7	
caterpillars, insects, spiders, snails, slugs, centipedes, berries	cavity usually in rotted snag 6–9 in. diameter, 5–25 ft above ground	9	
caterpillars, moths, beetles, aphids, spiders, seeds, berries	cavity 5–6 ft above ground in well-rotted tree, ≥4 in. diameter	14	
caterpillars, beetles, spiders, insect eggs, seeds, berries	cavity 5–25 ft above ground in rotten tree ≥6 in. diameter	11	

Species	Breeding Habitat	Area Requirements
chestnut-backed chickadee *Poecile rufescens*	moist coniferous or mixed forest	no information available
bridled titmouse *Baeolophus wollweberi*	oak or oak-pine forest, riparian deciduous woods	no information available
oak titmouse *Baeolophus inornatus*	oak forest, riparian mixed forest	no information available
juniper titmouse *Baeolophus ridgwayi*	pinyon-juniper forest, oak or oak-pine forest	no information available
tufted titmouse *Baeolophus bicolor*	deciduous or mixed forests with tall trees and dense canopy cover; shrublands	territory = 4–10 ac; in NJ, found in forests as small as 0.5 ac
verdin *Auriparus flaviceps*	arid shrublands with bare ground, few trees	no information available
bushtit *Psaltriparus minimus*	pinyon-juniper forest, shrublands, aspen-pine forest, riparian woods	territory = 1–3.5 ac
red-breasted nuthatch *Sitta canadensis*	coniferous or mixed forest	territory = 7.4 ac; in Vancouver, found in patches as small as 10 ac (smallest patch examined)

Feeding	Nesting	Conservation Status	Comments
caterpillars, moths, beetles, leafhoppers, scale insects, spiders, seeds, berries	cavity 2–20 ft above ground in rotted tree	15	
insects, seeds	cavity 4–30 ft above ground in dead limb or snag	WatchList 20	
caterpillars, beetles, leafhoppers, acorns	cavity in tree	WatchList 22	
caterpillars, beetles, leafhoppers, pinyon seeds	cavity in tree	18	
caterpillars, weevils, beetles, ants, wasps, bees, flies, spiders, seeds	cavity 20–65 ft above the ground (avg = 38 ft) in dead tree or limb ≥8 in. diameter	11	will use nest boxes (see Appendix 3)
aphids, caterpillars, scale insects, leafhoppers, spiders, berries	globe 4–12 ft above ground in thorny shrub, tree, or cactus	15	
insects, spiders	hanging cup 5–35 ft above ground	11	
insects, conifer seeds	nest cavity 5–100 ft above ground (avg = 15 ft) in snag or rotten tree, 6–9 in. diameter	9	

Species	Breeding Habitat	Area Requirements
white-breasted nuthatch *Sitta carolinensis*	mature deciduous or mixed forest, forest edges	territory = 1–37 ac, other estimates as high as 50 ac; in NJ, found only in forests >5 ac; in WI, found mostly in forests ≥3 ac
pygmy nuthatch *Sitta pygmaea*	open coniferous forest, especially yellow pines	territory = 1.6–3.7 ac
brown-headed nuthatch *Sitta pusilla*	open coniferous forest, especially pines	no information available
brown creeper *Certhia americana*	mature deciduous, coniferous, or mixed forest	territory = 5.7–16 ac; in Vancouver, found in patches as small as 10 ac (smallest patch examined)
cactus wren *Campylorhynchus brunneicapillus*	arid areas with scattered cacti (especially cholla) and thorny shrubs	no information available
rock wren *Salpinctes obsoletus*	areas of rock outcrops, canyons, with <40% forest canopy cover	no information available
canyon wren *Catherpes mexicanus*	arid, rocky canyons	territory = 2.2 ac

Feeding	Nesting	Conservation Status	Comments
weevils, beetles, tree hoppers, scale insects, ants, caterpillars, acorns, nuts	natural cavities or abandoned woodpecker cavities 15–65 ft above ground in tree	10	
beetles, wasps, caterpillars	cavity 8–60 ft above ground in dead limb, or snag > 18 in. diameter	16	
beetles, ants, grasshoppers, caterpillars	cavity 5–90 ft above ground in tree or snag, ≥8 in. diameter	WatchList 21	
insect eggs and pupae, weevils, beetles, leaf-hoppers, scale insects, aphids, spiders, caterpillars	behind loose slab of bark 5–65 ft above ground (avg = 36 ft), in snag ≥10 in. diameter with ≥40% of bark intact	13	
beetles, ants, wasps, grasshoppers	globe or cavity < 10 ft above ground in cactus or tree	15	
spiders, ants, grasshoppers, flying insects	open cup in rock crevice	13	
spiders and insects, including ants, termites, and beetles	open cup in rock crevice	14	

Species	Breeding Habitat	Area Requirements
Carolina wren *Thryothorus ludovicianus*	open or wooded areas with moderate to dense shrub cover, especially with water present	territory = 2.5–10 ac
Bewick's wren *Thryomanes bewickii*	mature pinyon-juniper forest, riparian woods, forest edges, areas with dense shrubs	territory = 1–11 ac
house wren *Troglodytes aedon*	deciduous or mixed forest edge, often near buildings	territory = 0.3–3.5 ac; in KS, found only in windbreaks >2.5 ac; in NJ, found in forests as small as 0.25 ac; in SD, found in shelterbelts as small as 0.6 ac
winter wren *Troglodytes troglodytes*	moist, dense coniferous forest with dense shrubs	in Vancouver, found in patches as small as 10 ac (smallest patch examined)
sedge wren *Cistothorus platensis*	wetlands with sedges or wet meadows with grasses >1 ft tall	territory = 0.5 ac
marsh wren *Cistothorus palustris*	wetlands with tall emergent vegetation (cattails, bulrushes, etc.)	territory = 0.01–0.9 ac; rarely found in wetlands <1 ac
American dipper *Cinclus mexicanus*	fast-moving, clear streams and rivers, <50 ft wide and <6 ft deep	territory = 400–2200 yd of stream (avg = 1200 yd)

Feeding	Nesting	Conservation Status	Comments
caterpillars, moths, leaf-hoppers, beetles, grasshoppers, forb seeds	cup (often domed) in tree cavity or other open cavity (among upturned tree roots, over-hangs, etc.); avg height above ground = 6 ft	11	
beetles, ants, wasps, caterpillars, grasshopper, spiders	cavity in snag 6–16 ft above ground	15	
caterpillars, grasshoppers, beetles, spiders	cavity up to 13 ft above ground in dead limb or snag, ≥8 in. diameter	7	
beetles, bugs, spiders, caterpillars	cavity in roots of upturned tree or stream bank	12	
spiders, insects	globe 1–2 ft above water or ground	18	
beetles, flies, moths, caterpillars, ants, grasshoppers	globe 1–3 ft above water	14	
adult and larval aquatic insects, including caddisflies, mayflies, midges, and stoneflies	globe of moss, grass, and leaves on rock face above fast water	17	will nest on bridges, pro-vided there is a horizontal ledge for nest sup-port

Species	Breeding Habitat	Area Requirements
golden-crowned kinglet *Regulus satrapa*	dense, mature coniferous forest with ≥40% canopy cover and little ground vegetation	territory = 2.3–6.3 ac (avg = 4 ac); in Vancouver, found in patches as small as 10 ac (smallest patch examined)
ruby-crowned kinglet *Regulus calendula*	coniferous (especially spruce) and mixed forest with 10–60% canopy cover	territory = 2.7–15 ac (avg = 7.2 ac)
blue-gray gnatcatcher *Polioptila caerulea*	pinyon-juniper forest, open deciduous forest with shrubs, riparian deciduous woods	territory = 1.7–7.4 ac; home range = 10 ac
California gnatcatcher *Polioptila californica*	dry areas of low (3–6 ft tall) shrubs, including sagebrush, buckwheat, salvia	density ≤1 pair per 5 ac
black-tailed gnatcatcher *Polioptila melanura*	dry areas of thorny shrubs and trees	io information available
eastern bluebird *Sialia sialis*	flat, open areas with few trees or shrubs, forest edges	territory = 2.5–3.5 ac
western bluebird *Sialia mexicana*	open areas with scattered trees and shrubs	territory = 1.5–5 ac
mountain bluebird *Sialia currucoides*	open areas with short grass, clusters of trees, and few shrubs	territory = 2–12 ac
Townsend's solitaire *Myadestes townsendi*	open coniferous or mixed forest with few shrubs and sparse ground vegetation	territory = 25–50 ac

Feeding	Nesting	Conservation Status	Comments
small beetles, gnats, caterpillars, scale insects, aphids, insect eggs	hanging cup 6–60 ft above ground	12	
spiders and their eggs, leafhopper, aphids, scale insects	open cup 3–6 ft from top of conifer tree (avg height above ground = 40 ft)	10	
leafhoppers, treehoppers, bugs, beetles, caterpillars, flies, spiders	open cup on branch, closer to tip than trunk; 3–80 ft high (avg = 30 ft)	10	
bugs, beetles, caterpillars, scale insects, wasps, ants, flies, moths	open cup <4 ft above ground in shrub	threatened 30	
beetles, bugs, caterpillars, wasps, ants, flies, moths	open cup <5 ft above ground in shrub	17	
grasshoppers, crickets, beetles, katydids	cavity <7 ft above ground in tree or fencepost	10	will use nest boxes (see Appendix 3)
grasshoppers, caterpillars, beetles, ants	cavity in live tree or snag	14	will use nest boxes (see Appendix 3)
spiders, beetles, grasshoppers, caterpillars	cavity in live tree or snag	14	will use nest boxes (see Appendix 3)
flying insects, caterpillars, beetles, ants, termites	open cup on the ground, usually under rock, log, or other pro-tective structure	13	

Species	Breeding Habitat	Area Requirements
veery *Catharus fuscescens*	moist deciduous or mixed forest with dense understory vegetation (1–10 ft high); riparian forest	territory = 0.1–3 ac
Bicknell's thrush *Catharus bicknelli*	moist coniferous forest	no information available
Swainson's thrush *Catharus ustulatus*	coniferous or deciduous forest with closed canopy	territory = 1.5–14.5 ac; in Vancouver, found in patches as small as 10 ac (smallest patch examined)
hermit thrush *Catharus guttatus*	deciduous, coniferous, or mixed forest with closed canopy, small brushy openings, thick leaf litter; forest edges	territory = 2–10 ac; in Vancouver, found in patches as small as 10 ac (smallest patch examined)
wood thrush *Hylocichla mustelina*	deciduous or mixed forest, with dense tree canopy (≥70%), dense shrub and sapling understory, leaf litter, <35% grass cover, wet soil available	territory = 1–7 ac; 0.2 ac of tree cover required in territory; in NJ, found only in forests ≥2 ac
American robin *Turdus migratorius*	open forest, forest edges, especially areas with short grass (2.5 in.), and where mud is available for nest construction	territory = 0.1–0.6 ac; in NJ, found in forests as small as 0.5 ac; in SD, found in the smallest shelterbelts examined (0.25 ac)
varied thrush *Ixoreus naevius*	dense, moist coniferous forest with dense low vegetation	in Vancouver, found in patches as small as 10 ac (smallest patch examined)

Feeding	Nesting	Conservation Status	Comments
beetles, caterpillars, spiders, berries	open cup on the ground or up to 5 ft above ground in shrub or tree	17	
ants, beetles, caterpillars	open cup <6 ft above ground in shrub or tree	WatchList 21	
insects, spiders, berries	open cup 2–20 ft above ground in shrub or conifer tree	13	
beetles, caterpillars, ants, earth-worms, berries	open cup on ground below shrub, small tree, or other vegetation; or up to 8 ft above ground in shrub or tree	11	
beetles, caterpillars, millipedes, ants, spiders, berries	open cup 2–70 ft above the ground (avg = 11 ft) in tree	WatchList 20	in Ontario, mostly absent from forests adjacent to high-density housing areas
insects, earth-worms, snails, spiders, berries	open cup 5–25 ft above ground in tree or shrub	6	will exploit abundance of insects ex-posed and/or injured by turf mowing
beetles, ants, caterpillars, crickets	open cup 5–15 above ground in tree or shrub	16	

Species	Breeding Habitat	Area Requirements
wrentit *Chamaea fasciata*	areas of dense shrubs, riparian shrubs	no information available
gray catbird *Dumetella carolinensis*	dense, shrubby thickets; will live in open forest or forest edges as long as dense shrubs are present	territory = 0.2–3.2 ac; in KS, found only in windbreaks >10 ac; in NJ, found in forests as small as 0.5 ac
northern mockingbird *Mimus polyglottos*	forest edges with areas of very short grasses	territory = 3–4 ac
sage thrasher *Oreoscoptes montanus*	areas with sagebrush	territory = 1.6–4 ac
brown thrasher *Toxostoma rufum*	areas with dense shrubs, coniferous or deciduous or mixed forest with dense shrubs, forest edges	territory = 1–3 ac; in KS, found only in windbreaks >0.75 ac; in NJ, found only in forests ≥2 ac (but more commonly in forests ≥10 ac)
long-billed thrasher *Toxostoma longirostre*	areas of dense, thorny shrubs, deciduous forest with thorny shrubs	no information available
Bendire's thrasher *Toxostoma bendirei*	open desert grassland with scattered shrubs, trees; avoids dense vegetation such as riparian areas	no information available
curve-billed thrasher *Toxostoma curvirostre*	arid, open and semiopen areas with thorny shrubs or cacti, scattered trees	territory = 2–11 ac

Feeding	Nesting	Conservation Status	Comments
ants, wasps, caterpillars, beetles, scale insects, leaf-hoppers	open cup 1–4 ft above ground in low shrub	19	
ants, beetles, grasshoppers, caterpillars, moths, berries	open cup 2–26 ft above ground (usually 2–8 ft) in shrub, small tree, or vines	15	
beetles, ants, bees, wasps, grasshoppers, earthworms, fruits	open cup 3–10 ft above ground in shrub, tree, or cactus	10	can be aggressive toward humans near the nest
beetles, ants, grasshoppers, spiders, wasps	open cup 0–3 ft above ground in shrub	15	
beetles, caterpillars, bugs, grass-hoppers, cicadas	open cup 0–25 ft above ground (usually <10 ft) in shrub, vines, or tree	17	
beetles, ants, bugs, moths, grasshoppers	open cup 4–10 ft above ground in tree, shrub, or cactus	WatchList 22	
grasshoppers, beetles, caterpillars, also some seeds and berries	open cup in shrub, cactus, or tree, 3–10 ft above the ground (avg 5 ft)	WatchList 23	
beetles, gastropods, and crustaceans	open cup 2–20 ft above ground (avg = 5 ft) in thorny shrub or cactus in open area	WatchList 18	

Species	Breeding Habitat	Area Requirements
California thrasher *Toxostoma redivivum*	open areas with dense shrubs, riparian shrubs	no information available
Crissal thrasher *Toxostoma crissale*	open areas with scattered shrubs; dense riparian shrubs	no information available
Le Conte's thrasher *Toxostoma lecontei*	sparsely vegetated, flat desert with scattered saltbush, shadscale, cholla cactus 3–6 ft tall, bare ground or sparse ground vegetation < 1 ft tall	territory = 9–44 ac (avg = 18 ac); home range up to 50 ac
American pipit *Anthus rubescens*	open areas with low vegetation, usually above treeline	territory = 0.01–0.4 ac; home range = 8–25 ac
Sprague's pipit *Anthus spragueii*	shortgrass prairie	no information available
cedar waxwing *Bombycilla cedrorum*	open forest, forest edges, riparian forest	territory = 0.1–1 ac
phainopepla *Phainopepla nitens*	arid areas with scattered shrubs, riparian deciduous forest	no information available
loggerhead shrike *Lanius ludovicianus*	open country with grasses and other short vegetation, scattered low trees and shrubs, especially if thorny	territory = 11–40 ac

Feeding	Nesting	Conservation Status	Comments
ants, wasps, bees, beetles, caterpillars, moths	open cup 2–10 ft above ground in shrub	WatchList 21	
beetles, grass- hoppers, ants, caterpillars	open cup 2–8 ft above ground in shrub	18	
grasshoppers, beetles, ants, moths, seeds	open cup 0–8 ft (avg = 2.5 ft) above ground in dense, thorny shrub or cholla cactus	WatchList 23	
flies, bugs, beetles, caterpillars, moths	open cup on ground, next to rock or hummock	13	
grasshoppers, crickets, moths, caterpillars, beetles, weevils	open cup on ground in grass tuft	WatchList 22	
berries, beetles, caterpillars, ants	open cup 6–20 ft above ground in tree	9	
berries (especially mistletoe), beetles, flies, caterpillars	open cup 4–50 ft above ground in shrub or tree, often in mistletoe clump	15	
grasshoppers, beetles, katydids, frogs, lizards, small birds, small mammals	open cup 3–10 ft above ground in thorny tree or shrub	17	

Species	Breeding Habitat	Area Requirements
European starling *Sturnus vulgaris*	urban areas, open forests, open areas near forest	no information available
white-eyed vireo *Vireo griseus*	dense shrubby areas including riparian areas, with dense shrubs ≤3 ft tall and scattered trees	territory = 2.5–3.2 ac; in FL, found only in habitat patches >5.7 ac
Bell's vireo *Vireo bellii*	dense shrubby areas including riparian areas, or young forest with dense shrubs 2–10 ft tall	territory = 0.3–4 ac
black-capped vireo *Vireo atricapillus*	shrubby areas (≥35% shrub cover, usually oaks <6 ft tall) with grasses and forbs, and few junipers	territory = 2.5–25 ac (avg = 7 ac)
gray vireo *Vireo vicinior*	arid thorn scrub, oak scrub, open coniferous or mixed forest, pinyon-juniper forest	territory = 5–17 ac

Feeding	Nesting	Conservation Status	Comments
wide variety of foods, including insects, fruits, seeds, human garbage	cavity 2–60 ft above ground (usually 10–25 ft) in tree, building, or nest box	6	introduced to the U.S. from Europe in 1890, this bird aggressively displaces native species such as bluebirds; should be discouraged from nesting whenever possible; unlike native birds, this species has no legal protection in the U.S.
moths, butterflies, caterpillars, flies, beetles, grasshoppers, spiders and their eggs, berries	open cup 1–7 ft above ground (avg = 32 in.) in shrub	16	
caterpillars, stinkbugs, bees, wasps, weevils, spiders	open cup in dense shrub or small tree, 1.5–5 ft above ground, often at the edge of the vegetation patch	WatchList 23	
caterpillars, beetles, moths, butterflies, spiders	open, hanging cup 1.5–6.5 ft above the ground in shrub	endangered 28	nests are often parasitized by cowbirds
beetles, caterpillars, moths, bugs, treehoppers	open cup 2–10 ft above ground in tree or shrub	WatchList 21	

Species	Breeding Habitat	Area Requirements
blue-headed vireo *Vireo solitarius*	moist, open coniferous or mixed forest	home range = 5–8 ac in high-density areas, 30–100 ac in low-density
Cassin's vireo *Vireo cassinii*	open oak forest	no information available
plumbeous vireo *Vireo plumbeus*	pinyon-juniper or open mixed forest	territory = 1–5 ac
yellow-throated vireo *Vireo flavifrons*	medium aged to mature deciduous or mixed forest in riparian or swampy areas with dense vegetation 1–3 ft tall, tall trees, and high, semiopen to closed canopy (30–90% closure)	territory = 7–10 ac; most common in forests >80 ac
Hutton's vireo *Vireo huttoni*	coniferous and deciduous (primarily oak) forest with moderate to dense canopy closure and understory	territory = 2.7–7.2 ac
warbling vireo *Vireo gilvus*	open deciduous or mixed forest with 40–85% canopy cover, trees >16 ft tall	territory = 3 ac; in KS, found only in windbreaks >2.5 ac; in SD, found in shelterbelts as small as 0.6 ac
Philadelphia vireo *Vireo philadelphicus*	deciduous forest with small to medium sized trees (especially aspen, birch, alder, and ash), shrubby areas	territory = 1.2–10 ac

Feeding	Nesting	Conservation Status	Comments
caterpillars, bugs, beetles, wasps, bees, moths	open cup 3–30 ft above ground (usually 4–12 ft)	13	
caterpillars, bugs, beetles, wasps, bees, moths	open cup 3–30 ft above ground (usually 4–12 ft)	19	
caterpillars, bugs, beetles, wasps, bees, moths	open cup 3–30 ft above ground (usually 4–12 ft)	17	
caterpillars, butterflies, moths, stinkbugs, scale insects, and beetles, captured in the mid to upper canopy	open cup 3–80 ft above the ground (avg = 35 ft) in tree near forest edge	15	formerly common in urban areas— its absence believed to be due to insecticide applications for Dutch elm disease; apparently sensitive to forest fragmentation
stink bugs, caterpillars, moths, beetles, spiders	open, hanging cup 3–45 ft above ground (avg = 16 ft) in tree, sometimes in shrub	17	
mostly caterpillars, also aphids, beetles, grasshoppers, ants, bugs, scale insects, flies	open cup 4–60 ft above ground (usually 30–60 ft)	12	
mostly caterpillars, also moths and butterflies	open, hanging cup near top of tree: 8–65 ft above ground (avg = 50 ft)	17	generally not found in urban areas

Species	Breeding Habitat	Area Requirements
red-eyed vireo *Vireo olivaceus*	mature deciduous or mixed forest with closed canopy, open understory with sparse ground cover	territory = 0.8–2.1 ac; in WI, most common in forests >40 ac; in NJ, found only in forests ≥2 ac (but more commonly ≥7.5 ac); in DE, found in woodlots as small as 2 ac
black-whiskered vireo *Vireo altiloquus*	mangrove swamps, deciduous forest	in FL, found in patches as small as 0.5 ac
olive warbler *Peucedramus taeniatus*	coniferous or conifer-oak forest	no information available
blue-winged warbler *Vermivora pinus*	areas of dense shrubs, streamside woods, forest edges	territory = 1–13 ac; in NJ, found only in forests ≥3 ac
golden-winged warbler *Vermivora chrysoptera*	open fields or bogs with dense patches of shrubs (covering about 50% of the area) and forbs, and with a forest edge	territory = 1–6 ac
Tennessee warbler *Vermivora peregrina*	moist deciduous, coniferous, or mixed forest with small openings, edges of dense forest	home range = 1–2 ac in very high-density areas, 5–12 ac in high-density , 40–60 ac in low-density
orange-crowned warbler *Vermivora celata*	dense shrubs especially with high humidity, including streamsides and mixed forest with shrubby understory	territory = 0.5–5 ac

Feeding	Nesting	Conservation Status	Comments
caterpillars, moths, beetles, wasps, bees, ants, flies, cicadas, scale insects	open cup 5–50 ft above the ground in a tree or shrub	10	sensitive to forest fragmentation; in DE, denser population in larger woodlots
spiders, caterpillars, earwigs, beetles, wasps, bees, flies, mosquitoes, berries	open, hanging cup 3–20 ft above ground in tree	18	
insects	open cup 30–70 ft above ground in tree	WatchList 20	
beetles, ants, caterpillars, grasshoppers, spiders	open cup on or near ground, in or under shrub or small tree	19	
moths, caterpillars, flying insects, spiders	open cup on the ground, at base of leafy or grassy vegetation	WatchList 25	
caterpillars, scale insects, aphids, beetles, flies, ants, leafhoppers, spiders	open cup on ground under shrub or grasses	15	
caterpillars, beetles, ants, other insects; also tree sap	open cup on ground or low in shrub, often on steep bank in gully	11	

Species	Breeding Habitat	Area Requirements
Nashville warbler *Vermivora ruficapilla*	open deciduous or mixed forests with shrubs	territory = 0.5–2.7 ac
Virginia's warbler *Vermivora virginiae*	areas with shrubs, pinyon-juniper forest	territory = 3–12 ac
Lucy's warbler *Vermivora luciae*	dense mesquite, streamside deciduous forest with shrubs	no information available
Northern parula *Parula americana*	dense, mature deciduous or coniferous forests along rivers, lakes, and swamps, with dense shrubs, >75% canopy cover, and abundant Spanish moss or hanging lichens	territory = 1 ac, home range = 2–40 ac; rarely found in forests <250 ac; in FL, preferred forests >50 ac
yellow warbler *Dendroica petechia*	riparian shrubs; young, open forest	territory = 0.1–3 ac
chestnut-sided warbler *Dendroica pennsylvanica*	open areas with shrubs or small trees; more common in areas with abundant shrubs >3 ft tall	territory = 1–2.7 ac, home range = 2–12 ac
magnolia warbler *Dendroica magnolia*	dense, young coniferous forest, or mature coniferous forest with dense understory	territory = 1.3–2.6 ac (avg = 1.8 ac)

Feeding	Nesting	Conservation Status	Comments
insects, including flies, grasshoppers, leafhoppers, caterpillars	open cup on ground, usually under shrub, log, or other structure, located at forest edge	15	
insects	open cup on ground under shrub and grasses	WatchList 21	
insects	cavity 5–40 ft above ground	WatchList 22	
mostly caterpillars and spiders	cup in mass of Spanish moss, beard moss, or lace lichen, 6–100 ft above the ground (avg = 13 ft) in tree	15	
mostly caterpillars, also mayflies, moths, mosquitoes, beetles, damselflies, treehoppers, spiders	open cup 2–60 ft above ground in tree or shrub	8	
caterpillars, moths, spiders	open cup 1–6 ft (avg = 2 ft) above ground in deciduous shrub or small tree	16	
caterpillars, weevils, beetles, leafhoppers, aphids, moths, scale insects, spiders	open cup 0.5–35 ft above ground (usually <10 ft) in conifer tree	11	

Species	Breeding Habitat	Area Requirements
Cape May warbler *Dendroica tigrina*	open coniferous forest	no information available
black-throated blue warbler *Dendroica caerulescens*	large patches of deciduous or mixed forest with dense shrubs <3 ft tall	territory = 2.5–10 ac; most common in forest patches >250 ac
yellow-rumped warbler *Dendroica coronata*	open coniferous and mixed forest, forest edges	territory = 1–2 ac
black-throated gray warbler *Dendroica nigrescens*	open coniferous and mixed forest, open areas with shrubs	in Vancouver, found only in patches ≥27 ac
Townsend's warbler *Dendroica townsendi*	dense coniferous forest	in Vancouver, found in patches as small as 10 ac (smallest patch examined)
hermit warbler *Dendroica occidentalis*	dense, moist coniferous forest	no information available
black-throated green warbler *Dendroica virens*	coniferous and mixed forest	territory = 0.6–1.2 ac; in ME, not found in island forests smaller than 0.9 ac
golden-cheeked warbler *Dendroica chrysoparia*	juniper forest with deciduous trees (oak, walnut, pecan, hackberry)	no information available
Blackburnian warbler *Dendroica fusca*	mature coniferous or mixed forest	territory = 1–2.7 ac

Feeding	Nesting	Conservation Status	Comments
caterpillars, wasps, flies, ants, bees, moths, beetles, spiders	open cup 35–60 ft above ground in tree	18	
caterpillars, moths, beetles, spiders	open cup low in shrub (avg height above ground = 17 in.), in area of dense shrubs	WatchList 20	
caterpillars, wasps, grasshoppers, gnats, aphids, beetles, spiders	open cup 4–50 ft above ground in tree	14	
caterpillars, other insects	open cup 7–35 ft above ground in tree or shrub	19	
caterpillars, bugs, beetles, leafhoppers	open cup 7–60 ft above ground in tree	17	
caterpillars, beetles, flying insects, spiders	open cup 20–40 ft above ground in tree	WatchList 23	
primarily caterpillars, also beetles, gnats, mites	open cup 3–7 ft above ground in conifer tree	16	
caterpillars, cicadas, beetles, ants, katydids, flies, moths, aphids, spiders	open cup in tree	endangered 29	
spiders, beetles, caterpillars	open cup 6–75 ft (avg = 33 ft) above ground in conifer	17	

Species	Breeding Habitat	Area Requirements
yellow-throated warbler *Dendroica dominica*	dense, mature deciduous forests in swamps or along rivers, also pine-oak forests	territory = 5.6 ac
Grace's warbler *Dendroica graciae*	pine-oak forest	territory = 0.6–2 ac
pine warbler *Dendroica pinus*	open pine forest	no information available
prairie warbler *Dendroica discolor*	young forest, openings in older forest, forest edges	territory = 1–8.6 ac (avg = 3.7 ac)
palm warbler *Dendroica palmarum*	open, boggy areas with scattered small coniferous trees and dense shrubs 3–6 ft tall	territory = 10 ac; home range = 25–100 ac
bay-breasted warbler *Dendroica castanea*	dense, mature coniferous (spruce-fir) forest, often near water	territory = 3.7 ac
blackpoll warbler *Dendroica striata*	coniferous forest	no information available
cerulean warbler *Dendroica cerulea*	mature deciduous forest with many trees >12 in. diameter and >60 ft tall, and >85% canopy closure	requires very large patches of forest

Feeding	Nesting	Conservation Status	Comments
beetles, moths, caterpillars, flies, grasshoppers	open cup, or pocket in Spanish moss, 10–80 ft above ground (avg = 40 ft) in tree canopy	17	
insects	open cup 20–60 ft above ground in tree	19	
grasshoppers, caterpillars, moths, beetles, ants, bugs	open cup 8–50 ft above ground (occasionally much higher) in tree	13	
caterpillars, moths, lacewings, beetles, ants, flies, spiders	open cup 1–45 ft above ground in tree	WatchList 20	
grasshoppers, beetles, caterpillars, mayflies	open cup on ground under small tree	17	
caterpillars, beetles, ants, moths, flies, spruce budworm	open cup 4–40 ft above ground (avg = 16 ft) in tree	19	
aphids, scale insects, caterpillars, beetles, gnats, mosquitoes, spiders, berries	open cup 2–12 ft above ground in tree or shrub	16	
insects, including caterpillars	open cup 15–90 ft above the ground (avg = 34 ft) in tree	WatchList 25	sensitive to habitat frag-mentation

Species	Breeding Habitat	Area Requirements
black-and-white warbler *Mniotilta varia*	mature deciduous and mixed forest with large trees, high percentage of canopy closure, and sparse shrub cover	territory = 2.2–16 ac; in FL, preferred forests >50 ac; in NJ, found only in forests ≥18.5 ac; in MD, found only in forests >35 ac
American redstart *Setophaga ruticilla*	mature deciduous and mixed forest with closed canopy and dense shrubs in swampy or riparian areas	territory = 1–1.5 ac; in WI, most common in patches >80 ac
prothonotary warbler *Protonotaria citrea*	mature deciduous forest with dense shrubs in swampy or riparian areas	territory = 2–6 ac (avg = 3.7 ac); in MD, found only in forests >170 ac
worm-eating warbler *Helmitheros vermivorus*	deciduous forest with dense shrubs, especially mountain laurel	in FL and MD, preferred forests >50 ac
Swainson's warbler *Limnothlypis swainsonii*	hardwood swamps and riparian forest with ≥75% canopy cover, tall trees (avg = 60 ft), some open areas, dense shrub cover, sparse ground vegetation, and thick leaf litter	territory = 0.3–8 ac (avg = 3 ac); in IL, found only in forests >850 ac

Feeding	Nesting	Conservation Status	Comments
primarily caterpillars; also ants, flies, beetles, weevils, spiders	open cup on the ground up against a shrub, tree, stump, log, or rock, often in a swampy area	14	
beetles, caterpillars, moths, leafhoppers, aphids, midges, spiders, berries	open cup 4–20 ft above the ground in small tree or shrub	12	
insects	cavity 5–10 ft above the ground in a live tree or snag, usually over water	WatchList 21	researchers have recommended that 100-yd wide riparian zones be protected for this species
insects; in spite of its name, does not eat worms	open cup on the ground	WatchList 21	sensitive to forest fragmentation; nests are usually >70 yd from forest edges
caterpillars, beetles, ants, spiders, crickets, grasshoppers, flies, other invertebrates captured on the ground or in shrubs	open cup 1–10 ft above ground (avg = 4 ft) in shrub or vine tangle, at edge of thicket, often <200 yd from water	WatchList 24	dense shrub understory may be the most important feature of this species' habitat; conservation activities center on encouraging dense growth of cane (*Arundinaria* spp.) in large tracts of mature forest

Species	Breeding Habitat	Area Requirements
ovenbird *Seiurus aurocapillus*	large patch of deciduous or mixed forest, with 60–90% canopy cover, 50–70 ft canopy height, low to moderate shrub density, and thick leaf litter	territory = 0.5–4.4 ac; in NJ, found only in forests ≥10 ac; in FL, preferred forests >50 ac; in PA, found only in forests >45 ac; but in DE, eight pairs found in a 20-ac woodlot
northern waterthrush *Seiurus noveboracensis*	streamsides, bogs, and swamps with trees or other woody vegetation, dense vegetation near ground level	territory = 1.2–2.5 ac
Louisiana waterthrush *Seiurus motacilla*	streamsides in deciduous or mixed forest with dense low vegetation	territory = 5–20 ac, 200–1000 yd of stream (avg = 400 yd); in MD, found only in forests >170 ac
Kentucky warbler *Oporornis formosus*	deciduous forest and swampy forest with semiopen canopy, and dense shrub and ground vegetation layers	in IL, found in forests ≥6 ac
Connecticut warbler *Oporornis agilis*	boggy areas in coniferous or mixed forest	no information available
Mourning warbler *Oporornis philadelphia*	open deciduous and mixed woods with 40–75% canopy cover and dense understory of shrubs and young trees	territory = 1.6–2.4 ac (avg = 1.9 ac)

Feeding	Nesting	Conservation Status	Comments
caterpillars, ants, and other insects	cup with a dome, on the ground where leaf litter is thick and shrubs are sparse	13	sensitive to forest fragmentation; usually does not build nest within 25 yd of forest edge
aquatic and terrestrial invertebrates, including beetles, flies, caterpillars, snails	open cup in cavity formed by upturned tree roots, or in fern cluster, or on ground in stream bank	12	
aquatic invertebrates	open cup on ground, typically in stream bank under roots or log	19	avoids open areas; avg distance from nest to forest edge = 64 yd
moths, bugs, ants, grasshoppers, beetles, caterpillars, aphids, spiders	open cup on ground under a tree, shrub, or in dense ground vegetation	WatchList 19	less abundant near forest edges
insects, including caterpillars, also spiders, snails	open cup on ground next to clump of grass or other vegetation	18	
caterpillars, beetles, spiders, other insects	open cup on ground in *dense* vegetation or low in a shrub	16	

Species	Breeding Habitat	Area Requirements
MacGillivray's warbler *Oporornis tolmiei*	dense shrubs (40–60% cover) in meadows, riparian zones, or forest (coniferous, deciduous, or mixed)	territory = 2–4 ac; in Vancouver, found in patches as small as 10 ac (smallest patch examined)
common yellowthroat *Geothlypis trichas*	wetlands with emergent vegetation, streamside shrubs	territory = 0.8–4.4 ac; in KS, found only in windbreaks >0.75 ac; in SD, found in shelterbelts as small as 0.75 ac
hooded warbler *Wilsonia citrina*	mature, often moist, deciduous forest with closed canopy and shrubby understory or small forest openings with shrubs	territory = 1–5 ac; in FL, not found in corridors <60 yd wide; recommended forest patch size >35 ac
Wilson's warbler *Wilsonia pusilla*	streamside shrubs, moist areas with shrubs	territory = 0.5–3.2 ac (avg = 1.2 ac); in Vancouver, found in patches as small as 10 ac (smallest patch examined)
Canada warbler *Wilsonia canadensis*	mature, moist, deciduous forest, streamside shrubs	no information available
red-faced warbler *Cardellina rubrifrons*	fir, pine, pine-oak, and aspen forests, especially in steep canyons, also streamsides with conifers	territory = 0.7–3.7 ac

Feeding	Nesting	Conservation Status	Comments
leafhoppers, beetles, bees, ants, wasps, weevils, caterpillars	open cup 0–9 ft above ground (avg = 18 in.) in grass clump or shrub	16	
grasshoppers, dragonflies, damselflies, mayflies, beetles, grubs, caterpillars, moths, spiders	open cup <3 ft above ground or water in shrub or emergent vegetation	13	
spiders, caterpillars, moths, grasshoppers, beetles, flies	open cup 1–5 ft above ground in shrub, often near small forest opening	18	sensitive to forest fragmentation
bees, wasps, beetles, caterpillars, aphids, spiders	open cup on or near ground, at base of shrub	13	
beetles, mosquitoes, flies, moths, caterpillars, spiders	open cup on or near ground	18	
mostly caterpillars, also flies, leafhoppers, other insects	open cup on ground with overhanging vegetation, rocks, or dirt; placed low on a slope, in the open or at the base of a tree	WatchList 23	very sensitive to habitat alteration— abandons areas where trees have been removed; wooded riparian corridor should be 100 yd on each side of stream

Species	Breeding Habitat	Area Requirements
painted redstart *Myioborus pictus*	oak and pine-oak forest, steamside deciduous and mixed woods	no information available
yellow-breasted chat *Icteria virens*	dense shrubs, especially along streams, ponds, or swamps	territory = 0.1–3.9 ac
hepatic tanager *Piranga flava*	open pine-oak or pinyon forest, with scattered tall trees	no information available
summer tanager *Piranga rubra*	open deciduous or mixed forest, streamside woods	territory = 4–25 ac; in FL, preferred forests >50 ac, and not found in corridors <60 yd wide
scarlet tanager *Piranga olivacea*	wet deciduous or mixed forest with high canopy closure, 8–14 in. diameter trees, dense shrub layer, and sparse ground vegetation	territory = 4.5 ac (MD); in NJ, found only in forests ≥7.5 ac; in WI, found only in forests ≥12 ac
western tanager *Piranga ludoviciana*	open coniferous or mixed forest	no information available
northern cardinal *Cardinalis cardinalis*	open forest or forest edges with dense shrubs (<10 ft tall)	territory = 1–7.2 ac (avg = 3.3 ac); in KS, found only in windbreaks >2.5 ac; in NJ, found only in forests ≥2 ac

Feeding	Nesting	Conservation Status	Comments
caterpillars, flies, beetles	open cup on ground with overhanging rock or other structure	19	
moths, beetles, ants, bees, wasps, mayflies, grasshoppers, katydids, caterpillars, spiders	open cup 1–8 ft above ground in shrub	14	
caterpillars, beetles, other insects, berries	open cup 15–50 ft above ground in tall tree	12	
bees, wasps, cicadas, spiders, caterpillars	open cup 4–70 ft above ground (avg = 25 ft)	15	
insects	open cup 4–75 ft above ground (avg = 21 ft) in tree	15	apparently sensitive to forest fragmentation
wasps, bees, ants, beetles, grasshoppers, termites, cicadas, berries	open cup 15–65 ft above ground in tree	15	
grass and forb seeds, buds, flowers, berries, beetles, grasshoppers, caterpillars, ants, spiders, centipedes	open cup 3–10 ft above ground in shrub or small tree	8	

Species	Breeding Habitat	Area Requirements
pyrrhuloxia *Cardinalis sinuatus*	open, arid areas with thorny shrubs	no information available
rose-breasted grosbeak *Pheucticus ludovicianus*	open deciduous or mixed forest, forest openings with shrubs	in NJ, found only in forests ≥3 ac, but more common in forests ≥25 ac
black-headed grosbeak *Pheucticus melanocephalus*	broad preferences, including coniferous, deciduous, or mixed forest, especially riparian areas and forest edges	territory = 1–10 ac (avg = 4.5 ac)
blue grosbeak *Guiraca caerulea*	field-forest edges and small, open woodlots with trees 9–12 in. diameter, few shrubs, and dense ground cover	territory = 3–15 ac
lazuli bunting *Passerina amoena*	open areas with dense shrubs, especially hillsides and riparian areas	territory = 3.5–12 ac
indigo bunting *Passerina cyanea*	brushy, relatively open areas; openings in deciduous woods; shrubby swamps	territory = 0.6–3.5 ac; in NJ, found in forests as small as 0.5 ac

Feeding	Nesting	Conservation Status	Comments
beetles, caterpillars, grasshoppers, forb and grass seeds, berries	open cup 4–15 ft above ground in shrub or small tree	17	
beetles, caterpillars, grasshoppers, spiders, snails, seeds	open cup 5–20 ft above ground in tree or shrub	15	in Ontario, was markedly less common in forests with adjacent high densities of houses
beetles, moths, caterpillars, berries, weed seeds mostly collected from foliage >10 ft above the ground, and on the ground	open cup 3–30 ft above ground (avg = 12 ft) in shrub or small tree, often near a stream	17	
grasshoppers, beetles, crickets, cicadas, caterpillars, snails, grass seeds	open cup 6 in.–25 ft above ground in small trees, shrubs, vines	11	
spiders, caterpillars, butterflies, grasshoppers, berries, forb and grass seeds	open cup 1–27 ft above ground (avg = 3.5 ft) in dense shrub	16	
spiders, insects, berries	open cup in shrub, <3 ft above ground	13	

Species	Breeding Habitat	Area Requirements
painted bunting *Passerina ciris*	shrubby areas in open forest or forest edges or forest openings	territory = 1.6–16 ac (avg = 7.8 ac)
dickcissel *Spiza americana*	open grassy areas	territory = 1–3 ac
green-tailed towhee *Pipilo chlorurus*	shrub-covered slopes, open forest with dense shrubs	home range = 5 ac
eastern towhee *Pipilo erythrophthalmus*	areas of dense low shrubs and/or small trees, and thick leaf litter; field-forest edges	territory = 0.5–17 ac; in NJ, found in forests as small as 0.5 ac
spotted towhee *Pipilo maculatus*	areas of dense low shrubs and/or small trees, and thick leaf litter; field-forest edges	territory = 1–5 ac; in Vancouver, found in patches as small as 10 ac (smallest patch examined)
California towhee *Pipilo crissalis*	areas of dense shrubs, pinyon-juniper forest	territory = 1–2 ac
canyon towhee *Pipilo fuscus*	desert scrub and other arid areas with dense patches of shrubs or low trees	territory = 1–7.5 ac

Feeding	Nesting	Conservation Status	Comments
grass and forb seeds, berries, beetles, caterpillars, grasshoppers, flies	open cup 3–10 ft above ground in shrub or tree	WatchList 21	
grasshoppers, crickets, caterpillars, beetles	open cup on or near the ground in dense ground vegetation	WatchList 20	
beetles, crickets, caterpillars, forb and grass seeds	open cup <3 ft above ground in shrub	16	
beetles, moths, caterpillars, grasshoppers, crickets, flower buds, seeds, berries	open cup on ground in area of dense shrubs, or up to 5 ft above ground in shrub or tree	15	
beetles, crickets, grasshoppers, caterpillars, moths, millipedes, seeds, berries, acorns	open cup on ground near edge of shrubby patch, or up to 12 ft above ground in shrub or tree	16	
caterpillars, beetles, other insects, forb and grass seeds	open cup 0–30 ft above ground (usually 4–12 ft) in shrub or small tree	18	
primarily forb seeds; also millipedes, grasshoppers, spiders	open cup 2–12 ft above ground in shrub, cactus, or tree	18	

Species	Breeding Habitat	Area Requirements
Abert's towhee *Pipilo aberti*	streamside woodlands with dense shrubs (including willows and mesquite)	territory = 3.7–5 ac
Bachman's sparrow *Aimophila aestivalis*	mature, open pine forest, >80 yr old, with dense grasses and forbs and few shrubs; also 1–5 yr old clearcuts	territory = 1.5–13 ac
Cassin's sparrow *Aimophila cassinii*	grasslands with scattered or fairly dense shrubs	territory = 15–20 ac
rufous-winged sparrow *Aimophila carpalis*	areas with tall grass and low shrubs, especially desert hackberry and mesquite	territory = 1–3 ac
rufous-crowned sparrow *Aimophila ruficeps*	open areas with scattered to dense shrubs, open pine-oak forest with shrubs, grassy and rocky areas with shrubs	territory = 1–4 ac
chipping sparrow *Spizella passerina*	open forest or forest edges	territory = 0.5–7.5 ac; in KS, found only in windbreaks >2.5 ac
clay-colored sparrow *Spizella pallida*	open areas with shrubs, streamside shrubs, forest-grass-land edges	territory = 0.1–1 ac
Brewer's sparrow *Spizella breweri*	open areas with sagebrush, pinyon-juniper forest	territory = 1.2 ac

Feeding	Nesting	Conservation Status	Comments
beetles, ants, caterpillars, grasshoppers, cicadas	open cup 4–8 ft above ground in tree or shrub	WatchList 22	sometimes found in suburban areas
grass and sedge seeds, beetles, weevils	open cup (sometimes with a dome of vegetation) on the ground at base of vegetation, especially clump of grass	WatchList 24	open forest can be maintained by burning at least once every 3 years
grasshoppers, caterpillars, moths, beetles, forb and grass seeds	open cup on or near ground, under shrub or in dense ground vegetation	WatchList 19	
caterpillars, grasshoppers, other insects, spiders, seeds	open cup <7 ft above ground in shrub or cactus	WatchList 23	
caterpillars, beetles, beetle larvae, grasshoppers, ants, spiders, seeds	open cup on or near ground under shrub or in dense grasses	18	
grasshoppers, caterpillars, beetles, leafhoppers, spiders, seeds	open cup 0–15 ft above the ground (occasionally much higher) in tree	11	
seeds of forbs and grasses	open cup in shrub, usually less than 1 ft above ground	WatchList 18	fairly tolerant of human activity; sometimes breeds in urban areas
beetles, beetle larvae, plant lice, caterpillars, seeds	open cup <4 ft above ground in shrub	WatchList 18	

Species	Breeding Habitat	Area Requirements
field sparrow *Spizella pusilla*	open areas with scattered shrubs or trees	territory = 0.75–4 ac
black-chinned sparrow *Spizella atrogularis*	arid areas with dense shrubs 3–7 ft tall, rocky terrain, scattered taller shrubs and trees	territory = 4–10 ac
vesper sparrow *Pooecetes gramineus*	open areas with grasses and forbs, also areas of bare soil	territory = 1–3 ac
lark sparrow *Chondestes grammacus*	open areas with scattered trees and shrubs, some areas of bare soil	territory = 3.4–8.8 ac; home range = 15 ac
black-throated sparrow *Amphispiza bilineata*	arid areas with scattered shrubs or cacti, very open pinyon-juniper forest	no information available
sage sparrow *Amphispiza belli*	open areas with shrubs, especially sagebrush	territory = 1.6–14 ac
lark bunting *Calamospiza melanocorys*	shortgrass prairie, grassy areas with widely scattered shrubs	no information available
savannah sparrow *Passerculus sandwichensis*	open, treeless areas with dense grasses and some forbs, especially near water	territory = 0.3–3 ac

Feeding	Nesting	Conservation Status	Comments
grass seeds, insects	open cup on ground in grass clump or under shrub	17	
adult and larval insects	open cup 0.5–5 ft above ground (avg = 2 ft) in dense shrub	WatchList 21	
beetles, grasshoppers, caterpillars, moths, spiders	open cup on ground next to clump of grass or other vegetation	14	
grasshoppers, beetles, caterpillars, grass and forb seeds	open cup on ground, or up to 7 ft above ground in shrub or tree	16	
insects	open cup <2 ft above ground in shrub or cactus, or on ground under shrub	14	
grasshoppers, beetles, leafhoppers, ants, spiders, seeds	open cup on ground or up to 4 ft above ground in shrub	WatchList 20	
grasshoppers, beetles, bees, ants	open cup on ground with overhanging vegetation	WatchList 19	
insects, including beetles, midges, flies, caterpillars, spiders, and small seeds	open cup on ground, often at base of grass clump or woody vegetation	12	sensitive to habitat fragmentation

Species	Breeding Habitat	Area Requirements
Baird's sparrow *Ammodramus bairdii*	open areas with tall grass, scattered tall forbs and shrubs	no information available
grasshopper sparrow *Ammodramus savannarum*	areas of dense medium to tall grasses with <35% shrub cover and patches of bare ground	territory = 0.8–3.3 ac; minimum recommended area = 75 ac
Henslow's sparrow *Ammodramus henslowii*	open areas with tall grass and forbs, scattered shrubs	territory = 0.8–3 ac
Le Conte's sparrow *Ammodramus leconteii*	open marshy areas with tall, dense grass or sedges	territory = 0.5 ac
saltmarsh sharp-tailed sparrow *Ammodramus caudacutus*	coastal marshes and wet meadows with abundant grassy vegetation	home range = 3–14 ac
seaside sparrow *Ammodramus maritimus*	salt marshes with medium-high vegetation (1.5–3 ft) and exposed muddy areas	territory = 0.7–16.8 ac
Nelson's sharp-tailed sparrow *Ammodramus nelsoni*	freshwater or salt marshes with tall grasses	no information available

Feeding	Nesting	Conservation Status	Comments
grasshoppers, caterpillars, moths, beetles, leafhoppers, spiders	open cup on ground	WatchList 23	
grasshoppers, beetles, caterpillars, ants, spiders	cup with grass dome, on ground at base of vegetation clump	16	may be sensitive to habitat fragmentation; will not nest within 50 yd of a habitat edge; habitat can be maintained by burning in late summer
crickets, grasshoppers, beetles, caterpillars, wasps, spiders	open cup on or near ground	WatchList 24	sensitive to habitat fragmentation
caterpillars, leafhoppers, stink bugs, spiders	open cup on or just above ground in grass clump	19	
beetles, crickets, grasshoppers, moths, ants, wasps, flies; also small mollusks	cup with overhanging grassy vegetation, just above ground	WatchList 25	
insects and insect larvae, spiders and their eggs, decapods, mollusks, marine worms	open cup with partial dome, 0–14 in. above ground (avg = 8 in.) in shrub or emergent vegetation	WatchList 21	
grasshoppers, beetles, caterpillars, ants, wasps, spiders, snails	open cup on ground	WatchList 24	

Species	Breeding Habitat	Area Requirements
fox sparrow *Passerella iliaca*	forest openings or edges with shrubs, riparian shrubs	territory = 0.6–2.5 ac
song sparrow *Melospiza melodia*	open areas with shrubs, forest edges with shrubs, riparian shrubs	territory = 0.1–1.5 ac; in NJ, found in forests as small as 0.25 ac; in SD, found in shelterbelts as small as 0.6 ac
Lincoln's sparrow *Melospiza lincolnii*	boggy areas with dense willow shrubs and sedges	territory = 0.2–2 ac
swamp sparrow *Melospiza georgiana*	freshwater marshes with emergent vegetation; riparian shrubs	territory = 5–10 ac
white-throated sparrow *Zonotrichia albicollis*	coniferous and mixed forest with dense shrubs in small openings, and forest edge with dense shrubs	territory = 0.1–8 ac
white-crowned sparrow *Zonotrichia leucophrys*	open, grassy areas with patches of dense shrubs and bare ground; water and tall coniferous trees nearby	territory = 0.3–2 ac
dark-eyed junco *Junco hyemalis*	openings in coniferous or mixed forest, forest edges	territory = 1.4 ac; in Vancouver, found in patches as small as 10 ac (smallest patch examined)

Feeding	Nesting	Conservation Status	Comments
beetles, flies, bugs, spiders, millipedes	open cup on ground under shrub, occasionally up to 8 ft above ground in tree or shrub	12	
beetles, grasshoppers, caterpillars, ants, wasps, spiders	open cup 0–10 ft above ground in (or under) shrub, tree, or emergent vegetation	11	
adult and larval insects, including beetles and moths	open cup on ground under a willow shrub	12	
beetles, caterpillars, grasshoppers, crickets, ants, spiders	open cup 0–5 ft above ground or water in emergent vegetation	14	
insects, spiders, millipedes, centipedes, snails	open cup on ground under shrub, grass, or other live or dead vegetation	11	
caterpillars, beetles, other insects	open cup on ground or 1–10 ft above ground in shrub, occasionally in coniferous tree	12	
caterpillars, beetles, grasshoppers, spiders, forb and grass seeds, berries	open cup on ground with overhanging rock, log, vegetation, or other structure	12	

Species	Breeding Habitat	Area Requirements
yellow-eyed junco *Junco phaeonotus*	coniferous and pine-oak forest	no information available
McCown's longspur *Calcarius mccownii*	shortgrass prairie with bare ground, cacti, scattered shrubs	territory = 1.5–3.5 ac
chestnut-collared longspur *Calcarius ornatus*	shortgrass prairie with scattered tall forbs	territory = 1–2 ac
bobolink *Dolichonyx oryzivorus*	grassy areas with some forbs, abundant vegetative litter	territory = 1–12 ac
red-winged blackbird *Agelaius phoeniceus*	wetlands, open areas	territory = 0.2–1 ac; will travel up to 1 mi from nest to find food
tricolored blackbird *Agelaius tricolor*	nests in wetlands with dense emergent vegetation; looks for food in open areas	no information available

Feeding	Nesting	Conservation Status	Comments
insects, flowers, buds, berries, seeds	open cup on ground with overhanging rock, log, vegetation, or other structure	17	
primarily grass and forb seeds, also grasshoppers, moths, beetles	open cup on ground, often next to grass clump, cactus, or shrub	WatchList 24	
forb and grass seeds, grasshoppers, crickets, beetles, spiders	open cup on ground next to vegetation clump or other structure	19	
forb seeds, beetles, caterpillars, moths, spiders	open cup on ground, sometimes with "roof," often placed under a large forb	WatchList 19	sensitive to habitat fragmentation; habitat should be mowed each year, after mid-July, or burned several weeks before adults return in spring (they return in early to mid-May)
beetles, caterpillars, grasshoppers, spiders, snails, grass and forb seeds	open cup 1–20 ft above ground or water in emergent marsh vegetation, tree, or shrub; or on ground in grasses; usually nests in colonies	11	may be the most abundant bird in North America; often considered an agricultural pest
caterpillars, grasshoppers, beetles, spiders	open cup in emergent vegetation	19	

Species	Breeding Habitat	Area Requirements
eastern meadowlark *Sturnella magna*	open areas with dense grass (4–12 in. tall) and abundant vegetative litter	territory = 3–15 ac
western meadowlark *Sturnella neglecta*	open areas with abundant grasses and vegetative litter	territory = 3–32 ac
yellow-headed blackbird *Xanthocephalus xanthocephalus*	wetlands in prairies, mountain meadows, and arid regions	territory around nest site = 0.03–1 ac, but adults may travel >1000 yd from the nest to find food
rusty blackbird *Euphagus carolinus*	at the edges of openings in swampy coniferous forests, with dense vegetation 6–12 ft above the ground	no information available
Brewer's blackbird *Euphagus cyanocephalus*	open areas, open forest, riparian woods	will travel up to 3.5 mi from nest to find food

Feeding	Nesting	Conservation Status	Comments
crickets, grasshoppers, caterpillars, cutworms, grubs	open cup in dense vegetation on ground, often covered by overanging grasses	14	mowing can improve habitat, but should be delayed until after nesting is complete (August), and only cut every 3–5 years
weed seeds, beetles, weevils, grasshoppers, crickets	open cup in dense vegetation on ground, often covered by overhanging grasses	15	
adult and immature aquatic and terrestrial insects, including damselflies, dragonflies, beetles, caterpillars, and cutworms	open cup 6–24 in. above water in emergent vegetation; avg water depth below nest = 16 in.; nests in colonies	17	
aquatic beetles, grasshoppers, spiders, snails	open cup 1.5–20 ft above ground in tree or shrub; sometimes over water	16	
grasshoppers, crickets, beetles, aphids, caterpillars, termites, spiders, grass and forb seeds	open cup on ground or up to 40 ft above ground in tree	12	

Species	Breeding Habitat	Area Requirements
great-tailed grackle *Quiscalus mexicanus*	riparian woods, open areas with shrubs, wetlands	no information available
boat-tailed grackle *Quiscalus major*	freshwater and salt marshes, open upland areas	no information available
common grackle *Quiscalus quiscula*	open areas with scattered trees; open forest	in NJ, found in forests as small as 0.5 ac; in SD, found in the smallest shelterbelts examined (0.25 ac)
bronzed cowbird *Molothrus aeneus*	open areas, forest edges, open forest	no information available
brown-headed cowbird *Molothrus ater*	grassy areas with scattered trees, and field-forest edges	territory = 10–50 ac; will travel up to 4 mi to find food

Feeding	Nesting	Conservation Status	Comments
insects, spiders, snails, tadpoles, fish, eggs and young birds, seeds, berries	open cup 2–20 ft above ground in shrub, tree, or emergent vegetation	8	
insects, crustaceans, mollusks, amphibians, reptiles, fruit, sedge tubers	open cup in emergent vegetation, or tree or shrub in or near water; nests in colonies with up to 35 nests (avg = 7)	14	
beetle larvae, grasshoppers, caterpillars, agricultural grain	open cup 1–75 ft above ground (avg = 12 ft) in shrub or tree (usually conifer)	11	considered an agricultural pest and nest predator whose population has grown unnaturally large due to forest clearing
caterpillars, beetles, flies, spiders, snails, grass and forb seeds	a nest parasite: it lays its eggs in the nests of other bird species, such as warblers and vireos, to be raised by them	13	
grass seeds and crop grains collected on the ground	a nest parasite: it lays its eggs in the nests of other bird species, such as warblers and vireos, to be raised by them	10	although a native species, this cowbird is responsible for declines in a number of other native songbirds; its breeding should not be encouraged

Species	Breeding Habitat	Area Requirements
orchard oriole *Icterus spurius*	riparian woodlands, open areas with scattered trees, patches of trees with grass and shrub layer around perimeter; prefers areas with dense 3–6 in. diameter trees	home range = 3–10 ac; in KS, found only in windbreaks >2.5 ac; in SD, found in shelterbelts as small as 0.5 ac
hooded oriole *Icterus cucullatus*	open deciduous forest, riparian forest	no information available
Baltimore oriole *Icterus galbula*	open deciduous or mixed forest, forest edges	in NJ, found in forests as small as 0.5 ac; in SD, found in shelterbelts as small as 0.75 ac
Bullock's oriole *Icterus bullockii*	open deciduous or mixed forest, forest edges	no information available
Scott's oriole *Icterus parisorum*	oak or pinyon-juniper forest, open areas with abundant yuccas or Joshua trees	no information available
pine grosbeak *Pinicola enucleator*	open coniferous forest	no information available
purple finch *Carpodacus purpureus*	moist coniferous or mixed forest	no information available

Feeding	Nesting	Conservation Status	Comments
invertebrates, including grasshoppers, spiders, beetles, and caterpillars; also berries and flower nectar	hanging pouch 10–70 ft above ground (avg = 30 ft); often nests in loose colonies (nests about 40 yd apart)	17	
caterpillars, beetles, wasps, ants, berries, flower nectar	hanging pouch 10–50 ft above ground in tree	18	often nests in urban areas, including golf courses
caterpillars, beetles, grasshoppers, wasps, spiders, berries, flower nectar	hanging pouch 6–60 ft above ground in deciduous tree	15	
caterpillars, beetles, grasshoppers, wasps, spiders, berries, flower nectar	hanging pouch 6–60 ft above ground in deciduous tree	15	
grasshoppers, beetles, caterpillars, berries, flower nectar	hanging pouch 4–20 ft above ground in tree	18	
conifer seeds, buds of deciduous trees, berries, insects	open cup 2–25 ft above ground in shrub or tree	13	
tree buds, blossoms, and seeds, also small fruits	open cup 2.5–60 ft above ground in coniferous (sometimes deciduous) tree	14	

Species	Breeding Habitat	Area Requirements
Cassin's finch *Carpodacus cassinii*	open coniferous forest	will travel up to 300 yd from nest to find food
house finch *Carpodacus mexicanus*	wide range of open habitats, with trees or shrubs available for nesting; common in urban areas	no information available
red crossbill *Loxia curvirostra*	mature coniferous forest	will travel over 500 yd from nest to find food; in Vancouver, found in patches as small as 10 ac (smallest patch examined)
white-winged crossbill *Loxia leucoptera*	conifer forests with abundant cone crops, especially spruce or tamarack	will travel up to 0.6 mi from nest to find food
pine siskin *Carduelis pinus*	coniferous or mixed forest, especially with clearings; forest edges	no information available
lesser goldfinch *Carduelis psaltria*	open forest or forest edge or shrubby areas close to open fields with abundant forbs	no information available
Lawrence's goldfinch *Carduelis lawrencei*	pine-oak forest, riparian woods, open coniferous forest, dry open areas with shrubs	will travel up to 1.3 mi from nest to find food

Feeding	Nesting	Conservation Status	Comments
tree buds, seeds, berries	open cup 6–90 ft above ground (avg = 36 ft) in coniferous tree	17	
buds, seeds, fruits of a wide variety of plants	open cup or cavity 12–15 ft above ground in tree, cactus, or building, protected by overhanging vegetation or other structure	8	a western species that has been artificially introduced into the East
conifer seeds (especially spruce, pine, Douglas fir, and hemlock); also aphids and insect larvae	open cup 7–70 ft above ground in conifer	13	
spruce and tamarack seeds; also fir seeds	open cup on limb of conifer tree (usually spruce), 3–65 ft above ground	13	
tree, forb, and grass seeds; buds, flowers, insects	open cup 10–40 ft above ground in tree	7	
forb seeds, tree flowers and buds, berries, small insects	open cup 5–30 ft above ground in tree or shrub	15	
forb seeds, insects	open cup 15–40 ft above ground in tree or shrub	WatchList 24	

Species	Breeding Habitat	Area Requirements
American goldfinch *Carduelis tristis*	open areas with low shrubs and scattered trees, especially with food sources such as thistles and Compositae	in SD, found in shelterbelts as small as 0.4 ac; will travel over 1000 yd from nest to find food
evening grosbeak *Coccothraustes vespertinus*	coniferous and mixed forest	no information available
house sparrow *Passer domesticus*	urban or rural areas— virtually anyplace with buildings	in SD, found in the smallest shelterbelts examined (0.25 ac)

Feeding	Nesting	Conservation Status	Comments
seeds from Compositae (many of which are considered weeds), grasses, small tree seeds (alder, birch, cedar, elm)	open cup in shrub or tree, shaded by leaves or needles	12	
tree seeds and buds, berries, insects	open cup 10–100 ft above ground in tree	9	
forb and grass seeds, insects, garbage	cavity in tree, building, or nest box; nests in loose colonies	10 should be discouraged from nesting whenever possible; unlike native birds, this species has no legal protection in the U.S.	introduced to the U.S. from Europe in 1850, this bird aggressively displaces native species such as bluebirds